PSYCHOLOGICAL PERSPECTIVES ON STRESS AND HEALTH

About the Editor

Girishwar Misra is Professor and Chairman of the Department of Psychology at Delhi University. Earlier he has taught at the Universities of Gorakhpur, Allahabad and Bhopal. Apart from numerous articles in journals, he has written or edited *Psychological Consequences of Prolonged Deprivation; Deprivation : Its Social Roots and Psychological Consequences, Foundations of Social Psychology. General Psychology; Applied Social Psychology in India. Psychology of Poverty and Disadvantage and Perspectives on Indigenous Psychology.* His areas of interest include cultural psychology, applied social psychology and human development. He is on the editorial board of *Psychological Studies* and *Culture and Psychology.* He was a Fulbright Fellow at Swarthmore College and the University of Michigan. He has received Radhakrishnan Award (1991) and Dr. Hari Singh Gaur Award (1992) form the Government of Madhya Pradesh for contributions to social science teaching and research. He is also on the executive committee of International Association of Cross-Cultural Psychology.

Psychological Perspectives on Stress and Health

Edited by

Girishwar Misra
Department of Psychology
University of Delhi, Delhi

CONCEPT PUBLISHING COMPANY, NEW DELHI - 110059

ISBN 81-7022-785-2

First Published 1999

Published and Printed by
Ashok Kumar Mittal
Concept Publishing Company
A/15-16, Commercial Block, Mohan Garden,
NEW DELHI - 110059 (India)

Phones : 5648039, 5649024
Fax : 091-11-5648053

Dedicated
To
The Memory of
Professor Durganand Sinha

Preface

The psychological study of stress and health, like many other fields of enquiry, is now quite developed and voluminous literature is avilable and being published to document the innovations in theroy, research and application in this domain. Also, many specialities like *health psychology, behavioural medicine and psychoneuroimmunology* are coming up to supplement the traditional domain of clinical psychology. Until recently these disciplinary developments were largely taken for granted as universals on the presumed ground that the positivist scientific method yields a context-free, abstract, acultural, and objective pool of knowledge. Perspectives from other cultures or traditions alien to the mainstream western thought were treated as non-scientific and looked at with suspicision. As a result they were largely ignored. However, serious investigations of the form and functioning of hardcore sciences have shown that science too is a kind of social construction and there are other and equally legitimate modes of rationality and reality construction. This, alongwith the realization of ambiguities in understanding the constraints on application to different cultures, created a need amongst the researchers to stay back from their work for a while and reflect upon some of the substantive issues. The main aim in preparing the present volume was precisely to do this in the growing field of stress and health.

For psychologists in a developing country like India which has a long past and now confronts the challenges of contemporary period life is full of complex demands. Individuals have to simultaneously appreciate and respond to local as well as global needs. The problem is made further complicated by the co-existence of different psychological worlds of the people from diverse ecological settings e.g. villages, cities and mega-cities. These sittings are interrelated but differ in terms of socio-economic and psychological complexion. The cultural life of the people of India also covers a broad spectrum ranging from the tribal to the most modern. This scenario necessitates a multi-pronged strategy on the part of academicians and professionals interested in the field of health.

In the last few decades the Indian social scientists have increasingly paid greater attention to the problems of stress and health. Several teams of researchers have been focussing on different aspects of the stress process and health behaviour in family and work settings. The present volume tries to bring together contributions from researchers who have shown sustained interest in exploring various aspects of stress and health in the Indian context. It tries to address several questions about stress and health. Some of them are : What is the significance of socio-cultural context for the conceptualization of well-being, illness and health behaviour? What are the indigeneous perspectives on health and stress? What are the salient concerns of Indian researchers in the field of stress and health ? What are the factors which moderate and mediate the effects of stress? What are the health problems of vulnerable groups like women and children? What are the coping strategies used in managing life stresses?

The contributions to the present volume were undertaken by the scholars independently, though in totality they enable the reader to have an overview of the work currently being undertaken by Indian researchers in the area of health and stress. The chief concern of the contributions to this volume has been to facilitate understanding of the dynamics of stress and health in the Indian socio-cultural context. However, it cannot claim to cover all aspects of health and stress, which has become an inter-disciplinary field of research in the true sense.

In the first Chapter of the book, Misra and Varma have outlined the pertinent conceptual issues for the study of stress and health. It sets the background for the volume. In Chapter 2, Palsane and Ram, have analyzed the socio-cultural context of health and stress. They argue that stress encompasses a variety of situations and circumstances. After presenting an overview of various concepts of stress they uphold the view that stress is a perceived transaction between a person and environment. The relationship between stressors and physical/mental wellness/illness is mediated by individual and socio-cultural variables (e.g. TABP, psycho-social competence, hardiness). It is argued that culture determines the worldview as well as the modes of treatment. Finally, the authors indicate the need for cross-cultural and long-term studies of stress and well being.

Sinha discusses the social psychological aspects of health behaviour in Chapter 3. He recognizes the need to go beyond the biomedical perspective and emphasizes the analysis of individual functioning in the social context. He traces the historical trends and indicates that the association between modern scientific psychology and health is very old. He draws attention to primary health care and recommends the biopsychological model. The problem of developing countries are pointed out and the diseases of poverty and affluence are discussed. In order to attain the objective of health for all more attention needs to be given to preventive and promotive aspects of health. The new challenges for psychology include collaboration with other disciplines and agencies.

Chapter 4, authored by Singh, and his colleagues examines the notion of health in the context of different systems of medicine. In the first part of the paper basic tenets of four systems of medicine viz., allopathy, ayurveda, homeopathy and unani—are presented. The second part of the paper illustrates the meaning of health and illness held by the practitioners of four systems of medicine mentioned above.

Naidu and Pande, in Chapter 5, have argued for expanding the discourse by looking at indigenous concepts. They report one effort in this direction by operationalizing an indigenous concept of non-attachment (*anasakti*) and have tried to empirically study its effect on stress, strain and the relationship between the two. Non-attachment was significantly negatively related to the experience of strain. The results tend to suggest that non-attchement is a moderator of stress-strain relationship.

In Chapter 6, Dalal examines the role of beliefs in coping with chronic illness which has increased in recent years. The personal meaning of illness and its implications for attribution of responsbility, affective reactions, compliance during treatment, managing pain and discomfort, and living with illness are discussed. The issues raised are relevant to intervention and rehabilitation of the chronically ill people.

Sharma has reviewed the studies related to social support as a complex and challenging construct in stress research in Chapter 7. He analyzes the concept of well being as perceived quality of life. He observes that, social support tends to vary across stages of life and examines the process of providing support. The structural and functional aspects of support are discussed and the level of analysis (individual vs. group), and relationship with disease prevention has been delineated. Finally, the cultural context with special reference to India has been highlighted.

Chakravarty and Misra in Chapter 8, examine the varied approaches to the understanding of coping with stress. The authors also illustrate the issues with the help of an empirical study on coping with life stresses across different hierarchical positions in a public sector undertaking.

In Chapter 9, Dwivedi has examined the effects of induced stress on human cognition. In particular, the relationship between sustained attention and skilled performance has been analysed. To this end, effects of electric shock and noise on short-term and long-term memory are examined. It is concluded that arousal is a non-specific unitary process. However, the type of stress manipulation produces differential effect on performance.

Chapter 10, authored by G.C. Gupta examines the stresses related to temporal regulation which are prevailing in developed countries. The problem of bringing organism into harmony with the surrounding world is discussed. It is proposed that designing of task and managing time are important strategies. Biological and general mechanisms are involved in tuning or interfacing with the temporal structure of environment.

Thakar and Misra have explored the implications of job for well-being amongst dual career women in Chapter 11. After examining the changing scenario emerging in the course of entry of women to the work force, the authors explore the meaning of work for these women and empirically assess the daily hassles experienced by them. Social support was found to moderate the effects of stress. Also, differential hassles were noted for women working at different job levels. The working women experienced greater well-being despite low social-support.

Chapter 12, authored by Nagar provides an overview of theory and research on environmental stressors. The changes at global level in a world encompassing diverse types and levels of human intervention are leading to a large number of problems. The human consequences of environmental stressors vary in terms of severity and time frame. Referring to work on ambient stressors and physiological and psychological perspectives on stress, Nagar, considers the problems of psychological mediation of environmental stressors. Finally, the research on residential design is discussed. The gaps in knowledge peraining to linkages between stress, cognition and health are pointed out.

In Chapter 13, Kapur has reviewed the work in the area of stress and health during childhood and adolescence. Based on the review of theoretical approaches and empirical studies, she observes that there is a need to explore the nature of association between chronic stressors, recent life events, and specific syndromes. It is indicated that the dimension of resilience and competencies in children need special attention. A longitudinal perspective and ethnographic approach is recommended for the study of stresses across age, gender and ethnic groups.

Sood and Misra, in Chapter 14, have reported the incidence of problem behaviours in primary school children. After discussing the difficulties in conceptualizing problem behaviour, the authors point out that socio-cultural norms play an important role in determining identification of problem behaviour. They also present results of a survey of behaviour problems in children and indicate important age and sex differences in the pattern of problem behaviours. The incidence of problem behaviours was related to a number of environmental variables and parental characteristics.

In Chapter 15, Rath has taken up the role of self-instructional training in promoting mental health in children. He discusses various aspects of VSI paradigm. Impulsivity, hyperactivity, aggressive behaviour and learning disability are various problems which have been handled under this paradigm. The author, however, concludes that considerable gap still exists between expectations and achievements in the field.

Saraswathi focusses on preventive mental health in Chapter 16. She recognizes the role of behavioural scientists in creating a better mental health care system, by providing a culturally and ecologically relevant understanding of psychopathology. She argues that the developmental dimensions must be adequately recognized. She advocates the building of a knowledge base so that environmental factors may be managed to ensure acceptable levels of quality of life.

In Chapter 17, Dalal has tried to identify some research issues which merit further investigation. He notes that the health related consequences of stress are contingent on the coping strategies used by the people. We need more careful studies to uncover flexibilities in the use of coping strategies. Similarly, the role of belief systems in managing tragic experiences and alleviating suffering is a potential area of research. Also multifacted studies of social support are needed to understand the nature and implications of motives and supportive efforts of the providers. Finally, the need for methodological shift is emphasised which may enable in-depth analysis of specific stressful episodes.

It is clear that there is a rich variety of challenges and opportunities for psychologists and other social scientists in theoretical and applied fields of health. They are now expected to play a more important role in every aspect of health. It is hoped that this volume would help to synthesize the burgeoning literature informed by the diverse perspectives that are available today so that a more complete understanding of the nature and implications of stress and health processes may be pursued.

Girishwar Misra

Acknowledgements

The present volume has its roots in a Seminar on Applied Social Psychology held a few years back at Bhopal University, Bhopal. This seminar was sponsored by the Madhya Pradesh Council of Science and Technology (MPCOST) and organized in collaboration with Academy of Administration, Bhopal. It provided an opportunity to deliberate on several issues including stress and health behaviour. It was decided during the seminar that a collection of essays on the current state-of the-art in the area of stress and health should be published. The participants in the seminar developed their arguments in the form of papers which were revised after peer review. In addition, several other contributions were specially commissioned to make the volume comprehensive. I would like to thank the distinguished colleagues and researchers for their contributions to this volume.

The enthusiasm of Shri Ashok Kumar Mittal was the primary factor that led me to choose Concept as publisher. His instant agreement that this kind of book was needed has created a compulsion to complete it. I am grateful to him for his keen interest.

During the work on this project I have received considerable support from my wife Madhuri. It's not possible to focus intently on an undertaking of this magnitude without inconveniencing family in many ways. So I am grateful that every body in my family was willing to put up with my schedule and obsessions. I thank them for allowing me to share with them the pains and excitement associated with this project.

While working on this volume many colleagues, students and researchers have helped out in numerous ways. I express my sincere thanks to all of them. I hope that the book will sensitize students, researchers and professionals to the pertinent issues and stimulate their interest in the area of stress and health.

This book is dedicated to the memory of Professor Durganand Sinha who was associated with this project since its conception. His contributions to the growth of psychology in India and bringing culture at the centre stage of psychological discourse and making psychological research relevant are widely recognized I take this opportunity to pay my tributes to him.

Girishwar Misra

CONTENTS

Contributors

Kohinoor Chakravarty holds a Ph.D. in psychology. Her areas of interest include well being and adaptation of migrants. She is currently a consultant based in California, USA. (Add: 2385 Shoreside Ct. Santa Clara, California 95054, USA).,

Ajit K. Dalal is Professor of Psychology at Allahabad University. He has worked extensively in the areas of attribution, multivariate methods and health psychology. He was a Fulbright Fellow at University of California, Los Angles. His publications include numerous journal articles and *Attribution Theory and Research* and *Human Resource Development and Psychology*. (Add: Department of Psychology, University of Allahabad, Allahabad - 211 002).

Chandra Bhal Dwivedi is Professor of Psychology at Banaras Hindu University. His areas of interest include cognition, stress, affective processes and indigenous psychology. (Add: Department of Psychology, Banaras Hindu University, Varanasi - 211 005).

G. C. Gupta has retired as a Professor of Psychology from Delhi University. He has worked in the areas of perception, cognition and consciousness. His publications include *Ecology, Cognition, Metacognition* and *Mind, Schooling : Shaping of the Mind, Linguistic Diversity* and *Issues in Cognitive Science*. (Add : 85, Vaishali, Pitampura, Delhi-110 034).

Malavika Kapur is Additional Professor of Clinical Psychology at NIMHANS. She has been a clinical psychologist at the National Health Services, Scotland; Senior Research Associate at the University of Edinburgh; and on the Faculty at KMC Hospital, Maniphal. She has contributed papers to national and international journals and authored *Mental Health of Indian Children and Mental*

Health in Indian Schools. (Add : Department of Clinical Psychology, National Institute of Mental Health & Neurosciences, Bangalore - 560 029).

Girishwar Misra is a Professor and Chairman of the Department of Psycholoy at Delhi University. Earlier he has taught at the Universities of Gorakhpur, Allahabad and Bhopal. Apart from numerous articles in journals, he has written or edited *Psychological Consequenees of Prolonged Deprivation, Deprivation: Its Social Roots and Psychological Consequences, Foundations of Social Psychology, Applied Social Psychology in India, Psychology of Poverty* and *Disadvantage and Perspectives on Indigenous Psychology.* He was a Fulbright Fellow at Swarthmore College and the University of Michigan. His areas of interest include cultural psychology, applied social psychology and human development. (Add : Department of Psychology, University of Delhi, Delhi - 110007).

R. C. Mishra is Professor of Psychology at Banaras Hindu University. He was at the Queen's University as a National Fellow, and later as Shastri Fellow. He has published extensively in the areas of perception, schooling and acculturation. He is author of *Ecology, Acculturation and Psychological Adaptation.* (Add: Psychology Department, Banaras Hindu University, Varanasi - 221 005).

Dinesh Nagar is Reader in Psychology at Bhopal University. He has worked in the area of spatial behaviour and environmental stress particularly crowding. He was a research fellow at University of Texas at Austin. Currently he is focussing on human resource development. (Add: Department of Psychology, Barkatullah University, Bhopal - 462 026).

R. K. Naidu has retired as Professor of Psychology from Allahabad University. He has been a Fulbright Fellow at Michigan University, Ann Arbor. His areas of interest are stress, well being, and indigenous psychology. (Add: Department of Psychology, Allahabad University, Allahabad - 211 042).

M. N. Palsane has retired as Professor and Head of Psychology Department from Poona University. He has worked and published in the areas of crowding stress, coping, meditation and health psychology. (Add: Department of Psychology, Poona University, Pune - 411007)."

Namita Pandey is Reader in Psychology at Allahabad University. Her areas of research interest are mediators of stress, and well-being, self processes and indigenous psychology. (Add: Department of Psychology, Allahabad University, Allahabad - 211 002).

Usha Ram is Reader in Psychology at Poona University, Her areas of interest are aggression, stress and personality dynamics. She has edited *Suffering and Stress and Management : West versus East* (Add: Department of Psychology , Poona University, Pune - 411 007).

Sudhakar Rath is Reader in Psychology at Utkal University. His main interest is in cognitive. style and interventions for overcoming cognitive deficits. (Add: Department of Psychology, Utkal University, Bhubaneswar - 751 004).

T. S. Saraswathi is a Professor of Human Development at M.S. University of Baroda. Her areas of interest are socialization, moral development and cross-cultural psychology. Books authored or edited by her include *Developmental Psychology in India : An Annotated Bibliography, Invisible Boundaries : Grooming for Adult Roles, Human Development and Family Studies in India* and *Culture, Socialization, and Human Development.* (Add: Department of Human Development & Family Studies, M.S. University, Baroda - 390 002).

Sagar Sharma is Professor of Psychology at Himachal Pradesh University. He was formerly Visiting Professor at the Universities of South Florida and Buffalow, and a Program Associate at the East-West Centre, Hawaii. His field of interest is stress and anxiety in the context of clinical, educational and cross-cultural perspectives. He has been UGC National Lectures in psychology and President of National Academy of Psychology, India. (Add: Department of Psychology, H.P. University, Shimla - 171 005).

Durganand Sinha was the founding Head and Professor of Psychology, Department of Psychology at the University of Allahabad. He was the President and Fellow of the International Association for Cross-Cultural Psychology. He had published on poverty and deprivation, cross-cultural psychology, and indigenisation in psychology. His publications include *Indian Villages in Transition, The Mughal Syndrome, Psychology in the Third World Country: The Indian Experience, Social Values and Development, Effective Organizations and Social Values,* and *Asian Perspectives on Psychology.* (Add: 8, Malviya Road, George Town, Allahabad - 211 002).

Tara Singh is a Senior Lecturer of Psychology at Bhopal University. He has published papers on cognitive development. He was also associated with project on coping with ecological crisis under the Partnership Programme of Shastri-Indo-Canadian Institute and did field work in British Columbia, Canada. (Add: Department of Psychology, Barkatullah University, Bhopal - 462 026).

Neelam Sood is a Fellow in the School and Non-formal Education unit of NIEPA. She has authored *Behaviour Problems in Children.* (Add: National Institute of Educational Planning and Administration, 17-B, Sri Aurobindo Marg, New Delhi - 110 016).

Gauri Thakar is Lecturer in Educational Psychology at NCERT. Her main area of interest is identity and well-being of Indian women. (Add: Department of Educational Psychology and Foundations of Education, National Council of Educational Research and Training. Sri Aurobindo Marg, New Delhi - 1 10 016).

K. N. Tripathi is a Reader in Psychology at Bhopal University. He has published in the areas of intrinsic motivation and goal setting. He has jointly directed the project on Longitudinal Study of MIC affected children at Bhopal, sponsored by NIPCCD, New Delhi. He has also worked on an Indo-Shastri project on coping with ecological crisis and did field studies in British Columbia, Canada. (Add: Department of Psychology, Barkatullah University, Bhopal - 462 026).

Sunit Varma is Lecturer in Psychology at Delhi University. His main areas of interest include theoretical developments in psychology, psychology of self, and health behaviour. (Add: Department of Psychology, University of Delhi, Delhi - 1 10 007).

1

Introduction : Concerns in the Study of Stress and Health

GIRISHWAR MISRA and **SUNEET VARMA**

The stressful events as causes of illness have a long tradition in human history. In contemporary societies, stresses of one or the other kind have become a common source of threat to mental and physical health and well-being of the people. They have become characteristic features of modern life. This situation has emerged in the context of unprecedented technological change, accompanied by industrialization and increasing attraction to consumerism as an ideal or functional form of life. Thus the life of an average urban person has become a constant struggle with pressures, conflicts and limits. The stresses are continuously evoked and escape from them has become impossible. These developments have made stress a central phenomenon of interest to the students of many disciplines namely medicine, psychology, sociology and anthropology (Ramlingaswami, 1990). While the contexts and sources of stress have been studied by different disciplines at different levels, its analysis remained the major concern of psychologists. As a result in the last few decades the nature and dynamics of stress and health have received considerable attention by psychologists around the globe.

Traditionally, the empirical study of stress and health has been undertaken within biological and psychological frameworks with little attention at integration of the two. Psychological researches on stress focus more on quantification which has often been done at the cost of oversimplification and disregard for the context and processes involved. The strategies to over come stresses have been major concerns of health practitioners. Recent analyses of stress phenomena are gradually moving toward identification of the mediators and moderators of coping and health related outcomes. Also, several individual difference dimensions have been uncovered, which influence the processes of stress and coping. Finer distinctions are being made between stress, stressors, strain and burnout, and diverse conceptualizations have been put forward.

The evidence emerging from these multi-faceted endeavours tends to suggest that there is no one-to-one correspondence between the objective stimulus conditions and stress/health related outcomes for the individual and group. It has now become amply clear that stress cannot be meaningfully viewed as some exogenous noxious stimulus or response of the body, rather it is the product of a dynamic mismatch between the individual and his/her environment. Many behavioural characteristics and dispositions define the structure of any environmental encounter or behavioural episode (e.g. *anasakti*, hardines, control, coping strategies, cognitive appraisal, etc.) and thus the personal conditioning variables become important. For instance, people with Type-A Behaviour pattern are more vulnerable to stresses than others. We live within the boundaries of our own cultural experiences. Hence personality and behavioural traits on the one hand, and social environmental characteristics on the other, determine the nature of one's experiences of stress and will-being.

It needs to be noted that stress is not always bad. It is, in fact, a basic ingredient of life. Our system is equipped with certain innate "stress alarms" that allow people to function effectively in many situations. Without undergoing any stress there would not be constructive or creative activity. What we need is to reduce the amount of negative stress (distress) enjoy and appreciate positive ~~ss (*eustress*). The meaning, mechanisms and management of stress are formed or construed in the socio-cultural context of the people. Societies with their divergent world-views have evolved different conceptualizations of stress, health, roles and responsibilities of a person. This along with particular ecological and social characteristics, determine the distribution of stressful experiences in different communities and groups.

The phenomenon of stress has largely been associated with affluence and western lifestyle. However, broad spectrum changes such as decline in the traditional family support system, migration and the influence of media are increasing the intensity and frequency of stressful experiences (Sinha, 1988). As a result, India is currently facing the problem of coping with the diseases of underdevelopment as well as the life-style diseases. The stresses arising from the rapid changes, competition, scarcity of resources, uncertainties, time pressure etc. are being experienced with increasing frequency and intensity. All this necessitates in-depth scientific studies of stress and related health problems in the Indian context.

As a concept 'health' is intimately related to the notion of self and the view held by the people. The current professional perspectives on health and stress are wedded to individualistic assumptions rooted in North American and Western European discourses wherein the complex influence of culture is largely ignored (Beardsby & Pederson, 1997; Capewell, 1994; Lewis-Ferandez & Kleinman, 1994; McName & Gergen, 1992; Tanaka-Matsumi & Draguns, 1997). Cultures such as ours, with notions of embedded or ensembled self, do not partition the world very neatly in terms of self and environment. Within such frameworks, both constitute each other (Misra & Gergen, 1993). Instead of control the goal is to maintain harmony with nature and play one's due role (Kiran Kumar, 1986; Landrine, 1992; Misra, 1994). The extremely hedonistic and individual — centred view which promotes growth, development and realization of potentials in an independent fashion holds true largely in the context of western societies (Markus & Kitayama, 1991). In the Indian context, appreciation of symbiotic relationship

(Sinha, 1990) is more prevalent and the person-environment unit is conceived to operate in a broader context.

Perspectives on Health

Though the importance of health and well-being is accepted by everyone, the identification of indicators that would give an accurate picture of the state of an individual's well-being and assessing reliably how a person is enjoying such a state has proved to be very challenging. It is generally held that if a person is healthy and happy he is free from ailments and has the means to meet his physical needs and other demands. But equating well being with lack of illness and economic conditon alone is taking a very partial and narrow view of the human situation. It ignores mental, psychological and social aspects of his or her existence. Though physical and material aspects are certainly important, we cannot meaningfully talk of well-being without taking into account the totality of an individual's existential condition (Sinha, 1990).

The most common way of thinking about health, based on the bio-medical model, is to view it as the absence of physical disease. Typically, an advanced stage of disease is indicated by certain physical symptoms or signs. This definition of health relies heavily on the medical model of health care and emphasizes the role of the physician in observing signs, evaluating symptoms and making an accurate diagnosis (a familiar example of this logic for psychologists is the classification of people by the DSM-IV criteria). It is also possible to define health as the absence of subjective feelings of illness or the absence of the sick role identity. While the theoretical framework for studying health is widened to include more than just the biological or physiological parameters (e.g. studying other factors besides physical disease symptoms), the problem of defining health is accerbated.

The usefulness of defining normal health as the biologically average state seems questionable because normal health can be expected to vary greatly, depending on culture, social class, and age. Since precise indicators of health are not enumerated in theoretical or statistical terms, the use of a dichotomous taxonomy (normal vs optimal) is of little help in clarifying definitional problems. However, a few helpful distinctions and clarifications are present in the literature. Twaddle (1969), for example, represented normal health and ill-health as adjacent categories on a continuum that spans perfect health and death. Mechanic (1986) emphasized the importance of viewing health within a given cultural context. A perspective further clarified by Coelho, Yuan, and Ahmed (1980), emphasizes the social functioning of a healthy individual since health always addresses certain goals and social groups. Thus definitions of wellness and illness take into account the specific roles the individual is expected to play in his cultural milieu, as well as the judgments that the individual himself and significant others in his social network make about the adequacy of his performance. In particular, effective functioning in the two social roles, the familial and the occupational, tends to be regarded as crucial to the well being of the individual and of his community. Sinha (1990) has stated that psychological well-being or good health are desirable but difficult to define. The latter is often negatively defined as absence of ill-health or as the relative absence of physiological malfunctioning in an organism. It has been taken to consist of freedom from any subjective feelings of discomfort or disability and from any disturbances of mental functions.

Biomedical and behavioural/social scientists have also made distinctions among various aspects of non-health. In this context, terms such as disease, illness, and sickness have been distinguished. "Disease" is a biomedical concept that refers to the physiological features of non-health. Being unhealthy frequently involves biological dimensions in which there is some alteration of bodily functions that results in reduced capacities or a shortening of the normal life span. "Illness" can exist whether or not disease is present. People often define themselves as ill because of certain subjective feeling states (e.g., pain, nausea, weakness). Persons reporting these feelings to others may be defined as unhealthy by others and by themselves. "Sickness" is viewed primarily by sociologists as a social identity, or role assumed by people who have been labeled as unhealthy. The social process of defining someone as "sick" can occur whether or not disease or illness is present.

In the formulation of "sick role" concept Parsons (1951) viewed sickness as a form of deviant behaviour that is characterized by a set of socially institutionalized expectations and obligations, viz.: (i) The sick person is entitled to some exemption from normal social activities based on the nature and severity of the condition. (ii) The sick person is not responsible for the condition and cannot get well by an act of decision and will power. (iii) The sick person must define the state of being ill as 'undesirable' and should want to get well. (iv) The sick person must seek professional, competent help and cooperate in getting well.

The concept of sick role can also be viewed in terms of adaptation because disease and sickness result from a person's inability to adapt to the environment. With every change in environment, new diseases develop because there are new adaptations to begin the accommodation of organisms to environmental change.

Antonovsky (1979), in a thoughtful analysis of health and disease concepts, argued that health cannot be understood using a pathologically oriented perspective. He suggested that health is a highly relative process rather than a state or static condition, influenced by the availability of genetic and major psychosocial resistance resources. Such resources include levels of social support, types of coping strategies (their degree of rationality, flexibility, and farsightedness), degree of commitment (level of continuance, cohesion and control), and level of ego identity. He also conceptualized health process as influenced by the specific social and cultural context. He concluded that a "sense of coherence" is the major determining factor in the person's overall health and disease status. The coherence concept appears to be related to other health-associated concepts, such as hardiness, learned helplessness, the type-A behaviour pattern, and giving up.

Antonovsky (1979) further tied the sense of coherence to his other major concept: breakdown (a synonym for health problem) which has four practical assessment criteria: (i) pain level (from none to severe), (ii) degree of functional limitation (from almost none to severe), (iii) prognostic implications (from minor to life-threatening), and (iv) action implications (from none to immediate action intervention). These considerations implicate that health involves the following features.

(1) It is very habitual, having to do with the persistent routine actions of people (e.g., eating, exercising, relaxing, relating to others).
(2) It is more encompassing than the absence of specific physiological pathology.
(3) It exists on a dynamic temporal continuum, fluctuating in response to the perceived demands (external as well as internal) over times.
(4) It cannot be understood independent of the particular social and physical context.
(5) It involves the available energy to perform certain tasks successfully.
(6) It "breaks down" (i.e., disease predominates with various symptoms occurring) when there is insufficient energy or skill to satisfy demands and maintain a sense of balance and harmony.

More recently, health has been conceptualized in more positive terms. The preamble of the Constitution of WHO defines health as a state of complete physical, mental and social well-being and not merely the absence of disease and infirmity. In this definition health is conceptualized as: (i) something which goes beyond the mere absence of disease, and (ii) that health has social and psychological characteristics. However, this definition has been criticized as too vague if not idealistic, leading some researchers to differentiate between "perfect or optimal health" and "normal health" (Coelho, Yuan, & Ahmed, 1980). Interestingly the WHO definition is very close to the definition of health in various treatises of Indian medical science. Sushrut, the ancient proponent of the traditional system of medicine, defined health as a state of delight or a feeling of spiritual, physical and mental well-being (Raina, 1990; Rao, 1983; Sharma, 1981).

Contemporary western thought and practice regarding health is plagued by 'scientism', an attitude which holds that science is the way to attain knowledge of reality. With this preconception and the subsequent employment of a reductionist-empiricist mode of science based on a positivist framework, a dualistic view of health has emerged. Thus physical health is regarded separate from mental health and the two domains are dealt with relatively independently. Such a criticism has led to a shift in focus from a purely biological approach to a bio-psycho-social approach towards the matters of health and disease. The latter approach has often been termed as 'holistic', a general label applied to any philosophical approach that focuses on the whole living organism. The basic axiom of the holistic position is that a complex phenomenon cannot be understood by an analysis of the constituent parts alone.

The traditional systems of medicine in the East, for example, Ayurveda in India are more holistic in their outlook towards matters of health and disease than the allopathic system of medicine. In this context, it needs to be pointed out that holistic medicine in the East goes beyond the whole living organism and views the individual's relationship with his/her social, cultural and spiritual ecology, as well as entire cosmos. In this view the person is embedded in his context.

The foundations of Western allopathic medicine are quite different from those of the indigenous science of Ayurveda. Consequently the structures of knowledge which arise from these two schools differ in many fundamental aspects. More specifically Ayurveda— the science of life, is based on the principle of five elements or the *panchammahbhuta siddhanta*. This principle states that all material reality is made up of the five basic elements—air, water, fire, earth and ether. These elements are organized in various forms, shapes and proportions thus giving rise to the diversity of the phenomenal world. The holistic perspective of Ayurveda is based on the philosophical foundation of the *samkhya, vaishesika* and *yoga* schools of thought. Western foundational theory, on the other hand, is atomistic. The basic differences between allopathy and Ayurveda have led to differences in the concepts found in the two sciences. The theories of causation of disease, pharmacology, dietics, nutrition, etc., are different in these two schools of medicine. For example, in indigenous pharmachology or *dravyaguna shastra*, the entire plant or its parts such as leaves, roots, bark etc., are studied as a whole in terms of their *in vivo* effects on certain parameters of health. In western allopathic medicine, on the other hand, active chemical substances are isolated and extracted from the plant and their *invitro* and *in vivo* effects on different parameters are studied (Shankar, Krishnakumar & Balasubramanium, 1991).

Current developments in scientific thinking also support a holistic outlook towards existence. Now-a-days, attention is getting refocussed on the links across mind-body-society and the larger universe. Views of reality derived from such a mode of thought resemble very closely with the views of reality held in the religion and philosophy of various ancient cultures (Capra, 1975). Matters of health and disease and knowledge of the human mind and body constitute an essential part of the natural philosophy of such cultures (Srinivas Murthy, 1991, 1993).

In traditional Indian treatise on medicine, the idea of maintaining balance has been repeatedly endorsed in the discussions of health and ill-health. Having various qualities in right or natural quantities (*sama*) is considered essential for health. Any distrubance (*asantulan*) in the equilibrium of *dhatu (vata, pitta,* and *kapha*) is considered disease, while the state of their equilibrium is health (Sharma & Dash, 1976; Sinha, 1990). In this analysis aspects of *sama* (in right or natural quantity) are emphasized. Essential features of a healthy person are that he possesses 'in right quantity' (neither too little nor too much) the defects or weaknesses (*samadosh*), digestive quality (*samagni*), semen (*samadhatuy*) and whose bodily functions are normal (*malakriya*).

Contemporary Indian Scenario

As noted above there is now growing awareness that there is intercultural and intracultural diversity in the meaning of health. Also, people employ different explanatory models of mental disorders across cultures. Therapy and healing practices also operate in the context of different discourses on health (Harwood, 1987; Kakar, 1982, 1991; McName & Gergen, 1992; Neki, 1973; Palsane, 1987, 1992; Ram, 1998; Udupa, 1985). All this indicates that the working assumptions in mainstream psychology regarding health represent one and not the only conceptual framework to understand and address health, and related phenomena. Indian thought systems clearly demonstrate a different and viable perspective.

The study of health and stress could only recently receive the attention of Indian psychologists. However, rooted in the western psychological tradition, majority of the published researches have shown little care for their cultural relevance and social applicability. The resulting "asymmetrical transactions," as Sharma (1988) has rightly remarked "have discouraged the growth of indigenous theoretical perspectives and methodologies" (p. 229). Thus the concepts and research tools used and problems pursued through them dealt with aspects of health and stress within western conceptual terms. We find considerable amount of research which tries to replicate the relationships observed in the western literature. But this situation is gradually changing and Indian researchers have started attending to indigenous constructs (Pestonjee, 1992; Prabhu, 1987; Sinha, 1990; Wig, 1990) and analysing the mental health problems and practices in the Indian context (Balodhi, 1990; Chakravarty, 1990; Evans, Palsane & D'Souza, 1983; Kapur, 1995; Nagendra & Nagarathna, 1988; Palsane & Lam, 1997; Satyavati,

1988; Singh, 1990; Srinivas Murthy & Wig, 1993; Verma, 1998).

The overall health scenario in India is not very encouraging and we are far away from the goal of health for all by 2000 A.D. Population growth, poverty, scarce resources, illiteracy, and poor infrastructual facilities are complicating the health care system (VHAI, 1992). Indian society is undergoing different types of transformation which have mixed implications for the quality of life of the people (Harwood, 1987). The introduction of technology, women's education and their entry into the work force, enhanced communication facilities, increased life expectancy and increased international collaboration in business and academic spheres are changing the tempo and complexion of life experiences of the Indian people. These macro level changes coupled with conflicts, dilemmas and frustrations and changes in the value system and life style, are leading to increased health related problems. Children and adolescents are becoming more vulnerable (Broota & Misra, 1997; Carstairs & Kapur, 1976; Dalal, In press; Mane & Ganderia, 1993; S. Malhotra, A. Malhotra & S. Verma, 1991; Tandon, 1994) and incidence of suicide, depression and juvenile delinquency is increasing.

Against this backdrop the students of stress and health have to share a dual responsibility. They have to articulate culturally appropriate concepts and theories which may offer alternate perspectives as well as to constructively inform the professional practices.

REFERENCES

Antonovski, A. (1979). *Health, Stress and Coping*. San Francisco : Jossey-Bass.

Balodhi, J.P. (1990). Psychotherapy based on Hindu philosophy. *Journal of Personality and Clinical Studies*, *6*, 7-12.

Beardsley, L., & Pederson, P. (1997). Health and culture - centered intervention. In J.W. Berry, M.H. Segall & C. Kagitcibasi (Eds.) *Handbook of Cross-Cultural Psychology (vol. 3) Social Behavior and Applications*. Boston : Allyn & Bacon.

Broota, K.D., & Misra, G. (1997). Mental health. In *Fifth Survey of Educational Research*, Vol. I (pp. 106-127). New Delhi : NCERT.

Capewell, S. (1994). Are health and illness defined by society or by doctor? *Proceedings of Royal College of Physicians Edinbarough*. 24, 181-186.

Capra, F. (1975). *The Tao of Physics : An Exploration of the Parallels between Modern Physics and Eastern Mysticism*. Boulder : Shambhala Publications.

Carstairs, G.M., & Kapur, R.L. (1976). *The Great Universe of Kota : Stress, Change and Mental Disorders in an Indian Village*. London : Hogarth Press.

Chakraborty, A. (1990). *Social Stress and Mental Health*. New Delhi : Sage Publications.

Coelho, G.V., Yuan, Ying-ying, & Ahmed, P.I. (1980). Contemporary uprooting and collaborative coping : Behavioral and social responce. In G.V. Coelho & P.I. Ahmed (Eds.), *Uprooting and Development : Dilemmas of Coping with Modernization* (pp. 5-17). New York & London: Plenum Press.

Dalal, A.K. (In Press), Health psychology. In J. Pandey (Ed) *Psychology in India Revisited : Recent Developments in the Discipline*. New Delhi: Sage Publications.

Evans, G.W., Palsane, M.N. & D'Souza, R. (1983). Life stress and health in India. *Indian Psychologist*, 2, 62-77.

Harwood, A. (Ed.) (1987). *Ethnicity and Medical Care*. Cambridge, MA : Harvard University Press.

Kakar, S. (1991). *The Analyst and the Mystic*. New Delhi : Viking-Penguin.

Kakar, S. (1982). *Shamans, Mystics and Doctors : A Psychological Inquiry into India and its Healing Tradition*. London : Unwin Paperbacks.

Kapur, M. (1995). *Mental Health of Indian Children*. New Delhi : Sage Publications.

Kiran Kumar, S.K. (1986). Belief, trust, impulse control and health. *Journal of Social and Economic Studies*, 3, 370-377.

Landrine, H. (1992). Clinical implicaitons of cultural differences : The referential versus the indexical self. *Clinical Psychology Review*. 12, 401-415.

Lewis-Fernandez, R., & Kleinman, A. (1994). Culture, personality and psychopathology. *Journal of Abnormal Psychology*. 103, 67-71.

Malhotra, S., Malhotra, A., & Varma, V.K. (1992). *Child Mental Health in India*. New Delhi : MacMillan India.

Mane, P. & Gandevia, K.Y. (Eds) (1993). *Mental Health in India : Issues and Concerns*. Bombay : Tata Institute of Social Sciences.

Mc. Name, S. & Gergen, K.J. (Eds) (1992). *Therapy as Social Construction*. London : Sage Publications.

Markus, H.R., & Kitayama, S. (1991). Culture and the self : Implications for cognition, emotion and motivation. *Psychological Review*. 98, 224-253.

Mechanic, D. (1986). Health and illness behavior. In J.M. Last (Ed.), *Public Health and Preventive Medicine*. East Norwalk, CT : Appleton-Century-Crofts.

Misra, G., & Gergen, K.J. (1993). On the place of culture in psychological science. *International Journal of Psychology*. 28, 225-243.

Misra, G. (1994). Psychology of control : Cross-cultural considerations. *Journal of Indian Psychology*. 12., 8-45.

Nagendra, H.R., & Nagarathna, R. (1988). *New Perspectives in Stress Management.* Bangalore : Vivekanand Yoga Research Foundation.

Neki, J. S. (1973). Guru-chela relationship : The possibility of therapeutic paradigm. *America Journal of Orthopsychiatry. 43,* 755-766.

Palsane, M.N. (1987). Yoga as psychotherapy. In M.L. Gharote & M. Lockhart (Eds.) *The Art of Survival.* London : Unwin.

Palsane, M.N. (1992). Normality, transcendence and meditation : Indian perspectives. In M. Blowo, & S. Srinivasan (Eds.) *Perspectives on Relaxation and Meditation* (pp. 177-195). Melbourne : Spectrum Publications.

Palsane, M.N., & Lam, D.J. (1997). Stress and coping. In D. Sinha (ed.), *Asian Perspectives in Psychology.* New Delhi : Sage Publications.

Parson, T. (1951). *The Social System.* Glencoe, Illinois : Free Press.

Pestonjee, D.M. (1992). *Stress and Coping : The Indian Experience.* New Delhi : Sage Publications.

Prabhu, G.G. (1987). Child and adolescent mental health research in India : An overview. *NIMHANS Journal. 5,* 79-89.

Raina, B.L. (1990). *Health Sciences in Ancient India.* New Delhi : Common Wealth.

Ram, Usha (1998) (Ed.) *Suffering and Stress Management : West Virsus East.* Pune : Deepa Publications.

Ramlingaswami, P. (1990). Social sciences in the health field in India. *Indian Journal of Social Science. 3,* 107-118.

Rao, S.K.R. (1983). The conception of stress in Indian thought : The theoretical aspects of stress in Samkhya and Yoga systems. *NIMHANS Journal. 2,* 115-121.

Satyavati, K. (1988). Mental health. In J. Pandy (Ed.) *Psychology in India: The State-of-the-art (Vol.2)* (pp. 217-288). New Delhi : Sage Publications.

Shankar, D., Drishnakumar, P.R., & Balasubramanium, A.V. (1991). Indigenous health sciences and western medical sciences : Foundational differences. *India International Quarterly. 18,* 21-25.

Sharma, P. (1981). *Charaka Samhita* (English translation). Varanasi : Chaukhambha Sanskrit Series Office.

Sharma, R.K., & Dash, B. (1976). *Charaka Samhita.* Varanasi : Chaukhambha Sanskrit Series Office.

Sharma, S. (1988). Stress and anxiety. In J. Pandey (Ed.) *Psychology in India : The State-of-the-art.* Vol. 1. (pp. 191-246). Delhi : Sage Publications.

Singh, S. (1990). *Organizational Stress and Executive Behaviour.* New Delhi: Shri Ram Centre for Industrial Relations.

Sinha, D. (1988). The family scenario in a developing country and its implications for mental health : The case of India. In P. Dasen, J.W. Berry & A. Sartorious (Eds.) *Health and Cross-cultural Psychology: Towards Applications.* Newbury Park : Sage Publications.

Sinha, D. (1990). Concept of psycho-social well-being : Western and Indian perspectives. *NIMHANS Journal. 8,* 1-11.

Srinivas Murthy, R. (1991). Holistic medicine : Contributions from behavioural sciences. *Indian International Quarterly. 18,* 205-215.

Srinivas Murthy, R. (1993). Evolution of the concept of mental health :

From mental illness to mental health. In P. Mane & K.Y. Gandevia (Eds.) *Mental Health in India : Issues and Concerns* (pp. 17-42). Bombay : Tata Institute of Social Sciences.

Srinivas Murthy, R., & Wig, N.N. (1993). Evaluation of the progress in mental health in India since independence. In P. Mane & K.V. Gandevia (Eds.) *Mental Health in India : Issues and Concerns* (pp. 337-405). Bombay : Tata Institute of Social Sciences.

Tandon, S.K. (1994). Perspectives of child psychiatry in India. *Indian Journal of Behavioural Sciences, 4*, 17-28.

Tanaka-Matsumi, J. & Draguns, J. (1977). Culture and psychopathology. In J.W. Berry, M.H. Segall & C. Kagitcibasi (Eds.) *Handbook of Cross-cultural Psychology (Vol. 3) Social Behaviour and Applications*. Boston: Allyn & Bacon.

Twaddle, A.C. (1969). Health decisions and sick role variations : An exploration. *Journal of Health and Social Behavior, 10*, 105-114.

Udupa, K.N. (1985). *Stress and its Management by Yoga*. Delhi : Motilal Banarasidas.

Verma, J. (1998). The state of a healthy mind : The Indian worldview. *Journal of Indian Psychology, 16*, 1-9.

Verma, R. (1991). *Psychiatric Social Work in India*. New Delhi : Sage Publications.

Voluntary Health Association of India (1992). *State of India's Health, (Ed.)* Alok Mukhopadhyaya. New Delhi : VHAI.

Wig, N.N. (1990). Indian concepts of mental health and their impact on the case of mentally ill. *International Journal of Mental Health, 18*, 71-80.

2

Illness and Well-being in Relation to Stress, Personality and Culture

M. N. PALSANE and **USHA RAM**

Health, be it mental and/or physical, has been found to be a culturally anchored concept. Culture often defines what is mental health and, as clinical psychologists have come to agree, mental illness or abnormality varies in its definition along the dimension of society and culture. Similarly, this concept has inter-individual and intra-individual variations. That is, while the idea of well-being varies from person to person, it changes within the same individual with age, information (knowledge) and personality variations.

WHO defined health as "a state of complete physical, mental and social well-being and not merely the absence of disease and infirmity". According to the Indian thought as mentioned in Ayurveda by Susruta (Sus. Sutra 15-44), "He that is possessed of the proper balance of the vitia, the metabolic heat, the body-elements and the excretory functions and who is possessed of absolute clarity of the spirit, the senses and the mind, is said to be enjoying perfect health' (cited in *Caraksamhita* vol. I, 1949, p. 577).

Society and culture have long been studied as some of the major determinants of an individual's personality. Personality in trun has been studied by clinical psychologists in their exploration of mental illness. A few psychologists like Rogers and Maslow ventured to understand the mentally healthy. Students of psychophysiological disorders appreciated the relation between socio-cultural and personality aspects in regard to physical and mental illness.

For over fifty years now psychological stress experienced by humans has drawn the interest of psychologists. Prolonged and/or intense stressful experiences have adverse effects on the experiencer's health, physical as well as mental. However, this experience and also its effects, vary from one personality to another just as personality is known to vary from culture to culture. All in all, the personality and culture is the focus and this is the sole theme of this paper.

Stress

Stress is an all-pervading phenomenon in life. It is necessary and useful for personality growth when in optimum quantity. When this optimum level, which varies from person to person, is exceeded, the costs are experienced in the form of health problems and illnesses besides many other consequences. Compilations of studies on stress-health relationship indicate that this area has been studied for long (e.g. Dohrenwend & Dohrenwend, 1974; Kaplan, 1996; Levine & Ursin, 1980; Rabkin & Struening, 1976; Selye, 1980).

Stress has been defined as a stimulus and also as a response. Stress stimuli or stressors are of three major types (Lazarus & Cohen, 1977) : major changes or events (e.g. wars, floods) that affect many; major changes or events (e.g. getting married, death of a family member) that affect one or a few; and daily hassles or incidents in daily living which irritate or distress one. Hence describing stimuli to be stressors would depend on the response elicited by the stimuli. This then refers to the relation between the stimulus (stressor) and person, emphasizing the person-characteristics. The stimulus-response approach to stress is circular as it asks what (stimulus) elicits a stress response and what (response) indicates a particular stressor.

Psychological stress then is a particular relationship between the person and the environment that is appraised by the person as taxing or exceeding his or her resources and endangering his or her well-being. This reiterates French *et al.*, (1974) concept of person-environment misfit occurring as a result of the environmental demands which are made on the person and being appraised as a threat, thus leading to stress, and affecting his or her well-being.

Stress may be operationalized, and measured by physiologically measures like blood-pressure, GSR, hormonal assays. Psychological measures include inventories of major life events, role stress, life change, occupational stress, environmental stress, daily hassles and so on.

Effects of Stress

Stress affects an individual in a variety of ways like narrowing the span of attention, bringing about certain cognitive deficits, inducing helplessness and irritability, affecting performance adversely, affecting physical and psychological health, and so on. This relationship between stress and its effects is complex. An inverted 'U' type relationship with performance indicates temporary improvement before deterioration begins. Chronic stress has costs which are cumulative in nature and this is most common in relation to physical and mental health.

Stress effects on individual's health may be of short-term or long-term nature. Elevation in blood pressure has been observed in cases of anger and anxiety, stressful interviews, loss of job, and natural disasters (Ax, 1953; Innes, Millar & Valentine, 1959; Kasl & Cobb, 1970; Ruskin, Board, & Schaffer, 1948). Prolonged rise in blood pressure is found in those who face stress for long periods as was seen in Kasl and Cobb's (1970) study of loss of employment.

Ulcers have been found twice as often among air-traffic controllers as among the pilots. That the latter have greater control over their planes than do the former is one of the probable reasons for this difference (Cobb & Rose, 1973).

As the duration of stress gets prolonged the individual's efforts and resources of coping start diminishing. This leads to psychopathology (Brown & Harris, 1978; Lazarus,

1977). Methods to cope with stress are varied and mental illness is just one of these (Cochrane, 1983). Similarly, schizophrenia has been found to be often preceded by stress occurring from recent life events (Spring & Coons, 1982). Prediction of schizophrenia in genetically high-risk males has been found to be an independent or an interaction effect of obstetric complications, maternal absence and institutional child-care (Beuhring *et al.*, 1982).

Social stress arising from marriage and parenting have been found to be closely related to depression (Ilfeld, 1977). One of the underlying factors in depression could be of a neurochemical kind, and neurochemical changes may be triggered off by stress (Anisman & La Pierre, 1982).

Adverse social conditions associated with stressors operate to create depression and these have been identified. Prolonged social conditions of the adverse kind tend to decrease the levels of self-esteem and self-confidence among people who tend to break down during difficulties (Brown & Harris, 1978). Similarly, higher degree of psychiatric symptoms were found to be more frequent among the lower class persons (Myers, Lindenthal & Pepper, 1974).

Frequent adjustment to changes in life because of the occurrence of life events increases the proneness to diseases as a result of lowering of resistance to diseases (Holmes & Masuda, 1984). Similarly, greater number of hassles of daily living also contribute to stress experiences (Kanner *et al.*,1981).

Along with changes or events, environmental and/or personal, is to be found the individual's life-style which includes eating habits, exercise, drinking habits, ways of coping with life, use of drugs and tobacco (Haggerty, 1977). The Type A Behaviour Pattern (TABP) (to be discussed later) has been found to have a cultural validity and predictability of coronary heart-diseases (CHD) (Rosenman & Chesney, 1982).

All these studies indicate a relationship between stressors on the one hand and physical and mental wellness or illness on the other. This is seen from Fig. 2.1.

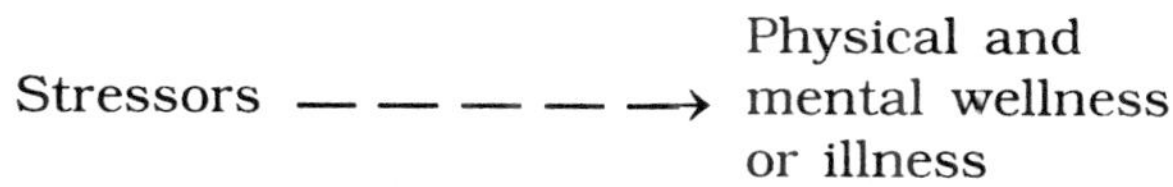

FIG. 2.1. Relationship between stress and health

The stressors in other words are related to physical and mental illness or well-being. There are, however, some intervening variables related to the strengths and weaknesses of individuals, groups or communities. These may be genetic, congenital, cognitive, motivational, social, and cultural in nature. Therefore, the intervening variables may fall into two major categories, i.e. individual variables, and social and cultural variables. This is seen in Fig. 2.2, a modification of Fig. 2.1.

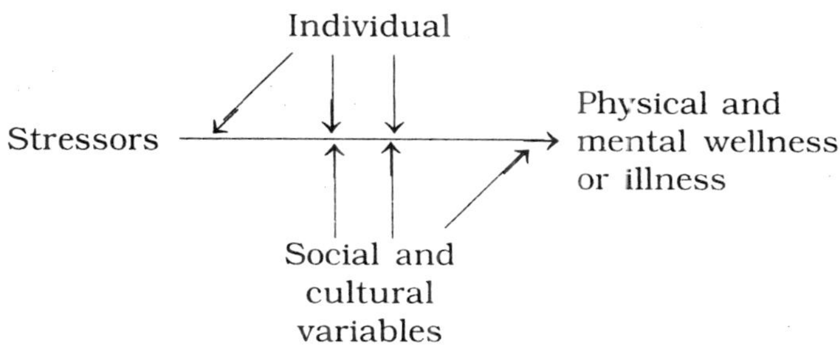

FIG. 2.2. Relationship between stress and health through individual and socio-cultural variables

The ultimate model may not be as simple as this one, but perhaps it serves the purpose in the present context. This model brings out the fact that the relationship between stress and illness is often mediated or moderated by the two sets of variables, those within and those outside the individual. These are briefly discussed below.

Personality

Wallace (1970) defined personality as "those ways of behaviour or techniques of solving problems which have a high probability of use by one individual". These comprise the intervening variables between stress and health.

The individual variables may be enduring motivational, attitudinal and personality characteristics as well as more temporary features like current cognitions, physical conditions and recently experienced stresses and hassles. In this paper, the individual variables are restricted to TABP (Friedman & Rosenman, 1974), psychosocial competence (Tyler, 1978) and hardiness (Kobasa, 1979).

Type A Behaviour Pattern (TABP)

Rosenman *et al.* (1964) described this coronary-prone behaviour pattern as being characterised by competitiveness (hard-pushing); multiphasic achievement orientation, that is, wanting to achieve and do more than one thing at a time; chronic activation, that is a tendency to stay active most of the time of the wakeful part of the day; a sense of time urgency, that is speed in almost everything done like eating, talking etc., as if time is running out on the person by the seconds; easy arousability, and hostility or anger. Hostility/anger dimension is the 'major' if not the 'only' coronary-prone element (Wright, 1988).

Psychosocial competence

The behavioural attributes of psychosocial competence have been described by Tyler (1978). This behaviour is characterised by active coping orientation, high initiative, realistic goal-setting, substantial planning, forbearance and effort to attain these goals, and a capacity to enjoy success, suffer failure and benefit from both. This is a fully developed process through which an individual interacts with his psychosocial environment. This environment includes events within his life space, including himself. It is an ongoing pattern which is both constructive and defensive, cognitive and affective, intrinsic and extrinsic, a process which is also structural. These skills, in fact, function as "energising, tempering and guiding qualities of human behaviour". They aim at mastery rather than "fit". These attributes do not get activated only in the face of stress nor are they restricted to any life stage, but "are a function of the individual's organic, psychological, and social development and current functioning" (Tyler & Pargament, personal communication, 1983).

Hardiness

A cluster of three traits, namely, commitment, control and challenge constitute the variable of hardiness according to Kobasa (1979). A person who is high in commitment tends to have a personal involvement in the performance of the activity rather than functioning in a detached, alienated way. Those with a high sense of control tend to believe that they have control and influence over most of the things happening around them. They, therefore, do not feel powerless vis-a-vis external force. People with hardiness also have a high sense of challenge in viewing life, and to them the changes in life are normal and they perceive these changes as a stimulus for growth rather than a "threat to security". Kobasa *et al.*, (Kobasa, 1979; Kobasa, Maddi & Courington, 1982; Kobasa, Maddi & Kahn, 1982; Kobasa, Maddi & Puccetti, 1982) have found through retrospective and prospective studies that hardiness functioning as buffer between stress and severity of illness symptoms, reduces the latter. Their studies show little relationship of hardiness to stressful life events, job, constitutional strengths, exercise, social support, age, education, marital status or religious practices. But hardiness in combination with constitutional strengths and exercise protect against ill health strongly. Hardiness along with certain social supports also seems to be effecitve against illness (personal communication, 1982).

Culture

Wallace (1970) defines culture as "those ways of behaviour or techniques of solving problems which, being more frequently and more closely approximated than other ways, (which) can be said to have high probability of use by individual members of society". These very 'ways' and 'techniques' comprise the intervening social and cultural variables in the stress-health relationship.

Culture consists of the customs, manners, values, beliefs, religious behaviours, social and intellectual characteristics of a society which mould an individual personality. As seen earlier personality characteristics are related to stress experience. And if personality is determined to a considerable extent by culture, the latter is related to stress through personality to affect one's well-being.

To say that human beings operate or function within the frame of society and culture would sound too simplistic to make any statement about socio-cultural effects on human behaviour. There are universals in beliefs, attitudes, values, motivations, cognitions, personality and, for that matter, the entire spectrum of behaviour of individuals. They have their origin in an individual's need to live in groups for his survival and these groups develop ways of adaptation appropriate to environmental demands which get stabilised over time. This being a continuous and dynamic process, the 'personality' of every 'culture' keeps changing with time and changes if the group decides to migrate to new place. Just as, for a psychologist, the terms society and culture are abstractions, it is possible to look at the individual also as an abstraction rather than a concrete reality for a simple reason that he shares with others common biological structures, common psychological, social and cultural entities of behaviour. It is this perspective that brings in the role of cultural variables in stress and illness. The discipline of medical anthropology deals with this subject matter.

By definition, culture is "that complex whole which includes knowledge belief, art, morals, law, custom and any other capabilities and habits acquired by man as a member of society" (Tylor, 1871, cited in Helman, 1984). Culture determines how an individual views his world and how he behaves in it in relation to other persons, natural and physical environment as well as supernatural forces. Management of the misfortunes is a part of cultural training, and there are institutionalised ways of dealing with stresses and sufferings of various sorts.

Most of the concepts which involve society and culture are necessarily defined by the given society and culture. Hence, culture-specific definitions are found of health, illness, abnormality and normality. For instance, it is a matter of greater prestige as the number of skulls strung around a hunter's neck increase in a hunting community while this would be deemed criminal in a civilized society. Even while diagnosing psychiatric or counselling cases it is necessary to consider the client's socio-cultural background as much as that of the psychiatrist or counsellor diagnosing them. An adolescent in urban India reacts rather less to directives from (authoritative) parents as against an American or European adolescent. Therefore, an American psychiatrist might find an Indian adolescent rather submissive and judge him so. Helman (1984) in fact found that the diagnostician's personality and experience, social class, ethnic and cultural background, political and religious following influence his/her diagnosis.

Modes of treatment also vary with the culture. There are popular methods of treatment as also folk and professional. In the popular method may be found self-treatment ranging from changes in food intake through fasting. In southern United States, a common folk usage is of acidic or astringent food like vinegar or lemon. "Bitters" and "tonics" are known to be used in Britain to regain health. Two common traditional treatments for the common cold may be found in India : if the cold has occurred due to exposure to cold wind, or rain, concoctions made from spices like dried ginger, corriander seeds, and pepper corns are consumed. If the cold has been contracted through stomach upset or indigestion, etc., the person may stay off regular food and consume a lot of warm, easy-to-digest fluids. In most traditional groups in several parts of the world are to be found home-remedies which are generally found in stock with the 'granny women'. Among the professional treatment are to be found besides the western allopathic and homeopathic, the Unani, the ayurvedic and the acupuncture methods, the latter three belonging to Asian sciences of medicine. Finkler (1981) found folk-healing to be useful for neurotic, psychophysiological and somatic disorders though not so for psychosis. The etiology of diseases is perceived in primitive cultures as wrath of a god, or a consequence of doing a wrong deed. Similarly, a religious view would attribute misfortune to "god's will".

Just as stressors would vary from one individual to another it could vary with cultural variations, too. The role of culture in experience of and response to stress could be protective or pathogenic. It influences the manifestation of stress response in a comprehensible 'language of distress' (Helman, 1984, p. 172) that is typical of a culture. Thus we find stress response varying though the stressor is same across cultures. Responses vary even within a cultural group and this may be attributed to personality factors. Guthrie *et al.*, (1975) in a study of some cultural groups found that Americans' response was in terms of more gastrointestinal symptoms, the French experienced changes in mood or thought, while Filipino women displayed more cardiovascular symptoms like increased heartbeat and shortness of breath. Women in all these groups studied reported dizziness, headaches, nightmares and muscle twitches. Guthrie *et al.* (1975) suggest that this may be so as 'in certain societies it may be less socially acceptable for males to admit and experience this constellation of symptoms'.

Cultures like Indian or Buddhist value meditation and contemplation more than competitive and materialistic achievements. Members of such cultures may be experiencing less stress and may be having greater stress-tolerance. This does not, however, over-rule the possibility or existence of stress in traditional and primitive societies. Stress is not a prerogative of modern society!

The ancient Indian society was in fact traditional and yet the then thinkers have delineated the concept, etiology and management of stress (Palsane *et al.*, 1986). Cultural beliefs, values, and practices play an important role in creating stressors as they do in preventing stress and therefore, certain types of stress are culture-specific. A culture specifies what is a good or bad event, a good deed or a bad deed, or success and failure, and variations among these are many in different societies. Every culture has norms of living and the members try to reach these standards. Therefore, "keeping up with the Joneses", or not "losing face" may be found in most cultures in some way or the other. Hence, failure to achieve the standards formulated within a given culture can become stressful. Possessing an 'X' model car may be prestigious in an urban modern society, while having 500 healthy cows may be so in a dairy-farming society.

Some belief in itself can be stressful as in case of the African tribals who practise and believe in 'voodoo' magic. Belief in curse can bring about adverse effects on the believers, almost as severe as death. But at the same time in some cultures along with the belief in curse are to be found ways of coping with it. For instance, in traditional Indian communities where such beliefs prevail may be found also ways of accepting the curse as part of one's fate or performing som rites to "undo" the curse. The latter could then function as "belief-in-action heals".

Examples of culturogenic stress are plenty in anthropological studies. For instance, 'magical death' which Landy (1977 p. 327) terms as socio-cultural death is found in Caribbean and Australia among the pre-industrial societies. In this, a person believes he is marked out for death and his group members perceive him as being doomed to death and soon withdraw from him telling him of his doom. Within 48 hours this person dies under the stress of the knowledge of being doomed to death. In modern societies, though of lesser intensity, culturogenic stress may be arising from the diagnostic labels. As Scheff (1966) pointed out, such labelling can affect the person's behaviour, social relationships, self-perception and others' behaviour towards him. The diagnostic labels could function as self-fulfilling prophecies to the person.

The cultural values of a group function as protection against stress. An example of this is the type of family. A cohesive, mutually supportive family can help its individual member to cope better with the problems of life (Helman, 1984). Bringing up children can be quite stressful in modern urban homes. But when this function is shared by several adults as in joint or extended families, it helps prevention of severe stress experience. The stress arising from uncertainty gets reduced when one belongs to a group and shares its value system, thus making life more meaningful and more controlled or predictable.

Other cultural values may include, beside the above, communal disturbances, wars, competition for marriage partner, dowry, materialistic acquisitions, and unequal distribution of wealth generating fear of the poor and poverty, thus leading to stress. Hence the significant role of culture in stress, personality and health.

Approaches to Study Stress Related Phenomena

Investigating into the relationship among stress, illness, well-being, personality and culture is complex. A continuous effort made by various disciplines jointly would provide meaning and depth to such a study. The disciplines like cultural anthropology, sociology and philosophy lend insight into the nature of values, beliefs, and practices of the different peoples from various societies while psychology would delve into the behaviour being affected by these factors. The medical sciences would be required to study the epidemiology of the health-illness dimension. All these disciplines have studied stress-health independently for some time now. For a better understanding of the relationship a greater interaction between the workers from all these disciplines is necessary. This will then generate an inter-disciplinary approach to the study and perhaps this will pave the way to the ultimate holistic approach to health.

Cross-cultural studies are an inevitable aspect of stress-health research. As has been seen from the discussion earlier, culture affects both personality and health. Though relationship between culture and health has been established for long, this cannot be generalized. For instance, in some of the industiral societies the values may be very materialistic and therefore the members experiencing stress in the race to attain higher materialistic levels may be prone to heart diseases. In some other cultures the incidence of heart diseases may be very low but that of gastro-intestinal diseases may be higher. The specificity of illness in a culture cannot be generalized. Though there are similarities in cultures, the differences are many. It is then the cultural dimension that brings about the variations in the experience of both stress and health. These differences in cultures along with similarities are therefore, important in the understanding the stress-health relationship through personality. Most of the studies are undertaken in small localized areas and are essentially monocultural. Considering the cultural variations in the concepts, the processes as well as the outcomes, such studies need cross-cultural validation for the purposes of theory construction.

Epidemiological effects of stress take their toll over long periods. Hence the need for long-term studies, that is, longitudinal studies. The studies conducted in this field have been largely cross-sectional and mostly of the correlational nature. The cause-effect relationships require long-term follow-up studies. Such studies are prospective rather than retrospective and methodologically superior. Continuous follow-up gives a more elaborate profile of the process and the intermediate outcomes or effects.

The preceding discussion of methodologies indicates major lacunae in the present designs. However, it is far more difficult, time-consuming and expensive to adopt the suggested methodologies. This is precisely the reason why they are used less often. They are suggested only to indicate the present deficiency. Unless these are made up, the theory construction in this field may not progress much.

REFERENCES

Anisman, H., & La Piere, Y. (1982). Neurochemical aspects of stress and depression : Formulations and caveats. In R.W.J. Neufeld (ed.) *Psychological Stress and Psychopathology*. New York : McGraw-Hill.

Ax, A.F. (1953). The physiological differentiation between fear and anger in humans. *Psychosomatic Medicine, 15*, 433-442.

Beuhring, T., Cudek, R., Mednick, S.A., Walker, E.F., & Schulsinger, F. (1982). Vulnerability to environmental stress: High-risk research on the development of schizophrenia. In R.W.J. Neufeld (ed.) *Psychological Stress and Psychopathology*. (pp 67-90). New York : McGraw-Hill.

Brown, G.W., & Harris, T. (1978). *Social Origins of Depression : A Study of Psychiatric Disorder in Women*. London: Tavistock.

Carakasamhita. Vol. I (1949). Jamnagar, India : Shree Gulabkunverba Ayurvedic Society.

Cobb, S., & Rose, R.M. (1973). Hypertension, peptic ulcer, and diabetes in air traffic controllers. *Journal of the American Medical Association, 224*, 489-493.

Cochrane, R. (1983). *The Social Creation of Mental Illness*. London: Longman.

Dohrenwend, B.S., & Dohrenwend, B.P. (eds.) (1974). *Stressful Life Events : Their Nature and Effects*. New York : Wiley & Sons.

Finkler, K (1981). Non-medical treatments and their outcomes. Part two : Focus on the adherents of spiritualism. *Cultural Medical Psychiatry, 5*, 65-103.

French, J.R.P., Jr., Rodgers, W.L., & Cobb, S. (1974). Adjustment as person-environment fit. In G.V. Coelho, D.A. Hamburgh, & J.E. Adams (eds.), *Coping and Adaptation*. (pp 316-333). New York : Basic Books.

Friedman, M. Rosenman, R.H. (1974). *Type A Behavior and Your Heart*. New York : Knopf.

Guthrie, G.M., Verstraete, A., Deines, M.M., & Stern, R.M. (1975). Symptoms of stress in four societies. *Journal of Social Psychology, 95*, 165-172.

Haggerty, K. (1977). Changing life styles to improve health. *Preventive Medicine, 6*, 276-289.

Helman, C. (1984). *Culture, Health and Illness*. Bristol : Wright PSG.

Holmes, T.H., & Masuda, M. (1984). Life change and illness susceptibility. In B.S. Dohrenwend, & B.P. Dohrenwend (eds.) *Stressful Life Events : Their Nature and Effects*. (45-86) New York : Wiley & Sons.

Ilfeld, F.W. (1977). Current social stressors and symptoms of depression. *American Journal of Psychiatry, 134*, 161-166.

Innes, G., Millar, W.M., & Valentine, M. (1959). Emotion and blood pressure. *Journal of Mental Medicine, 105*, 840-851.

Jenkins, C.D. (1975). The coronary-prone personality. In W.D. Gentry & R.B. Williams (eds.). *Psychological Aspects of Myocardial Infarction and Coronary Care*. St. Louis : Mosby.

Jenkins, C.D., Zyzanski, S.J., & Rosenman, R.H. (1979). *Jenkins' Activity Survey (Form C): Manual.* New York: Psychological Corporation.

Kaplan, H.B. (1996). *Psychosocial stress.* New York : Academic Press.

Kasl, S.V., & Cobb, S. (1970). Blood pressure changes in men undergoing job loss: A preliminary report. *Psychosomatic Medicine, 6,* 95-106.

Kobasa, S.C. (1979). Stressful life events, personality and health: An inquiry into hardiness. *Journal of Personality and Social Psychology, 37,* 1-11.

Kobasa, S.C., & Maddi, S.R. (1977). Existential personality theory. In R. Corsini (ed.), *Current personality theories.* (pp 243-276). Itasca, Ill.: Peacock.

Kobasa, S.C., Maddi, S.R., & Courington, S. (1981). Personality and constitutional mediators in the stress illness relationship. *Journal of Health and Social Behavior, 22,* 368-378.

Kobasa, S.C., Maddi, S.R., & Kahn, S. (1982). Hardiness and health: A prospective study. *Journal of Personality and Social Phychology, 42,* 168-177.

Kobasa, S.C., Maddi, S.R., & Puccetti, M.C. (1982). Personality and exercise as buffers in the stress-illness relationship. *Journal of Behavioral Medicine, 5,* 391-404.

Landy, D. (ed.) (1977). *Culture, Disease and Healing: Studies in Medical Anthropology.* New York: Macmillan.

Lazarus, R.S. (1977). *Psychological Stress and the Coping Process.* New York: McGraw-Hill.

Lazarus, R.S., & Cohen, J.B. (1977). Environmental stress. In I. Altman, & J.F.Wohlhill (eds.), *Human Behavior and the Environment: Current Theory and Research.* (pp 90-127). New York: Plenum.

Lazarus, R.S., & Folkman, S. (eds.) (1984). *Stress, Appraisal, and Coping.* New York: Springer.

Levine, S., & Ursin, H. (1980). *Coping and Health.* New York : Plenum.

Myers, J.K., Lindenthal, J.J., & Pepper, M.P. (1974). Social class, life events, and psychiatric symptoms : A longitudinal study. In B.S. Dohrenwend, & B.P. Dohrenwend (eds.), *Stressful Life Events : Their Nature and Effects.* (pp. 191-205). New York : Wiley & Sons.

Neufeld, R.W.J. (ed.) (1982). *Psychological Stress and Psychopathology.* New York: McGraw-Hill.

Palsane, M.N., Bhavsar, S.N., Goswami, R.P., & Evans, G.W.

(1986). The concept of stress in the Indian tradition. *Journal of Indian Psychology, 5*, 1-12.

Rabkin, J.G., & Struening, E.L. (1976). Life events, stress, and illness. *Science*, 1013-1020.

Risenman, R.H., & Chesney, M.A. (1982). Stress, Type A behavior and coronary disease. In L. Goldberger, & S. Breznitz (eds.), *Handbook of Stress*. (pp 547-565). New York: Free Press.

Rosenman, R.H., Friedman, M., Straus, R. Wurm, M., Kositschek, R. Hahn, W., & Werthessen, N.T. (1964). A predictive study of coronary heart disease: The western collaborative group study. *Journal of the Medical Association, 189*, 15-22.

Ruskin, A., Board, O.W., & Schaffer, R.L. (1948).Blast hypertension: Elevated arterial pressure in victims of the Texas city disaster. *American Journal of Medicine, 4*, 228-236.

Scheff, T.J. (1966) *Being Mentally Ill: A Sociological Theory*. Chicago : Aldine.

Selye, H. (ed.) (1980). *Selye's Guide to Stress: Research Vol. I*. New York: Van Nostrand.

Spring, B., & Coons, F. (1982). Stress as a precursor of schizophrenic episodes. In R.W.J. Neufeld (ed.) *Psychological Stress and Psychopathology*. New York: McGraw-Hill.

Tyler, F.B. (1978). Individual psychosocial competence: A personality configuration. *Educational and Psychological Measurement, 38*, 309-323.

Tyler, F.B., & Pargament, K.I. (1983). The behavioral attributes of psychosocial competence. Mimeographed paper received through personal communication.

Wallace, A.F.C. (1970). *Culture and Personality*. New York: Random House.

World Health Organization (1946). *Constitution of the World Health Organization*. Geneva: The Author.

Wright, L. (1988).The Type A behaviour pattern and coronary artery disease: Quest for the active ingredients and the elusive mechanism. *American Psychologist, 43*, 2-14.

3

Social Psychology and Health Behaviour

DURGANAND SINHA

In recent years the most exciting development in psychology has been the demolition — or more appropriately, expansion — of its traditional boundaries through its interface with other disciplines. One such interface is with health where the union appears to be most auspicious. Association of psychological functioning with health has been recognized in India since ancient times. Sushrut, the ancient proponent of traditional system of medicine, has defined health as *prassannanmendriyamanah swastha*, i.e., health is a state of delight or feeling of spiritual, physical and mental well-being. This was many centuries before the WHO conceptualized it as a positive state of complete physical, mental and social well-being and not simply as absence of disease. Such a characterization at once suggests a model that goes beyond the more prevalent bio-medical approach to health and puts emphasis on entire individual and his social functioning.

Psychology is at once a science and a profession. Unlike many other social sciences, the link between the two is more intimate and inseparable. Therefore, it is not at all surprising that almost from the very beginning, there has been association of modern scientific psychology with health. Historically, a number of things have happened that have ensured the place of psychology in the area of health. Mental testing, entry of psychology into hospital and clinical setting, especially since the Second World War, and the introduction of counselling in educational and other spheres have provided a strong impetus to the psychodiagnostic approach. But these professional areas traditionally have induced primarily the delivery of mental health services to individuals typified by doctor-patient relationship, with emphasis on diagnosis, therapy and care, leading to the improved health and development of the individual.

Psychological factors in the treatment and care of individual patients is a vigorous field of research and practice. Though it represents largely a medical approach, it has seriously shaken the concept of disease as being purely bio-medical, and has led to what has been called the *bio-psychological* point of view. This is more in the case of Primary Health Care (PHC) work that has now expanded to cover the entire health system. PHC faces an increasing number of complex socio-cultural and economic problems. As pointed out in a WHO/SEORO publication (1986, pp. 7-8), "even when easily available, some maternal and child health and family planning services were under-utilized. Even when medically successful, expanded immunization programmes and tuberculosis and leprosy treatment programmes encountered distressingly high drop-out rates. And even with all the best intentions, community participation in major campaigns, such as malaria control and water and sanitary programmes, proved much more difficult to achieve than originally thought. *Health, it turned out, required more than health services* (Emphasis is author's)". Control of smoking which is not only carcinogenic but also associated with hyper-tension, is another case in point. Smoking is often a socially accepted habit and is enmeshed in cultural tradition. Among elite groups, it is even considered as an assertion of status. Therefore, any programme for the control of smoking must understand the social aspects of the behaviour before any effective programme for it can be designed.

Underlying the bio-psychological perspective, there are two major premises: (a) health is not a bio-medical problem but one which is influenced by cultural, social, economic and psychological aspects of the life of the people concerned; and (b) most causes of illness and total well-being are not genetic in origin but environmental, and thus controllable by human society. In other words, health and illness are not simply a bio-medical problem but have psychological, social and economic dimensions as well. Full understanding of health requires a holistic concept — as indicated in the definitions of Sushrut or the WHO — which provides due recognition of socio-cultural aspects.

Preventive and Promotive Aspects of Health

Importance of cultural and psychological factors comes out more prominently in the preventive and promotive aspects of health. From earlier concern for mental health and well-being of the individual and individual psychotherapy the acceptance of the goal of HFA (Health for All by the year 2000) as embodied in the Alma Ata Declaration of the WHO has made the contribution of psychology to health of the community of signal importance. Four factors exert influence and finally determine the health status of a person. These are the effects of the environment, the behavioural patterns and lifestyles of the individual, development and provision of health services and the hereditary and genetic constitution. The final outcome of health status is determined by the interplay of these four factors. In other words, illness is not only a medical but a socio-psychological phenomenon. Much of what is experienced as illness stems largely from the *behaviour* of the individual rather than simply from pathogens of a biological origin. Such health related behaviours as smoking, drug and alcohol abuse, overeating, excessive use of salt, failure to use safety belt, failure to seek medical care, and engaging in highly stressful lifestyle are but a few 'behaviour pathogens' responsible for serious illness.

Scientists who have worked in third world countries like India and the Philippines (Guthrie, 1988) have observed that behaviour pathogens are often responsible for malnutrition, higher fertility and spread of infectious diseases. Folk beliefs and practices, for example, often lead to denial to the baby of mother's milk which is not only high in nutrient qualities but also provides immunity conferring agents. There is resistance to reliable method of contraception due to unreal fear of side effects. Similarly, people's belief system and general apathy have been responsible for distressingly high drop-out rates encountered in immunization, tuberculosis and leprosy treatment programmes.

In developing countries like India, widespread poverty and paucity of resources create difficulties for proper treatment and health care for large masses of people. Government expenditure on health has been negligible. Individual health care is expensive and much beyond the means of a vast majority of the population. If Health for All is our accepted goal, emphasis has to be not only on the individual and curative aspects of illness but more on *promotion of health* and *prevention of illness*. Since they involve the community and society at large, it is a fertile area for social psychology to operate. Recent advances in health care have reinforced the belief that the promotion of health and prevention of illness can be significantly enhanced by incorporating the scientific findings and modern technology of psychology.

Diseases of Deprivation and Affluence

The epidemiological picture in India has changed. Certain disturbing trends are emerging with respect to both communicable and non-communicable diseases. Though economic development has taken place, acute poverty and miseries associated with it still remain. This has produced a paradoxical scenario. Comparison of the latest census figures with those of earlier years reveal that India has the unique distinction of having high incidence of the diseases of deprivation as well as those of affluence. Malnutrition, and respiratory, digestive and parasitic diseases which are aggravated by poverty and lack of environmental hygiene remain rampant. Malaria and some other vector-borne diseases which were almost eradicated about a couple of decades back, seem to be making a vigorous come-back in many developing countries. Resistance to DDT that mosquitoes have developed is not the only reason. There are linkages between the patterns of socio-economic development and the epidemiology of malaria. Rapid increase in irrigational facilities and factors associated with Green Revolution that have changed the ecology have created optimal conditions for the resurgence and spread of malaria and some other vector-borne diseases. People's belief system, attitudes and behaviour in this regard stand in the way of programmes for the control and elimination of these diseases.

On the other side, there is alarming increase in cardio-vascular ailments, cancer and disabilities and deaths due to accidents. Change in lifestyle with economic prosperity has made the population highly susceptible to diseases of affluence. Socio-economic and psychological factors are to a considerable extent responsible for it. The belief of health psychologists that lifestyle and health are correlated closely is generally accepted. At the present time, most serious diseases in the highly industrialized countries are chronic conditions which may be prevented or modified by changing behaviour that generates ill-health. These ailments are neither infectious nor contagious, nor are there vaccines or pharmacological *cures* for them. But they invariably have a behavioural correlate which can be modified and controlled. In fact, behavioural research that involves persuading groups of people to change their behaviour in order to ascertain whether modifying a risk-factor can alter the incidence and the cause of disease has become a promising area of research for psychologists and behavioural scientists. Behavioural epidemiology is the obvious outcome.

Coronary-prone Behaviour Pattern

Identification of "coronary-prone behaviour pattern" or *Type A* behaviour has been a signficant step in this direction. The pattern of behaviour that is observed in a lot of coronary cases is characterized by excessively competitive drive, impatience, hostility and quick movements. Realization of this has not only an impact on the case of individual patient, but has led to programmes for the prevention of one of the main "killers" in industrially advanced countries. High level of stress is the general outcome of the pattern of behaviour exhibited by *Type A* people. Further, with development and modernization, both physical and psychological stressors have increased with resultant rise in the incidence of cardio-vascular and stress-related ailments. Environmental stressors also, like noise, over-crowding, temperature, air pollution, and innumerable daily hassles have gone up abnormally. These constitute the objective dimensions of stress-related diseases. But the effects are not simply linked with the physical characteristics of the environment. Equally important is how the individual perceives and interprets these potential stressors and emotionally responds to them. In other words the kind of coping mechanism for these noxious stimuli that he develops constitutes an important element in the curative factors of stress-related illnesses.

There are many other sources of stressors in our personal, social and work environment. Work overload and work schedules, meeting deadlines, roles in social and organizational functioning that are often ambiguous, if not conflicting, social relations at work, organizational climate, speed and hustle that are associated with urban living, and innumerable other aspects of so-called modern life singly as well as cumulatively make the life of the individual stressful. Health psychologists have analysed the kind of coping responses the individual develops to these stressors, and their linkage with health. The way one learns to cope with these stressors and social and familial support systems in this regard have been found to be significant moderators in the relationship between stress induced effects and various stress-related diseases. In this context, the age old adage to be concerned with the *process* of work and not its *outcome* may have positive prophylactic influence (Pande & Naidu, 1986). The part played by the kind of almost obsessive concern for *result* that modern management practices borrowed from the West in episodes of cardio-vascular ailments and incidence of by-pass surgeries in young and aspiring business executives in their thirties and early forties cannot be lightly brushed aside. On the other hand, the social support system that has generally existed in Indian society— though it is already showing signs of waning — is supposed to serve as a cushion to stress factors.

The role of psychology and other behavioural sciences in checking the incidence of cardio-vascular illness and promoting health in an entire community have nowhere been brought out so convincingly as in North Korelia Project in Finland. Though a largely rural community and depending for its livelihood on agriculture and forests, the incidence of cardio-vascular ailments was extraordinarily higher in the region than elsewhere in Finland. In the project, beginning in 1972, very high rate of smoking and a few other aspects in the life style of the community were observed. With the aid of a team of social scientists, a community based large-scale educational intervention programme was launched. Among other things, it brought about over a period of five years drastic reduction in the level of smoking and other cardio-vascular risk factors (i.e., hypertension, elevated cholestrol and so on) among the population. The project demonstrated how many of our daily habits and elements in our lifestyle make us prone to certain ailments which could be successfully located, altered and controlled by the application of psychological technology. The emphasis in North Korelia Project was not simply on health education, but bringing about a change in the lifestyle using the principle of social learning, community organization, communication-persuasion efforts and behaviour modification techniques. It demonstrated conclusively that the health of the community could be improved and incidence of killer diseases could be drastically brought down by modifying the lifestyle of people in the health enhancing direction.

Psycho-social Factors in Malnutrition

Malnutrition is world's most serious health problem. It is especially the case in the developing countries where 75 per cent of children live. More than half of them are short and underweight for their age. Many ailments are the consequences of malnutrition which lowers the resistance and makes the child more vulnerable to communicable diseases. Poverty and lack of resources are the main causes of malnutrition. The problem, however, gets aggravated by the fact that due to ignorance and lack of information, mothers adopt practices that are at times unhygenic and stand in the way of utilizing the available indigenous resources to combat malnutrition. For example, mother's milk especially at delivery and in the ensuing weeks provides important immunity-conferring agents and is an invaluable protection against the infections of the neonate, and is also uniquely suited to the digestive capabilities of the human infant. But certain prevalent beliefs and mistaken ideas have often been responsible for the sudden termination of lactation to the detriment of the nutritional status and health of the infant.

Studies have shown that mere possession of information and knowledge about baby feeding does not materially improve the situation. Information does not necessarily get transformed into actual behaviour, nor does the effectiveness of knowledge always increase with education (Guthrie, 1988).

Compliance Problem

Similar is the case with over-eating, over-weight, smoking, heavy consumption of alcohol and of drugs, absence of physical exercise that are correlated with non-communicable diseases like cancer, hypertension, and cardio-vascular ailments. The problem is not lack of information or knowledge. We know the health hazards to which we expose ourselves due to these habits. People do not easily alter their behaviour and lifestyle to ward off the dangers. This inability of the person to change his behaviour in the best interest of his health (as in the case of Filipino mothers for the sake of nutrition and health of the child), is indeed a manifestation of what can be called "compliance problem" (Guthrie, 1988, p. 9). As has been pointed out, people of all ages fail to follow sound practices which they understand and accept. Even in the face of life threatening hazards, they continue destructive practices. Essential regimen of medication is not followed, regulation in diet is ignored, and there is failure to regulate one's lifestyle despite doctor's advice. It is not an indication of failure to understand, nor of indifference to their health and welfare, nor due to low educational level. It is just not complying to the information or advice inspite of the danger that looms large.

In India and many Asian countries with collectivist orientation, an individual does not make health decisions alone. Unlike in the West, there is family and even community involvement in illness and influential decisions are made by the senior members through consensus, or on the advice of experienced neighbours. Patient's behaviour is group-oriented rather than individualistic. Therefore, it is suggested that in understanding and controlling health behaviour, due cognizance has to be taken of the role of the family and the community. For any preventive and promotional programme, the best entry point is the family and/or the community.

Behaviour Modification Technology

The problem of compliance involves modification of person's habit and behaviour pattern. Psychology in this respect provides the technology. Applying the principle of contingent reinforcement, appropriate habit of baby feeding can be inculcated and maintained (Guthrie, 1988). Effectiveness of reward hinges on proximity to the activities it seeks to strengthen. Since the benefits of change, for example, in baby feeding, diet or resorting to daily exercise are not immediately visible, nor experienced by individual, the effectiveness of contingent reward is greatly reduced. There are however, subtle and innovative ways of linking reward with modification in behaviour. With poor rural Filipino mothers, "trading stamp strategy" was found useful. Mothers who altered their behaviour in line with the baby feeding practice calculated to ensure infant's health and nutrition could earn health coupons which, in turn, could be traded for T-shirts, soap, sugar or other kinds of consumer items prized in the community (Guthrie, 1988, pp. 9-10). Similar strategies can yield desired results with regard to modifying and maintaining proper diet and lifestyle. Principles of reinforcement, group or social pressure, conformity principles, and various persuasion devices have been utilized in different spheres of health and illness with beneficial results. These include compliance of people with health regimens, pain and stress management and control, rehabilitation and the like.

Health Research in India

So far as researches in India are concerned, we have mostly towed the West and are busy preparing personality profiles of cancer, cardiac and accidents cases, and analyzing patients' attributions. Concentrating on patients and curative aspects has limited utility because our problems of health and disease are massive. The focus of health research, therefore, has to be more on the preventive and promotive aspects. Experience with primary health care has demonstrated that the local cultural context, community conceptions, beliefs, attitudes, norms, institutions and behaviour, need to be understood if health status has to be improved.

Role of Psychologist

Psychology has evolved over the past three decades or so substantial theoretical and methodological armamentarium and assessment tools. A psychologist has at his disposal special training in social scientific methods, communication skills and technology of behaviour modification both at the individual and the community level, as well as appropriate tools for surveying the belief and attitudinal systems and disease-generating and disease-preventive behaviour that are indigenous to the community. Indigenous resources could be harnessed to promote health and well-being of the individual and the community and prevent stress. Community psychologists have already proved their utility in conducting surveys of resources of the community, assessing the beliefs, attitudes and needs of its members with regard to health and illness, analyzing sources of high stress, and aiding community leaders in developing intervention programme and social action aimed at improving the health and quality of life for the entire community.

A psychologist can do his best by working not in the secure and often "unreal world" of academic psychologising, but by learning to work closely and better with policy- makers and the community and its leaders, as consultants and participants in the design, implementation, monitoring and evaluation of various health promotion programmes and health delivery services aimed not only at the traditional medical intervention points of the individual, but also at the level of the family and the community. Cooperation with other disciplines working towards identical objective of health for all is essential. In the area of health, psychologists should not only tolerate but learn to have *active* collaborative relationship with other disciplines.

REFERENCES

Guthrie, G.M. (1988). Six to eighteen — the perilous months. *Nutrition Today, 23*, 4-11.

Pande, N., & Naidu, R.K. (1986). Effort and outcome orientations as moderators of stress-strain relationship. *Psychological Studies, 31*, 207-214.

WHO/SEORO (1986). *Concepts of Health Behaviour Research.* SEORO Regional Office for South East Asia, New Delhi.

4

The Notion of Health in Theory and Practice : A Study of Four Medical Systems

T. SINGH, K.N. TRIPATHI, S. VARMA and **R.C. MISHRA**

Achieving a state of health is an important goal at the individual as well as societal levels of human functioning. However, the meaning of health is construed differently across different cultures. Also, the various systems of medicine offer different views of health and illness and nurture different types of beliefs and practices pertaining to health. This paper has twin goals i.e. to describe the theoretical perspective and to present an account of the views expressed by practitioners drawn from allopathic, Ayurvedic, homeopathic and Unani systems of medicine on the meaning of health and illness.

DIVERSE SYSTEMS OF MEDICINE : AN OVERVIEW

Ayurveda

Ayurveda, the ancient system of medicine, is prevalent in India particularly in villages. One of its basic concepts is that the body consists of three humours— *Vata, Pitta* and *Kapha.* Psychological and physiological functions depend upon the organization and integration of these three humours. Even when well integrated, there is a predominance of one of the humours that characterizes the personality of a person causing *vayu prakriti, pitta prakriti* or *kapha prakriti.* These constitutional peculiarities decide one's vulnerability towards the development of the corresponding physiological or psychological disturbances due to morbid imbalance of the healthy humoural equilibrium under physical or mental stress. The selection of the viscera and the type of disturbance depends upon the *prakriti* and external factors. The treatment of resultant disorder consists of re-organization of disturbed humoural functions by drugs and various practices.

The Ayurveda pharmacopoeia describes the use of different parts of a variety of herbs, plants, minerals, and animal substances from which drugs are prepared by special processes. Each drug may act on different viscera differently depending upon the patient's *prakriti* and therefore, the usual Ayurvedic prescription consists of a mixture of drugs for their synergistic action on the disturbed bodily or mental functions and minimum side effects on the body as a whole. Thus, Ayurvedic therapy does not affect the diseased viscera only. It is holistic in approach and recognizes the role of social and psychological factors in the development of disease.

Many misconceptions are also prevalent. For instance, somatic expression of psychiatric disorders is very common and it is related to the misconception that *vayu* (gas) circulates in the body and might be localized in certain parts giving rise to bodily disturbances. Also, many sicknesses are explained in terms of the weakness of semen or loss of semen due to sexual excess which might lead to illnesses ranging from impotence to psychosis and from headache to tuberculosis or cancer. Thus, many drugs in Ayurveda have been prescribed for strengthening semen.

The medical model of health has been the framework for several decades and now a considerable part of the health and welfare budget is utilized for treatment of disease by way of allopathic medicine. Despite this trend, the traditional holistic practices of health care derived from Ayurveda are still carried out in many Indian households and form an integral part of the Indian way of life. Such practices are interwoven into the fabric of daily life and are a part of the larger social and religious traditions and rituals. For example, fasting on certain specified days of the week is a common ritual among the Hindus. Such fasts serve a dual purpose. From the health point of view, fasting provides a period of rest to the digestive system and aids to the process of purification of the body. At the same time, it must be noted that such fasts are addressed to specific gods and goddesses and thus serve religious and spiritual functions as well.

The noteworthy feature of the Ayurvedic approach to health is its holistic orientation. Matters of health and disease are not isolated from other aspects of bodily functions and are considered as part of the larger mind-body-cosmic system. Due consideration is given to the various interlinkages and complexities. This system deals with problems of health and disease in their natural setting which provides more balanced solutions. Unlike the allopathic approach, Ayurveda emphasizes on maintaining the essential unity of the human organism while treating illnesses.

> "Thus science is dependent on *yukti* which is the intellect that perceives the phenomenon brought into existence by the coming together of the multitute of causes of which the phenomena, are, in turn, constituted. Again, having perceived the multiplicity of causes behind a phenomenon, *yukti* is necessary to bring together the appropriate actions and materials at the appropriate time and place... Thus, the traditional system, even in its theoretical formulation, seeks to find means of healthy living in this world rather than dissecting it or bringing about major changes" (Shanker, Krishnakumar & Balasubramanium, 1991).

As an illustration of the holistic orientation of Ayurveda, the principle of *rtu-satmya* is found to be useful. *Rtu-satmya* means "appropriate to the articulation of time" (Zimmerman, 1979, 1980). Here, time refers to the seasonal cycles. In India, it is common knowledge that certain foods and drinks serve to compensate for the imbalance caused by the extreme conditions of specific seasons. For example, during summer it is a common practice to consume *panah*, a drink made from half-ripe mangoes, which has a cooling effect on the body. In Ayurveda, foods and drinks are understood not only in terms of their nutritive value but also in terms of other attributes such as "hotness" or "coldness" etc., which refer to their effect on the body. Different seasons of the year have different effects on the body which at times lead to various discomforts and can even cause sickness. On such occasions appropriate diets and herbal medicines are administered to restore balance in the body.

Based on the same reasoning, various ailments are treated in Ayurveda in accordance with the principle of *rtu-satmya*. Certain elements and activities as well as environmental configurations are considered appropriate for the restoration of health because they compensate for the deficiencies in the body. In addition to a diet and herbs regimen, other prescriptions include specific physical exercises, rest, sleep, specific physical conditions of the surrounding environment etc. Zimmerman (1980, p. 100) has elaborated on the virtues of the principle of *rtu-satmya* as practiced in Ayurveda and emphasises that "This kind of therapy aims to modify the idiosyncrasies of the patient by giving him/her good habits. The means of effecting this sort of appropriateness are of two sorts, food and medications on the one hand, their action being of the same order (assimilation by the organism of substances bearing therapeutic virtues)— and bodily techniques on the other hand (physical exercises, daytime rest, functions, etc.)."

The point to be noted from the above discussion is the recognition of the organic and holistic relationship between man and his natural ecological environment. Certain displaced configurations in the man-environment system lead to disharmony within the human organism. Harmony can be restored by rearranging certain elements which are crucial for maintaining balance in the man-environment system from the point of view of the human organism.

Ayurveda is based on the *panchamahabhuta siddhanta* or the principle of five elements. Good health results from a proper balance among the five elements (*bhutas*)— air, water, earth, fire and ether; and the three humours (*doshas*)— wind (*vata*), bile (*pitta*), and phlegm (*kapha*). This balance takes palce at a number of levels, viz. physical, physiological, psychological and spiritual. As Murthy, (1991), "the five elements give rise to three humours— *vata, pitta* and *kapha* which govern all physical and mental functions. In the cosmos, when the five elements are in equilibrium, there is a cosmic balance and harmony; whereas when their balance is deranged they cause catastrophes. Similarly, the three humours of the body, when in equilibrium, create harmony and good health whereas their imbalance and derangement leads to various disorders".

Each of the three humours are composed of one or more of the five elements. For example, *vata* is composed of ether and air; *pitta* is derived from fire. The function of each humour is related to the element or elements of which it is composed. The entire manifest world is made up of the five elements and, therefore, everything in it is endowed with humoural qualities. The food we eat as well as our surrounding environment, both physical and socio-psychological, continuously interacts with the humours of our bodies. For this reason, various herbal medicines are prescribed in Ayurveda which help in restoring the humoural balance of the body.

The three humours relate more closely to bodily states whereas the three *gunas* (attributes) — *satva* (clarity or light), *tamas* (inertia) and *rajas* (activity) — are related to the characteristics of the mind. A state of health results from a proper balance between the three humours and the three attributes of the mind. In Ayurveda, it is held that a healthy state of being results from (i) normal digestion; (ii) unimpaired excretion; (iii) clarity of the senses, mind and soul; and (iv) possession of complete tranquility. It recognizes the fact that the mind (*manas*) can have an adverse effect on health despite the normal functioning of the humours and other bodily elements (Murthy, 1991).

Ayurveda is not based on a mind-body dichotomy which forms an essential part of the contemporary medical model of health (Murthy, 1993). It believes that longevity and quality of life are influenced by an interplay of two factors — *daiva* (fate) and *puruskara* (personal effort). This clearly indicates that Ayurveda is not deterministic because it holds that health can be improved by one's own efforts. Although the Indian system of medicine stresses on maintaining a balance between the person-society-cosmos system to ensure good health, it also takes into account illness caused due to attacks by micro-organisms. It is emphasized that an individual is susceptible to external attacks only when inner harmony is disrupted due to negligence on the part of an individual.

Unani

The origin of the Unani system of medicine can be traced to Hippocrates of Greece (460 B.C.). Later, this system spread to the Middle East where Al-Razi (A.D. 850-923) and later Ali-Ibn-e-Sina (A.D. 980-1037) are given credit for developing the system and presenting it in a book form. Unani Tibb was introduced in India by the Arabian and Persian invaders and it developed further with the inclusion of various herbal medicines.

As given by Hippocrates, Unani medicine is based on the humoural theory according to which four humours are present in the human body—blood, phlegm, yellow bile and black bile:corresponding with four basic temperaments—Sanguine, Phlegmatic, Choleric and Melancholic. Every individual possesses a humoural constitution unique to him which represents his balanced or healthy state. All ailments result from a disturbance of this balanced state. The body has an in-built mechanism for restoring balance and the role of the physician is to facilitate this mechanism with the help of various methods including herbal medicines.

According to the Unani system of medicine, the human body is made up of seven components (*Umoor-e-Tabiya*), all of which play an important role in the maintenance of health. These are : *arken* or the four elements — air, water, fire and earth; *mizaj* or temperament; *akhlat* or the bodily fluids such as hormones and enzymes; *aza* or the organs of the body; *arwah* or the spirits which are the life force; *qua* or the faculties; and *afal* or the various bodily functions and movements. In this system the treatment of diseases comes under two categories—preventive and curative. The preventive measures include exposure to clean unpolluted air; intake of clean and hygienic food and drinks, proper exercise and rest; exposure to pleasant company, beautiful scenery etc., in the case of psychological ailments; normal sleep, and proper functioning of the excretory process. All the above must be ensured for a state of good health. Curative treatment includes (i) regimental therapy (*Ilaj Bid Tadbir*) or use of special physical techniques for various ailments, e.g., *takhriq* or sweating, *dalak* or *massage*, *taleek* or *leeching*, etc. (ii) diet therapy (*Ilaj Bil Khiza*) where certain illnesses are treated by the intake of specific diets, (iii) drug therapy (*Ilaz Bid Dawa*) which consists of the administration of various herbal medicines as well as certain drugs of animal origin and (iv) surgery (*Ilaz Bil Yed*) in which special techniques and instruments were developed by Unani physicians who were pioneers in the field.

Homeopathy

Homeopathy is a system of medicine introduced by a German physician, Samuel Hahnemann. He set forth the principles on which this system is based. These include the following : (i) Morbid conditions are cured by the same medicines which would produce the disease in healthy bodies, in accordance with the old belief expressed by the Latin phrase *similia similibus curenture* (let like be cured by like). (ii) That the drugs administered should be simple and not compounded. (iii) That in most cases only very small quantities of the drug should be given, on the theory of dynamization, or increase of force with diminution of matter. Such dynamization, it is alleged, being produced by titration (i.e., grinding to a fine powder) and by extreme dilution. Homeopathy is not a traditional or indigenous medicine like Ayurveda or Unani system.

It is interesting to note that in Ayurveda too, there is a mention of the *similia principle*. In this principle, the disease is produced by influences which act similar to the effects of the remedy and the disease condition is removed through remedies which produce similar symptoms to the disease. Thus, by similar things disease is produced and by similar things administered to the sick they are healed of their disease. Thus the same thing which will produce some thing stranger, when it does not exist, will remove it when it does. In the same way, a cough can be provoked and cured by the same medicine.

Homeopathy adopts a psychosomatic approach based on the concepts of holistic medicine as against the analytic approach which asserts the role of component parts or organs of the body. One of the greatest advantages of Homeopathy is the freedom from introgenesis, or the harmful side effects of medicine which are prevalent with allopathic drugs. It does not cause catastrophic effects that may occur with other types of medicines.

The approach of treatment in this system is very different from allopathy. A homeopath treats the patient who has the disease whereas the allopath treats the disease the patient has. Hahnemann placed strong emphasis on individuality and on individualizing the disease. Each person suffers "from a nameless disease, which never before occurred in the same way, in the same person, under the same circumstances, and which never again can occur in exactly the same way". It has been said that if one removes the effects, one removes the disease—the cause of the effects. This has been very aptly put in Latin as *Cessateffectus cessat cause*. If the effects, which are the symptoms, are cured in entirety (not suppressed) then obviously the causative factor must have been removed or normalized.

In taking the history of a patient, considerable attention is paid to patient's interaction with environment, weather conditions, cravings and aversions in food, emotional states, loves and hates, fears, frame of mind, life style, domestic and office atmosphere, sexual habits, state of sleep and even dreams. This process is not an attempt to get a sort of personality profile and a holistic understanding of an individual, apart from diagnosing the disease. Hahnemann mentioned that "no true cure can take place without rigid personal treatment (individualization) of each case".

Allopathy

The term allopathy is usually applied to an orthodox method of therapeutics as opposed to homeopathy. Hahnemann, viewed allopathy as a method of treatment of disease consisting of the use of medicines the action of which upon the body produces morbid phenomena different from those of the disease treated. It treats diseases with the contrary rather than similar drugs. Being reductionist in its approach this model views the human body as a complex machine made up of a number of component parts. Treatment of diseases within the medical model of health is undertaken by physical means such as surgery etc., or by chemical means such as the various allopathic drugs. Such treatment serves to counteract or block the negative or toxic effects of the disease.

This system of medicine does not take into consideration the organic relationship between man and his surrounding environment, be it the social environment or the physical environment. The human organism is viewed as complete in his/her self and illness is understood in terms of the malfunctioning of certain bodily components or mechanisms caused by external attacks of micro-organisms or due to the breakdown of the body parts themselves. Such a piecemeal and molecular analysis overlooks the relationship of the affected or diseased parts with the larger system and consequently, a variety of negative side effects arise from the chemical and physical interventions applied within this framework. It considers sickness in terms of biologically and physically determined conditions. The disease/health process is localized in the organism. Its origin is traced back to ancient Egyptian medicine. Hippocrates evolved the theory of four humours to explain health and disease. Subsequently Galen investigated the functions of different parts of the body. Knowledge of anatomy and blood circulation and surgery gradually made this system very effective. The discovery of vaccinations and bacteria as a cause of disease have provided sound basis to this system.

Other examples also serve to illustrate the reductionist orientation of the medical model of health. Within this model, a human being's interaction with the physical environment is understood only at a chemical and molecular level. Food substances are analyzed in terms of their nutritive values, i.e., in terms of proteins, carbohydrates, fats etc., which they contain. The effect of dietary factors on other aspects of the mind-body system are largely ignored. There is little awareness in modern medicine about the effect of certain foods on emotionality and other attributes relating to temperament as well as the palliative action of certain foods in specific ailments. The relationship between psycho-social aspects of life and onset of illness is largely ignored within the medical model of health and disease. Modern medicine has paid scant attention to the relationship between life events and onset of illness. Folk wisdom, on the other hand, has always taken this relationship as significant.

HEALTH BELIEFS OF MEDICAL PRACTITIONERS : AN EMPIRICAL STUDY

This study aimed at understanding the meaning of health as conceived by the practitioners of allopathic, Ayurvedic, Unani and homeopathic systems of medicine. As noted in the previous section these systems construe health and disease in different ways. This raises the question whether and to what extent these conceptual notions are shared by these practitioners.

Four hundred medical practitioners (male and female both), 100 each from allopathic, Ayurvedic, Homeopathic and Unani systems of medicine drawn from different parts (urban and rural both) of Uttar Pradesh, participated in the study. Their ages ranged from 23 to 87 years with professional experience of 2 to 45 years (M = 21 years). Except some Unani practitioners, all others had medical qualifications which were recognized by the state and or central government.

In order to explore the health beliefs a questionnaire measure was prepared dealing with : (i) meaning of health, (ii) characteristics of a healthy person, (iii) ways to maintain health, (iv) factors responsible for ill-health, (v) distinguishing features of the system, (vi) attitude towards other systems of medicine, (vii) application of other systems of medicine in clinical practice, (viii) attitude towards integration of different systems of medicine, and (ix) adoption of other medicinal systems. The questions were open ended and the responses obtained from the participants were content analyzed. The major findings emerging from the study are as follows.

Meaning of Health

Table 4.1 shows that majority of the practitioners (50.18%) describe meaning of health in terms of well-being, fitness and healthy condition of an individual. The second largest set of responses described health in terms of normalcy of behaviour, appearance and age appropriate feeling and experience (29.70%), followed by absence of disease (20.07%). Some differences in the pattern of responses were also observed among the four groups of medical practitioners. While describing the meaning of health, allopathic practitioners have responded more in favour of the well-being component (60.00%); followed by absence of disease (24.11%) and normalcy (15.71%) components. A similar pattern emerged in the case of Homeopathic practitioners. The Ayurvedic practitioners gave greater emphasis on well-being (51.54%) component, followed by normalcy (29.82%) and absence of disease (18.64%). Practitioners of Unani system also shared the pattern of Ayurvedic practitioners. Majority of the Unani practitioners viewed health in terms of well-being (44.20%), followed by normalcy (43.99%) and absence of disease (11.81%), respectively.

TABLE 4.1 : Meaning of Health

Components of Health	Allopathic	Ayurvedic	Homeopathic	Unani
Well being/Fitness or Healthy condition	168 (60.00)	235 (51.54)	85 (47.75)	217 (44.20)
Absence of disease	68 (24.11)	85 (18.64)	71 (39.89)	58 (11.81)
Normalcy of behaviour, appearance, feeling and experience according to age	44 (15.71)	136 (29.82)	22 (12.36)	216 (43.99)

Note : Figures in bracket indicate percentages.

Characteristics of a Healthy Person

Medical practitioners were asked to enumerate the characteristics of a healthy person. The responses thus obtained were categorized and the results are presented in Table 4.2. It is clear that among the allopathic practitioners, majority of the respondents viewed well-being (38.22%) as a characteristic of a healthy person; followed by activity level (16.81%), appearance, satisfaction and happiness (13.48%); behaviour and adjustment (10.34); normal physical/bodily conditions (7.64%) and normal physiological functioning (6.29%). Ayurvedic practitioners emphasized activity level (23.34%); followed by normal physiological functioning (18.30%); appearance, satisfaction and happiness (14.99%); normal physical/bodily conditions (13.64%); behaviour and adjustment (11.06%); well-being (9.21%) and absence of disease (5.53%).

Homeopathic practitioners viewed normal physiological functioning as a major characteristic of a healthy person (31.84%); followed by normal physical/bodily conditions (20.52%); well-being (17.69%); behaviour and adjustment (8.96); absence of disease (8.49%); activity level (6.32%); and appearance, satisfaction and happiness (6.13%). Unani practitioners have viewed normal physiological functioning

(44.97%) as a major characteristic of a healthy person; followed by activity level (22.91%), appearance, satisfaction and happiness (20.39%); well-being (6.42%); and absence of disease (3.63%).

TABLE 4.2 : Characteristics of a Healthy Person

Characteristics	Allopathic	Ayurvedic	Homeopathic	Unani
Normal physical/bodily conditions	34 (7.64)	111 (13.64)	87 (20.52)	6 (1.68)
Normal physiological functioning	28 (6.29)	149 (18.30)	135 (31.84)	161 (44.97)
Normal daily routine	7 (1.57)	32 (3.93)	— (0.00)	— (0.00)
Well being (mood, sociability, capability, positive status etc.)	170 (38.20)	75 (9.21)	75 (17.69)	23 (7.42)
Absence of disease/illness	28 (6.29)	45 (5.53)	36 (8.49)	13 (3.63)
Activity level/work/ vitality	72 (16.18)	190 (23.34)	27 (6.37)	82 (22.91)
Appearance/satisfaction and happiness	60 (13.48)	122 (14.99)	26 (6.13)	73 (20.39)
Behaviour and adjustment	46 (10.34)	90 (11.06)	38 (8.96)	— (0.00)

Note : Figures in bracket indicate percentages.

Factors Responsible for Ill-health

Views of the medical practitioners regarding factors responsible for ill-health appear in Table 4.3. It is evident that all the four groups of practitioners have viewed individual and family level factors more responsible for ill-health of individuals as compared to societal and environmental factors.

Largest percentage of responses of this type were given by Ayurvedic practitioners (77.77%). Percentages of Allopathic, Homeopathic and Unani practitioners viewing individual and family level factors as responsible for ill-health were 57.35, 58.51, and 59.87 per cent, respectively. Similarly, largest percentages of responses were given by allopathic (42.65%) and homeopathic (41.49%) practitioners describing societal and environmental factors as responsible for ill-health; followed by Unani (30.13%) and Ayurvedic (22.23%) practitioners.

TABLE 4.3 : Factors Responsible for Ill-health

Factors	Allopathic	Ayurvedic	Homeopathic	Unani
Individual and family	242 (57.35)	710 (77.77)	244 (58.51)	276 (69.87)
Societal/Environmental	180 (42.65)	203 (22.23)	173 (41.49)	119 (30.13)

Note : Figures in bracket indicate percentages.

Ways to Maintain Good Health

Responses indicating various ways to maintain good health are presented in Table 4.4. The category of life style, environment, cleanliness, and sanitation were viewed most important by practitioners of all the four systems. Barring the homeopathic practitioners, the second largest response category was quality of food and water/diet, for maintaining good health; followed by temperament, work and exercise, and treatment and prevention. The category of knowledge and education as a way to maintain health was viewed important by allopathic practitioners only.

TABLE 4.4 : Ways to Maintain Health

Ways	Allopathic	Ayurvedic	Homeopathic	Unani
Quality of food, water and diet	130 (23.42)	272 (29.63)	62 (18.18)	121 (26.30)
Life style, environment, cleanliness and sanitation	191 (34.41)	360 (39.22)	180 (52.79)	289 (62.83)
Treatment and prevention, and no intoxication	89 (16.04)	115 (12.53)	20 (5.87)	7 (1.52)
Temperament, work and exercise	122 (21.98)	171 (18.63)	79 (23.17)	43 (9.35)
Knowledge and Education	23 (4.14)	— (0.00)	— (0.00)	— (0.00)

Note : Figures in bracket indicate percentages.

Distinctiveness of the System

The practitioners were asked to give their views regarding the distinctiveness of their own system as compared to other systems of medicine. The obtained responses are given in Table 4.5.

TABLE 4.5 : Distinctiveness of the System

Speciality	Allopathic	Ayurvedic	Homeopathic	Unani
Scientific basis	204 (24.11)	66 (8.37)	— (0.00)	— (0.00)
Advancement	218 (25.77)	— (0.00)	— (0.00)	— (0.00)
Unique medicines	44 (5.20)	287 (36.38)	106 (55.50)	213 (71.00)
Unique treatment	238 (28.13)	393 (49.81)	85 (44.50)	87 (29.00)
Advanced level of surgery	120 (14.18)	— (0.00)	— (0.00)	— (0.00)
Treatment without surgery	— (0.00)	21 (2.66)	— (0.00)	— (0.00)
Rehabilitation and prevention	22 (2.60)	9 (1.14)	— (0.00)	— (0.00)
Suitable to Indian conditions	— (0.00)	13 (1.65)	— (0.00)	— (0.00)

Note : Figures in bracket indicate percentages.

It is clear that majority of the allopathic practitioners have viewed speciality of treatment method (28.13%) as a characteristic of their system. They have described that their system is advanced (25.77%) and has a scientific basis (24.11%). Advanced level of surgery as well as medicine were reported by 14.18 per cent and 5.20 per cent of the allopathic practitioners considered rehabilitation and prevention as a speciality of their system. A large section of Ayurvedic practitioners has viewed speciality of their system in terms of uniqueness of treatment mode (49.81%) and types of medicines (36.38%) used. As this is the oldest, none of the Ayurvedic practitioners has viewed their system as advanced. However, some of them did describe their system as grounded in scientific principles (8.37%). Also, it is special and peculiar in the sense that there is provision of treatment without surgery (2.66%) and emphasis is given on rehabilitative and preventive aspects (1.14%). An important speciality of the Ayurvedic system which was not viewed by other practitioners, is its suitability to the tropical Indian conditions. Speciality of the homeopathic system of the medicine as viewed by homeopathic practitioners was in terms of type of medicine (55.50%) and treatment (44.50%). Similar views were also given by Unani practitioners where they had described special characteristics of their medicine (71.00%) and treatment (29.00%).

III
CONCLUSIONS

The present excursion into the four medicinal systems demonstrates both similarities and differences in the views of the practitioners of allopathy, Ayurveda, homeopathy and Unani systems. Although most of the practitioners have endorsed the view that health stands for well-being, fitness and healthy condition of people, their preferences did show variation. Thus major emphasis on these components was given by allopathic practitioners followed by Ayurvedic, Homeopathic and Unani practitioners. Absence of disease as a major dimension of health was viewed by Homeopaths followed by allopathic, Ayurvedic and Unani practitioners.

The present results indicate considerable degree of congruence in the views of allopathic and homeopathic practitioners who have emphasized absence of disease to a greater extent than Ayurvedic and Unani practitioners. In contrast, normalcy of behaviour, appearance, and feelings according to age as components of health were emphasized more by Ayurvedic and Unani practitioners. Also, well-being, fitness and healthy condition of individuals as major aspects of health received more favour from allopathic and Ayurvedic practitioners than from Homeopathic and Unani practitioners. The overall view of the practitioners indicated well-being, fitness and healthy conditions of individuals as critical aspects of health. The category of normalcy of behaviour, appearance and feelings according to age was regarded as a major component of health while absence of disease ranked third in the priority order. In regard to the characteristics of a healthy person, well-being emerged as the most important characteristic. However, Homeopathic and Unani practitioners viewed normal physiological functioning as most important characteristic of a healthy person. Homeopathic practitioners had expressed their views in terms of activity level, work and vitality as most important characteristic of a healthy person while this was considered as the second most important characteristic by the allopathic and Unani practitioners. Ayurvedic practitioners considered normal physiological functioning as the second most important characteristic of a healthy person. Homeopathic practitioners have viewed normal physical/bodily condition as the second most important characteristic. Appearance, satisfaction and happiness as important characteristics was endorsed more strongly by Unani practitioners followed by Ayurvedic, allopathic and homeopathic practitioners. More allopathic and Ayurvedic practitioners were in favour of behaviour and adjustment categories in comparison to Homeopaths while Unani practitioners gave importance to behaviour and adjustment characteristics of a healthy person less strongly. No importance was given to normal daily routine by homeopathic and Unani practitioners. However, some responses given by Allopathic and Ayurvedic practitioners were in favour of this characteristic. These findings indicate major differences in the viewpoints of practitioners in characterizing a healthy person.

Irrespective of their systemic background, all the practitioners viewed ill-health as determined by individual and family level factors more than broader social and environmental factors. However, Ayurvedic and Unani practitioners gave relatively greater stress on them than Homeopathic and allopathic practitioners. Societal and environmental factors were viewed more strongly by allopathic and Homeopathic practitioners as compared to Ayurvedic and Unani practitioners whose viewpoints were less in favour of these factors.

It was also observed that except Homeopaths all practitioners had similar views regarding the ways to maintain good health. In this context, living style, environment, cleanliness and sanitation were viewed most important. Second largest group of responses dealt with quality of food, water and diet as important for maintaining good health, except by Homeopathic practitioners who favoured temperament, work and exercise as important for maintaining good health. Although, all the four groups of practitioners viewed treatment and prevention as important for maintaining good heath, it was more strongly favoured by Allopathic practitioners, followed by Ayurvedic and Unani ones. The most important finding in this regard was about the knowledge and education for maintaining good health which was referred to by the allopathic practitioners only.

In regard to speciality of treatment methods the findings indicated that allopathic practitioners strongly hold the view that their system is advanced and has a scientific foundation. They have viewed the speciality of their system more strongly in terms of uniqueness of medicine, diagnosis and treatment, advanced level of surgery and provision of rehabilitation, prevention and health education. Ayurvedic practitioners have expressed the speciality of their system more strongly in terms of the nature and quality of medicine and treatment. Also, they claim that their system has a scientific basis. Two other specialities of Ayurvedic system consisted of treatment without surgery and appropriateness of the system to suit Indian conditions. On the other hand, Homeopathic and Unani practitioners have viewed the speciality of their system strongly in terms of type of medicine as well as treatment. They did not express any other feature of their system.

In general, the majority of practitioners of the four systems of medicine appear to view health in terms of well-being, fitness, and healthy life conditions of individuals; followed by normalcy of behaviour, appearance, and experience of feelings according to age, and absence of disease. In regard to the characteristics of a healthy person, largest responses were in favour of normal physiological functioning followed by preference for activity level, work and vitality; well-being; appearance, satisfaction and happiness; normal physical/bodily conditions; behavioural adjustment; and absence of disease and illness. Normal daily routine was the least preferred response. Practitioners of all four systems of medicine viewed individual and family level factors as more responsible for ill-health than environmental and societal level factors. In view of the practitioners, life-style, environment, cleanliness and sanitation are most important ways to maintain good health followed by quality of food, water and diet; temperament, work and exercise; and treatment and prevention. Very few practitioners (only allopathic) considered knowledge and education as an important way to maintain health. Majority of the practitioners have described the speciality of the system in terms of treatment followed by the type of medicine used, scientific foundation and advanced nature of the system.

REFERENCES

Murthy, R.S. (1991). Holistic medicine : Contributions from behavioural sciences. *India International Quarterly, 18*, 205-215.

Murthy, R.S. (1993). Evolution of the concept of mental health—from mental illness to mental health. In P. Mane and K. Gandevia (Eds.), *Mental Health in India : Issues and Concerns* (pp. 17-42). Bombay : TISS Publication.

Shankar, D., Krishnakumar, P.R., & Balasubramanium, A.V. (1991). Indigenous health sciences and western medical sciences : Foundational differences. *India International Quarterly, 18*, 21-25.

Zimmerman, F.B. (1979). Remarks on the body in Ayurvedic medicine. *South Asian Digest of Regional Writing, 18*, 10-26.

Zimmerman, F.B. (1980). Rtu-satmya : The seasonal cycle and the principle of appropriateness. *Social Science and Medicine, 14B*, 99-106.

5

Anāsakti : The Indian Vision of Potential Human Transcendence Beyond Mechanistic Motivations

R.K. NAIDU and **NAMITA PANDE**

This is a historical account of how work with an Indian concept of motivation evolved over a period of nearly a decade. It is also an account of the intellectual struggles which a training in the mechanistic Western psychology triggered off in the mind of the first author who was born and nurtured in a spiritual tradition. Against this backdrop, a review of studies of Anāsakti and a description of the steps taken to operationalise this concept are presented here. In Indian spiritual lore, *Anāsakti* means detachment of the spiritual principle, the basis of consciousness, from the body and ego. Anāsakti or detachment is a means towards self realisation and it is also an end state because a realised soul is spontaneously anāsakt or detached.

As a student of postgraduate classes, the first author imbibed great enthusiasm and excitement from his teachers. They taught with pride a psychology imported almost totally from the United States of America. On this Campus, to be associated with the Psychology Department automatically bestowed an aura of being modern enlightened and elitist. The teachers of this Department had a robust optimism about the capacity of mainstream Western 'scientific' psychology to come up with creative and adequate solutions for human problems. Had not the other sciences-physics and chemistry-revolutionised human life? Why would this young science fail to deliver the goods particularly when it so faithfully and blindly follows in the footsteps of its elders—the physical sciences?

These teachers preached 'scientism' with a missionary zeal. Such zeal is always associated with iconoclasm. New structures are not built by assimilating them into the old structures. One fired with a missionary zeal first tries to destroy the old structures. The new is then built over the debris. The missionaries of scientific psychology followed the same strategy.

Psychology, they declared could solve all human problems. But to possess this 'mahamantra', they admonished, one first had to get rid of certain mental infirmities like philosophy and religion. In the classrooms of sixties, students often heard condescending and derogatory observations about philosophers, faith, ancestors, and one's own culture and heritage. Using the metaphor of maps for education, Schumacher (1977) graphically describes these attitudes : "The maps I was given advised me that virtually all my ancestors, until quite recently, had been rather pathetic illusionists . . . our entire past was today fit only for museums. . ." (p. 1, 2).

The initial euphoria of studying an elitist science effectively prevented the first author from perceiving the deeper issues hidden under the attitudes constituting this superficial scientism. Some of these issues bear upon the capacity of psychology as a discipline to adequately describe the totality of human experience and behaviour while there were some other issues related to certain unintended effects on the shaping of the minds of young Indian students.

Some of the issues bearing on psychology as a discipline may be raised as the following questions : Are the models of man underlying behaviouristic and cognitive psychologies adequate to account for the entire range of human experience and behaviour? Is man merely an enormously complex assemblage of reflexes or merely an information processing machine? By merely using different words and talking about 'goal directed behaviour' are the questions about human will, purpose, and choice just magically wished away? Personalities such as Ghazzali, Christ, and Ramakrishna are examplers of the ultimate in human ethical refinement. They are as much or even more committed to truth as any professional scientist. All of them declared in one voice (thereby satisfying the scientific requirement of consensual validation) that the core of human personality is spiritual.

None of the mainstream scientific psychologies thought it fit to even pause and consider the possibility of the spiritual element in humans, let alone developing concepts and methods to address that domain of human experience. Is that an academically sound attitude towards some of the most profound human issues?

Let us now look at one important feature of Western scientific psychology. It seeks objective knowledge. How is objectivity ensured? The answer to this question would be repeatability of observations and consensus among observers. Consensus ensures commonality of experience. But commonality is not necessarily the proof of truth. Often it only represents the lowest common denominator. If commonality were the only test of truth, intellectual progress of any kind-scientific or otherwise-would not be possible except when an entire community of observers collectively experience a new perception or a community of thinkers simultaneously have a collective new insight. In all these cases, collective elevation of consciousness is involved. Such a phenomenon is unknown, at least in the recorded history of human thought.

Even within a given Zeitgeist, it is the specially equipped individual mind which succeeds in grasping a new thought or a novel perception. The requirement of consensual validation would condemn all these acts of creation as merely non-valid and untrue.

When a student is trained in the objective ways of science, among other things he is advised to restrain his biases while making scientific observations, and use the objective scientific style recommended by the American Psychological Association (APA) while writing the report.

This style is characterized by unemotional descriptions, impersonal narrations, and whenever possible, replacing qualitative statements by quantitative statements.

An objective state of mind cannot be induced by a mere admonition to keep the biases at bay. Often one is not even aware of one's biases. Before one can control the impact of biases, one has to become aware of them. How else is this to be achieved except by systematically learning to look within or in other words by introspecting or reflecting on the inner thoughts and feelings? This is hardly ever taught in psychology courses. Why? Just because of the mindless position taken by Watson and our blind following of that tradition?

As regards the APA style of writing, it is sufficient to point out that a study does not become objective merely by the eschewal of personal pronouns while writing the report. The mainstream Western psychology with its insistence on the outward looking objective methods and denial of the spiritual element in man, is a partial and truncated discipline. The need to move away from this tradition and towards a transpersonal position was strongly felt by us.

There was yet another reason to question the mainstream psychology which claims to be only an intellectual enterprise. Every body of knowledge has political implications. "Whether he wants it or not, or whether he is aware of it or not, anyone who spends his life studying society and publishing the results is acting morally and usually politically as well" (Mills, 1973; p. 90). It is this realisation of the invisible political impact which gave rise to the indigenous movement, particularly in countries which were erstwhile colonies of Western powers.

When viewed in this context, no self-respecting nation can really afford to teach an entirely imported discipline to its youth. Every concept has a cultural and value context. A university course may ostensibly claim to teach merely a set of concepts. But when those concepts are taught to impressionable and growing minds, we believe that the values of the culture of the origin of those concepts are also communicated. This subtle, surreptitious and unconscious value indoctrination becomes a 'hidden agenda' of education. This agenda serves to alienate a student from his own culture.

Dissatisfaction with the mechanistic psychology discussed earlier and the realisation of the political implications of an imported (mainly American) psychology made the first author search for transpersonal and indigenous alternatives. In 1980 he happened to listen to a lecture by Swami Chinmayananda who described the *Gita* as 'The best manual for sound mental health'.

This single sentence initiated a programme of research which is still in progress. A brief review of that programme is presented here.

The first *Gita* based document on this subject was a two page research proposal entitled "Psychological Costs of Being Concerned About Partially Controllable Events" written by the first author in March 1981. This paper argued that outcome concerns would impede task performance and also impair health and that these effects be empirically examined. This proposal was presented in a social psychology course conducted by Dr. Phillip Brickman at the University of Michigan.

This proposal was followed, strangely enough, not by an empirical study of the hypothesised relationships between outcome concerns, task performance and health, but by a more thoroughgoing theoretical analysis of these and other psychological concepts embedded in the *Gita* by Thapa (1983). This postdoctoral dissertation gave a detailed theoretical analysis of the concept of anāsakti or non-attachment (particularly with the gross material phenomena and the outcomes of one's actions) delineated in the *Bhagavad Gita* (in this chapter detachment and non-attachment have been used as synonyms). Thapa analysed the dimensions of the concept, traced their linkages with current motivational concepts and came up with the first draft instrument for assessing effort and outcome orientations as an individual difference variable.

The first major empirical work on anāsakti was a doctoral research by Pande (1990). This study consisted of two separate empirical investigations which were carried out to examine the moderator role of anāsakti in the stress-strain relationship. In the first study, an effort and outcome orientation scale was developed to assess the relative emphasis which students place on either task related activities or the anticipated outcomes. It was found that students high on outcome orientation perceived greater distress when they encountered stressors and manifested greater symptoms of strain compared to students high on effort orientation. In the second study, a scale measuring the other aspects of anāsakti (besides effort and outcome orientations) was developed and administered on an adult sample. The major finding of this study was that although people who were high and those who were low on anāsakti did not significantly differ from each other in terms of the number of stresses which they had encountered, yet those who were more anāsakt felt significantly less distressed and exhibited fewer symptoms of strain.

Three papers covering the various findings of Pande's research were published (Pande & Naidu 1986, 1992; Naidu & Pande, 1990). Generally it was found that anāsakti or non-attachment was a health promoting attitude. An equally important psychological finding was the existence of individual differences in this variable. The distributions of anasakti scores were generally found to be normal but tended to be leptokurtic. The larger implication of this research is being presented here.

According to the Indian spiritual tradition, the human personality is a multilayered hierarchical structure which extends from the gross physical through the subtle mental to the non-physical spiritual element which is the subtlest of all (Sinha & Naidu, 1994). According to this view, the deterministic causal laws apply most effectively to the gross physical level and the applicability of these laws gradually tapers to utter unapplicability at the spiritual level. The level at which an individual functions depends upon the extent to which his consciousness has evolved. Mechanistic causal principles of behaviourism will effeciently predict the behaviour of a person who identifies himself primarily with his body and is psychologically speaking, a being of reflexes.

The causal principles apply a little less to the mental level because the mind is a mix of both matter and spirit. If in an individual the lower mind consisting of the bodily appetites dominates, the mechanistic laws would predict his behaviour to that extent but even in such an individual there is room for the exercise of inner volition which is the expression of his spirituality. That is why there is greater uniformity of the leaning of responses to aversive stimuli among animals and very small children but not so with adult human subjects. Underwood (1968) points out that conditioning of a human child's withdrawal response is a more predictable phenomenon whereas, "with adult subjects in the laboratory, conditioning is a different problem since the voluntary control may inhibit the occurrence of the desired response" (p. 346).

An individual whose consciousness dwells primarily in the higher mind of concepts and ideals would be able to bring the impulses of the body and ego under the subordination of his will. The behaviour of such a person would transcend the predictive powers of mechanistic psychology. The consciousness of a self-realised individual after having detached itself from the body, mind and ego dwells entirely within the realm of the spirit. The spirit revels within itself. Such a person is autonomous, not subject to the usual environmental, bodily and libidinal influences. The Western mechanistic psychology is totally inappropriate for such a person. In other words that variety of psychology is inappropriate to a person to the extent he has become truly human.

Tripathi, Naidu, Thapa and Biswas (1993) studied the impact of various professional and personal life stresses on the health and performance of police personnel in Uttar Pradesh. This study was supported by the Bureau of Police Research and Development. Attachment to the immediate surroundings was measured by a brief five item scale. Attachment in this context, may be viewed as a concept reciprocal to anāsakti in the sense, reverse scoring of these items would have yielded a measure of anāsakti.

It was found that those high on attachment were characterized by higher Type A Personality scores, greater depression, fear and guilt and reported more daily hassles.

A cross-cultural study of the moderator role of anāsakti was conducted by the first author and Dr. Ira Roseman of Rutgers University, Camden, U.S.A. In this study 140 American and 287 Indian University students served as subjects. The anāsakti scale had 22 items. For both the American and Indian samples, it was found that anāsakti was associated with lower level depression and anxiety. Though anāsakti did not account for a major part of stress-strain relationship, it did buffer it to a small but significant extent. The report of this study is still under preparation. Currently work is in progress which examines the relationship between anasakti and mood fluctuations and further work on the impact of this attitude on performance of certain physical and mental tasks is at the stage of planning.

A distinctive feature of this research programme is empirical examination of a concept which belongs to the domain of spirituality. Therefore, the process of operationalisation of this indigenous concept is explicated in greater detail in the following section.

Measuring Anasakti

The *Bhagavad Gita* is not only a metaphysical treatise (*darsana sastra*) but also a treatise on ethics (*nitisastra*). The Samkhyan metaphysical dualism which the *Gita* embodies explains material phenomena of the manifest world (*jagat*) as modifications (*vrittis*) of the primordial matter (*prakriti*). *Prakriti* reinforces a sense of mistaken identity (*mithya bodh*) with matter (*anna*), mind (*manas*), intelligence (*vijnana*) and egotism (*ahamkara*); perpetuates ignorance (*avidya*) and renders the recognition of the real self (*Purusa*) improbable. However, it is the ethical conduct of life which the teachings of *Bhagavad Gita* systematically deliberate that has made its philosophy more comprehensible to the common man. Elaborating *Karma Yoga*, the *Gita* prescribes anasakt *karma* (non-attached action) to a spiritual seeker which can help him avoid bodily excesses of indulgence and resist external distractions to become harmonized (*yukta*) with his actions and get detached from all desires for their fruits (*karma phalasa*).

The *Gita* contends that action performed with a sense of duty enables man to achieve control over the modifications of his mind. Besides explaining the ideological imports of this prescription, the *Gita* portrays the characteristic attitudes, feelings, and actions of the *sthitaprajna* (the man of stable wisdom) who is the ideal practitioner of anāsakti or *niskama karma*. The *sthitaprajna* is a human being who has transcended the usual human levels of experience and behaviour. To operationalise anāsakti, descriptions of the attitudes and behaviours of the *sthitaprajna*, as set forth by the *Bhagavad Gita*, were examined. This description also formed the source for the items of the Anasakti Scale.

Characteristics of the Sthitaprajna

In the second adhyaya (chapter) of the *Bhagavad Gita*, Arjuna asks Krisna to reveal the various qualities which characterise the man of stable wisdom. He asks Krisna

> 'Sthitaprajnasya ka bhasa samadhisthasya Kesava
> Sthitadhih kim prabhaseta kim asita vrajeta kim'
> (*The Gita*, 2 : 54).

"What is the description of the man who has this firmly founded wisdom, whose being is steadfast in spirit, O Kesava (Krisna)? How should the man of settled intelligence speak, how should he sit, how should he walk?" (Radhakrishnan, 1948, p. 122). While answering these questions, Krisna presents a detailed description of the various qualities which a sthitaprajna possesses. A very brief description of those qualities is presented here.

According to the *Gita*, the most dominant value which a sthitaprajna holds is duty. He believes that one should perform his duties without being concerned about the consequences (*'Karmanyeva' dhikaraste ma phalesu kadhacana*', 2:47) and that one should be willing to sacrifice his life in fulfilling the duties which are ascribed to him depending upon his station in life (*'svadharme nidhanam sreyah paradharmo bhayavahah*', 3:35). He performs his duties with complete involvement (*'Karmany abhipravrtto*', 4:20) even though it may involve personal costs. Such an effort orientation results because a sthitaprajna acts without any mental attachment to the fruits of action (*'tyaktva karma phalasangam*', 4:20). He does not depend upon the consequences to direct the course of his action (*'anasritah karmaphalam*', 6:1), so much so, that he even renounces the '*samkalpa*' — the formative will-towards the fruits of his actions (*'sarvasamkalpaamnyasi*', 6:4). Since he has no egoistical goals to achieve through his actions, he takes no pride in what he accomplishes (*'nirahamkarah*', 2:71) and is not jealous of people who may have materially succeeded in their lives (*'vimatsarah*', 4:22).

Another dominant characteristic of a sthitaprajna refers to the ability to appraise dualities with a sense of sameness and remain emotionally poised. For him ". . . a clod, a stone and a piece of gold are the same . . ." (Radhakrishnan, 1948, p. 191; '*samalostasmakanchanah*', 6.8). He is sans-attachment success and failure with an even mind (`*siddhyasidhhyoh samo bhutva*', 2:48). He remains unruffled in facing the auspicious and the inauspicious. He is one "... whose mind is untroubled in the midst of sorrows and is free from eager desire amid pleasures . . . " (Radhakrishnan, 1948, p. 123;) '*duhkhesv anudvignamanah sukhesu vigatasprhah*', 2:56) and he ". . . does not rejoice or loathe as he obtains good or evil... " (Radhakrishnan, 1948, p. 124; '*. . . prapya subhasubham na bhinandati na dvesti. . .*', 2:57). He has his senses under his own control and therefore he indulges into sense experiences and withdraws himself away at his own will (*'visayan indriyais caran aatmavasyair. . .*', 2:64).

This impulse control enables him to ultimately relieve himself from longings for material possessions ('*tyaktasarvaparigrahah*', 4:21). He leads a life of intense activity in the interest of society but at the same time remains ever contented ('*nityatrpto*', 4:20) only to enjoy a state of profound peace.

The Behavioural Referents of Anasakti

The qualities defining the sthitaprajna helped in the indentification of the behavioural referents of anāsakti which formed the core of items of the anasakti measure. These behavioural referents will be presented in terms of characteristics which an anasakt individual is likely to manifest in the conduct of his degree of anāsakti will—

(i) perceive his work as duty. He is likely to discharge his duties scrupulously without mental attachment to the consequences,

(ii) show a lack of concern for the consequences of action. An anasakt person is likely to act without much insistence for rewards,

(iii) appraise his success and failure in objective rather than in egoistical terms,

(iv) be less governed by external standards such as social approval or censor. His behaviour will be guided by his own internal standards about correctness of conduct and excellence in performance,

(v) not experience strong negative emotions such as passion, fear or anger ('*vitaragabhayakrodhah*', 2:56),

(vi) not insist on seeking pleasure and avoiding pain. At the physical level, an anasakt person is expected to show greater endurance for pain than others. At the social level, he is expected to overcome temptations and resist hedonistic compulsions. As a result of these, it is anticipated that an anasakt person would be able to exercise ethical choices more readily against various appetites and aversions (Naidu, Thapa & Das, 1986),

(vii) show an absence of egotism or sense of mineness. He would perhaps be able to replace his smaller personal motives by larger impersonal goals,

(viii) maintain an emotional equipoise in the face of positive as well as negative experiences. He would maintain equanimity of emotions while facing the desirable and the undersirable and would remain imperturbed by success or failure, auspicious or inauspicious, pleasant or unpleasant events,

(ix) show total absorption in the task at hand. He would manifest complete involvement in all kinds of tasks that he may undertake, dissolving the past fears and future expectations (Swami Chinmayananda, 1975),

(x) show heightened concentration. An anāsakt person would be able to focus on the task at hand and would not be easily distractable. He would concentrate on any task with a relative ease regardless of what be its affective value for him, and

(xi) make an effort toward achieving task excellence. Under no circumstances, an anāsakt person would compromise with lower standards of task excellence.

Illustrative Items of Anasakti Measure

Items of the anasakti measure were written in Hindi. They were generically related to the behavioural referents of anāsakti but were more narrow and specific in their meanings. The English equivalents of a few items of the measure are being presented here for the purpose of illustration.

An anāsakt person is highly effort oriented. He places greater emphasis on effort rather than on its consequences or extrinsic rewards. Items such as '*I like doing those tasks which may yield benefits quickly*' or '*while I am engaged in an important task at that time I repeatedly ask myself whether I would succeed or fail*' were framed to measure how much emphasis one places on his efforts rather than on consequences which those efforts may yield.

Effort orientation is also related to the importance which one assigns to his duties with full conviction even when they turn out to be expensive ventures or invite social criticisms. While fulfilling his duties he is expected to be less concerned about whether or not he would be rewarded in return. Items such as '*I hesitate in fulfilling a duty if I find it an expensive venture*' measured the emphasis which an individual places on carrying out his duties.

Another important aspect of effort orientation refers to how intensely an individual attends to the tasks that he undertakes. While attending to a task, effort oriented individuals are expected to control fluctuations of attention and resist minor distractions more easily than others. Items like '*While I am engaged in an important task at that time I get distracted by small happenings around me*' and '*I work hard even on small tasks' were framed to measure attention control and effort after excellence*, respectively. An anasakt person is not only highly effort oriented but also emotionally stable. Because he does not place much emphasis on consequences while he attends to a task, he acquires the necessary strength to maintain emotional poise when consequences eventually appear. Such a person feels neither too happy when he obtains rewards nor too unhappy when he experiences failure. Items like '*generally I remain peaceful*' and '*I feel depressed when I lose*' were written to measure equipoise in the face of success or failure.

Restriction of pleasure seeking impulses is another important facet of anasakti. To the extent an individual is anasakt, he acquires the inner strength to resist temptations and restrain himself from indulging in sensory pleasures. Such items as '*I do not long for physical pleasures*' measured the degree to which an individual can resist hedonistic compulsions.

Besides these, anasakti also relates to an individual's

psychological orientation towards living in the present and not in the past or future. It also relates to an absence of such concerns as comparing one's performance with the performance of others or seeking their approval. Items like '*Generally I live in the present*' and '*I often think whether my work is better or worse in comparison to others*' were framed to measure present orientation and concern for social approval.

The extent to which an individual has internalised the ideal of anasakti gets reflected in the general philosophy of life to which he subscribes and his work related attitudes. Accordingly, the items of the anasakti measure were kept in two sections. The first section consisted of items which intended to measure the respondent's global orientation towards life in general. Examples are '*generally I do not think about the past days*' or '*I hesitate in fulfilling a duty if I find it an expensive venture*'.

In the second section, the remaining items were subsumed under the stem : '*While I am engaged in an important task at that time*'. Here are a few examples of items with their stem : While I am engaged in an important task at that time '*I am not aware of how much time has passed*' or '*My effort does not decrease even when success is at a distance*'.

Respondents were asked to indicate to what extent behaviours contained in these items were applicable to them on a five point rating scale ranging from 1 (not at all applicable) to 5 (entirely applicable). Reverse scoring was done for items which were negatively cued. A higher score on this measure indicated a higher degree of anasakti.

If after reading this chapter other investigators get a little more interested in indigenous and spiritual concepts which are psychologically significant and feel inclined to work on them and thus contribute to the creation of a psychology with a distinct Indian flavour, we would have been amply rewarded.

REFERENCES

Mills, C.W. (1973). *The Sociological Imagination*. New York : Penguin Books.

Naidu, R.K., & Pande, N. (1990). On quantifying a spiritual concept : An interim research report about non-attachment and health. *Abhigyan*, 1-18.

Naidu, R.K., Thapa, K., & Das, M.M. (1986). On measuring detachment : An example of a scientific analog of an indigenous concept. Unpublished manuscript, University of Allahabad, Allahabad.

Pande, N., & Naidu, R.K. (1986). Effort and outcome orientations as moderators of stress-strain relationship. *Psychological Studies*, 31, 207-214.

Pande, N. (1990). Studies on differential vulnerability to stress: The impact of detachment on health. Unpublished Doctoral dissertation, University of Allahabad, Allahabad.

Pande, N., & Naidu, R.K. (1992). Anasakti and health: A study of non-attachment. *Psychology and Developing Societies*, 4, 89-104.

Radhakrishnan, S. (1948). *The Bhagavad Gita*. Bombay: Blackie.

Schumacher, E.F. (1977). *A Guide for the Perplexed*. New York Harper Colonphone Books.

Sinha, D. & Naidu, R.K. (1994). Multilayered hierarchical structure of Self and Not-Self: The Indian perspective. In M. Bouvy *et al.* (Eds.). *Journeys into Cross-Cultural Psychology*. Amsterdam : Swets & Zeitlinger.

Swami Chinmayananda, (1975). *The Holy Gita*. Bombay : Central Chinmaya Trust.

Thapa, K. (1983). Effort-consequence orientation as a moderator variable of stress-strain relationship. Postdoctoral dissertation, University of Allahabad, Allahabad.

Tripathi, R.C., Naidu, R.K., Thapa, K., & Biswas, S.N. (1993). *Stress, Health and Performance : A Study of Police Organisation in Uttar Pradesh*. University of Allahabad, Allahabad.

Underwood, B.J. (1968). *Experimental Psychology*. Bombay : The Times of India Press.

6

Health Beliefs and Coping with Chronic Illness

AJIT K. DALAL

With the increase in life expectancy in recent times, the prevalence of chronic diseases is also on increase. Chronic diseases, such as arthritis, asthma, tuberculosis, heart attack, diabetes are more common today than ever before. These chronic diseases and their subsequent complications cause death in almost 70 to 75 per cent of the cases world-wide. It is thus quite probable that one day some doctor would tell us that our illness is chronic and cannot be cured.

Once an illness is diagnosed as chronic and the realization dawns that one has to live with it, a new phase of crisis begins. Though much depends on the severity of the sickness and prior anticipation, patients experience disorientation, anxiety, fear and loss of control, as if life has slipped out of their hands. The distressing physcial symptoms, pain and long drawn treatment regimen drains away not only one's economic and social but also psychological resources. Patients are frequently required to mobilize all their external and internal resources to combat the disease and pain. Most of the patients only gradually reconcile to the fact that the chronic disease has become part of their existence and they cannot wish it away. In some cases, as in the case of heart attack, the immediate concern in the crisis phase is of hospitalization and saving life; psychological considerations are secondary in this initial phase. In most of the other illnesses people get forewarning signals and have some degree of preparedness.

The diagnosis of a chronic disease triggers several major worries. One needs to ascertain how much the illness will impair their functioning. How can it be integrated with their lives in the long term perspective? What kind of adjustments they would be required to make in their occupational and social life? Generally, patients get enough time to ponder over the illness and its consequences, test their naive theories of illness and recovery, form some stable opinion about the causes of the illness and about appropriate coping strategies. These inquisitive exercies, which Lazarus (1983) has called secondary appraisal, clears some of the mist shrouding the illness.

The patient's progress from initial crisis phase to physical and psychological rehabilitation is fraught with many setbacks, fight backs, forward leaps and uncertainties. A recovery apparently smooth and steady may suddenly nosedive creating an emergency, or a life threatening condition may suddenly brighten up. A large variety of factors would play an important role at each stage. The background of the sick person— age, gender, socio-economic status; personality characteristics-intelligence, emotional maturity, self-esteem; social factors— social support, family network, etc., greatly influence one's capacity to cope with the illness. There is enough research evidence to throw light on these aspects. This chapter is not intended to discuss the role of these factors but aims at examining some of the health related beliefs which a sick person holds and the extent to which these beliefs play an important role in shaping the health practices. It is recognised that the patients' own beliefs about their health and treatment regulate their health behaviour to a far greater extent than the doctors' beliefs or objective medical data (Roberts, *et al.*, 1984). Though there has been a spurt of research examining these health beliefs in recent years, no clear pattern in terms of their implications for recovering from the illness has emerged.

Much of the research focusing on health beliefs share some common understanding about human nature. First, human beings have enormous capacity to withstand severe personal tragedies and illnesses, even for a prolonged period. This has a psychological cost, but it does not diminish the adaptive potential. Second, people are motivated to make efforts to recover from the crisis situation. In fact, it is assumed that the efforts to recover begin with the onset of the tragic happening. Third, people are not only motivated but also possess a self-curing mechanism. In the crisis situation, this mechanism gets activated and people on very rare occasions need institutional support to deal with the psychological crisis. People not only recover or successfully adjust but also learn to be more resourceful in facing a similar crisis in future. Fourth, people can be helped and trained to cope with the adversities by bringing appropriate changes in their own beliefs and attitudes.

When do people realize that they are chronically sick?

In some cases of coronary heart disease the impinging reality leaves no scope for speculations. However, in most of the other instances it takes quite long for the patients to reconcile with the fact that they are chronically sick. People tend to believe, even in the face of hard evidence to the contrary, that they will be fully cured. When the disease is diagnosed as chronic, there is a tendency to explore the possibility of error in the diagnosis. People are very susceptible at this stage to suggestions that the disease is curable. Even patients at the advanced stage of cancer are found to be hopeful of complete cure (Kubler-Ross, 1969).

People assign meaning to their illness in many different ways. As pointed out by the medical sociologist Parsons (1972), the sick role is necessarily socially deviant and society will permit it only after the doctor legitimizes the patient's need, both to regress and accept the sick condition. Psychologists, however, take a different view point. Herzlich's (1973) empirical study focused on the social psychological meaning and implications of health and illness as stages of being. The respondents regarded illness as an intrusion, an external imposition which renders a person passive and powerless. Herzlich observed that when people face an illness, particularly a long term one, their self-perceptions are blurred. To regain some sense of self-sensibility, they need to make sense out of their illness. Sometimes, the need to understand the illness is so compelling that it actually overshadows the desire to be cured.

Ostensibly, the meaningful understanding that a sick person seeks is not limited to the medical explanations of one's sickness. Patients extend their formulations to embrace social-psychological implications for themselves and their family. This view is contrary to the view held by psychoanalysts who regard illness as 'motivated' (Lipowski, 1970). The cognitive view advocated here considers it unlikely that many people actively seek illness. It is possible that some patients may impart neurotic meaning to it, for example, they may view illness as a punishment or as an escape from the rigours of life.

Taking Lipowski's (1970) categorization of the concepts of illness, Schussler (1992) found in a study of chronic patients that those who perceived illness as challenge, as enemy, or as punishment resorted to negative emotional coping, those who viewed their illness as relief, as a strategy resorted to immature defenses (somatization, regression, etc.), and those who viewed their illness in terms of value, and internal control showed evidence for cognitive reconstruction. The meaning of illness was thus found closely associated with the nature of coping.

In the Indian setting, it is generally not through the routine check up that the disease is detected. When people observe some unusual symptoms or bodily changes, they confide it to their close relatives and friends, who help in interpreting the symptoms to arrive at a naive diagnosis (Singh, 1987). These are the people in the close social network who provide initial interpretations about the possible implications of the symptoms. Those who appraise the illness as still at the initial stage may try domestic remedies. In quite a number of cases formal medical check up does not take place to arrive at a diagnosis

(Chandrasekhar, Isaac, Kapur & Parthsarthi, 1981). There is a greater degree of reliance on the diagnosis made by elders, priests and paramedical personnel.

Why Me? The Causal Search

Once a diagnosis of the chronic disease dawns upon the patient, a very natural reaction is that of fear and anxiety. The patient is uncertain as to how to handle the anxiety. An easy way out is to refuse to accept the diagnosis or to delink symptoms from the illness, and thus unconsciously block any cognizance of the illness. This state, however, cannot last long, for the reality may be too volatile to be swept under the rug. The other option for the patient is to accept the diagnosis but resort to other ego-defences, such as rationalization, compartmentalization, isolation, displacement, projection, and the like. These patients belittle the significance of the symptoms, delay seeking medical care, or fail to comply with treatment regimen and rehabilitation programme. One such example is of heart patients who at times procrastinate in seeking diagnosis, and thereby jeopardize their chances of survival.

There is enough research evidence to suggest that people spontaneously engage in causal search in their everyday life. In a review of published research works, Weiner (1985) found strong evidence for causal thinking. However, this causal thinking does not trigger on every conceivable occasion. Wong and Weiner (1981) and Weiner (1985) found that casual search is activated when the outcome is negative and unexpected. The experimental studies of Dalal and Agrawal (1987) on student sample also confirmed that the negative outcome promotes causal search. Gerard (1963) showed that the situation of high uncertainty is another precondition for causal thinking. The motivation to find causes of the illness was recognised in many early clinical studies of cancer patients (e.g., Bard & Dyk, 1956). Patients were found to be reporting perceived cause of their illness when questioned at any point in time, following their diagnosis. In the researches which had assessed patients months and years after diagnosis, the number of patients who report causal attributions range between 69 to 95 per cent (Affleck, *et al.*, 1985; Lowery & Jacobson, 1984). In one study, Taylor, Lichtman & Wood (1984) found that a majority of cancer patients, their spouses, relatives and close friends do report the causes of cancer. However, the frequency of causal attributions vary with the type of illness. Lung cancer patients were less likely to report causes of their illness than were myocardial infaraction patients (Mumma & McCorkle, 1982). Frequency of the attributed causes also depend on the severity of the illness. Cardiac patients with more severe symptoms, during recovery reported greater number of causal attributions (Affleck *et al.*, 1985).

Stuides conducted on Indian hospitalized patients present a somewhat different picture. Studies, by Dalal and Pande (1988), and Dalal and Singh (1992) on orthopaedic and tuberculosis patients, respectively, addressed this issue. The results showed that the causal thinking was not very frequent among orthopaedic patients with accidental injuries. The patients were asked if they contemplated why this mishap has happened only to them. Most of the answers fell in the categories 'never' (1) and 'seldom' (2) on a 5-point scale. When the patients were asked to mention the causes of the accident, most of them gave one or two causes, permanently disabled listing less causes than the temporarily disabled. In the second study on tuberculosis patients, it was found that very few patients mentioned more than one cause. In another study by Agarwal and Dalal (1993) on heart attack patients, a similar pattern was observed.

It is, however, argued that the low evidence for causal thinking does not necessarily imply absence of causal beliefs. A number of causal beliefs are part of the cultural belief system, deeply ingrained in the process of socialization. In all the three studies referred above, God's will and *Karma* were more frequently mentioned as causes by the Hindu patients implying greater acceptance of their fate, rather than questioning it. This finding is corroborated in earlier studies also (e.g., Minturn & Hitchcock, 1966). The theory of *Karma* is not only the corner stone of Hindu religious philosophy but also much of its social theory (Gokhale, 1961; Radhakrishnan, 1926). This theory has profound influence on Indian thinking, providing readily available causal explanations to a wide range of life events, including tragic ones. According to this theory, all good or bad deeds accumulate across all previous births and the present suffering could be due to the misdeeds of previous births.

Whether causal search is present or absent, the evidence is overwhelming that the patients who have causal explanations are better adjusted than those who have no causal explanation (Bulman & Wortman, 1977; Dalal & Pande, 1988; Lowery & Jacobson, 1984; Silver & Wortman, 1980).

Why do people need to have causes of their misfortune and suffering? There are several tentative answers. People generally do not want to believe that the world around them is chaotic and unlawful where events occur randomly. They need to find some order and meaning in the things happening to them and others. Frankl (1963) in a study of people who survived in the concentration camps during the Second World War found that this search for meaning in life was a major preoccupation of the prisoners. Those prisoners who could find a positive meaning in their suffering did cope better than the others. Paranjpe (1984, 1987) noted that the search for explanations of sufferings has been the cornerstone of Indian philosophical traditions. By understanding the causes of an event, one may also begin to understand the significance of the event and what it symbolizes about one's life (Taylor, 1983). This understanding helps one to adjust to the new realities of life.

The other function which causal attributions serve for the patient is of assigning moral responsibility for the events. People generally want to believe in a just world (Lerner, 1975), where people get what they deserve and deserve what they get. It was observed by Lerner and his colleagues in a series of experiments (Lerner, 1975; Lerner & Mathews, 1967) that people have a tendency to blame the victims for their misfortunes. Bulman and Wortman

(1977) found that the spinal cord injury patients who blamed themselves for the accident showed better coping than those who blamed others. Surprisingly, good copers also believed that the accident was unavoidable. Bulman and Wortman explained it in terms of the fact that the patients believed that they were voluntarily engaged in the activity that led to the accident. The motivation to make attributions appears much more complex in view of the finding that those accident victims who attributed their accident to the Karma showed better recovery (Dalal & Pande, 1988); whereas, in the case of tuberculosis patients this was not the case (Dalal & Singh, 1992).

Attribution to Karma implies blaming oneself in causal but not in moral terms. In few studies the distinction between causal and moral responsibility is maintained. It is quite possible to blame oneself in a causal sense but not in a moral sense (Kanekar, 1988). For example, when you ignore normal health precautions, violate normal procedures, you feel responsible but not morally. The essence of this aspect of explanation is the question of what you ought to have done, rather than the consequences or what you did. In a study of accident victims Brewin (1984) found greater causal self-blame associated with victims feeling less anxious and tense, whereas greater moral self-blame was associated with a more rapid return to work.

Quite often, making attributional judgments is a public activity and people are supposed to explain why they fell sick. People generally want to present themselves favourably in the eyes of others and make esteem enhancing, self-protective attributions. Snyder, Stephan & Rosenfield (1978) refer to this tendency as egotism and suggest that when faced with the possibility of failure on a task, people may apply the tactics of not trying, of giving up prematurely. This has the advantage that people can attribute their failure to lack of effort, a less distressing cause than lack of ability. Jones and Berglas (1978) found the evidence of people using various self-handicapping strategies to have some face saving causal attributions.

Belief in Personal Control

Personal control refers to belief in one's ability to influence intended outcomes by participating in decision making and carrying out those decisions. One aspect of personal control involves a sense of freedom of choice, being aware of the opportunities to select preferred goals and means (Janis & Rodin, 1979). Personal control is integral to self-concept and self-esteem (Bandura, 1977; deCharms, 1979; White, 1959). The feeling of control is presumed to reduce the experience of stress, facilitate coping with unavoidable, unpleasant events and perhaps even enable people to live longer. For example, cancer patients who believed that they had control over their illness were better adjusted to their illness than patients without such beliefs (Taylor, Lichtman & Wood, 1984). In another study, the results suggested that when the illness condition was perceived as being modifiable and under one's control, the recovery from mycoardial infraction was enhanced (Bar-on, 1987).

It may be mentioned here that belief in control does not imply real control. Even in case of cancer, findings show that mothers of children with leukamia blame themselves for having it (Chodoff, Friedman, & Hamburg, 1964). Langer (1975) termed this phenomenon as illusion of control. Many such beliefs in control persist even in the face of contrary evidence. Lazarus (1983) argued that many of these illusions of control indeed have positive consequences and lead to better psychological adaptation. Such illusions are pervasive in day-to-day activities. Lazarus termed them as *healthy illusions.*

A chronic illness undermines one's sense of control over one's body and over life in general. Patients need to regain some degree of personal control to plan future actions. An inference about what caused the disease facilitates the adjustment process and helps to manage or prevent the disease from getting worse. Taylor (1984) found that among cancer patients, 37 per cent believed that they had a lot of control. She found that both the belief that one can control one's own cancer, and the belief that physician or treatment mode can control it, were strongly associated with overall positive adjustment, and both together were even better. Thompson (1981) after reviewing a series of studies observed that those who had a sense of personal control were less distressed than those who had experienced a lack of control.

People can control the course of their illness in many ways. Thompson (1981) has identified five types of control beliefs which patients can exercise in a crisis situation. One is behavioural control, which is the belief in one's ability to take some steps to reduce the intensity of the illness, make it less frequently occurring, or alter its timing and duration. Patients believe that by taking appropriate actions, negative consequences of the prolonged sickness can be averted. To be effective, behavioural control need not be real. The belief that one can take steps to control one's illness is sufficient to reduce distress. Second is *cognitive control*, which is availability of some cognitive skills to think differently about the illness. For example, a hospitalized patient about to undergo a painful diagnostic medical procedure may be instructed to focus on the benefits of the procedure rather than on the current discomfort. Third is *decision control* which refers to the belief in ability to make decisions about the future course of action. The patients believed that they have options to choose from; are capable of making their own decisions. The fourth is *information control*, which is a sense of control achieved when one acquires sufficient information about the abnoxious event itself. A patient awaiting surgery, for example, may have all post-operative side effects carefully explained, so that when they occur, it will not be distressing. The fifth is *retrospective control*, a term coined by Thompson, to refer to the belief that the event which just occurred was controllable, thereby implying that its reoccurrence can be controlled in future.

Thompson's conceptualization of control was further extended by Rothbaum, Weisz and Snyder (1982) in their two process model of control. According to them, control can be primary or secondary, i.e., one can change the aversive situation itself (primary control) or one can strive to bring oneself in line with the aversive situation (secondary control). If the attempts for primary control fail or are perceived as likely to fail, then the person may respond with secondary control. Like primary control, secondary control may also assume many forms, such as predictive control, illusory control, vicarious control, and interpretive control. Rothbaum *et al.* (1982) have presented an impressive body of research evidence to suggest that behaviours like withdrawal, passivity, and inaction can, in fact, be secondary control restoring efforts, not necessarily indicative of helplessness.

Attribution of Responsibility

Brickman and his associates have further extended the research in this direction by incorporating causal attribution and control in a unifying model. Brickman, *et al.* (1982) have made a distinction between attribution of responsibility for the problem and for its solution. This model was initially propounded to predict helping behaviour but can be easily applied in cases of chronic illness. Four alternative situations are possible, giving rise to 4 different models. People may hold themselves responsible for both the cause and the solution (moral model); for causing the disease only but not for the solution (enlightenment model); not for causing the problem but for its solution (compensatory model); neither for causing nor for the solution of the problem (hospital model). The behavioural sequence in these four situations would vary. In the study by Dalal and Singh (1992) on tuberculosis patients, both causal and recovery beliefs were studied,i.e., beliefs about the factors causing illness and beliefs about the factors facilitating recovery. It was observed that recovery beliefs had higher correlation with psychological adjustment than causal beliefs. In a study conducted on surgical patients (Dalal & Singh, 1992) the trend was reverse, i.e., causal beliefs were more closely associated with surgical recovery than the recovery beliefs. In fact, the attending surgeons were attributed most of the recovery.

Health Beliefs and Affective Reactions

A wide variety of reactions are observed when people are told about the diagnosis of a chronic illness. Quite often the initial reaction is that of denial or disbelief which averts the onset of any emotional crisis. Denial also gives some time to adjust to the impinging reality. Other typical reactions are of high anxiety and emotional disturbance, clouding clear thinking. On the other hand, there are people who accept the diagnosis rather stoically. Chronic illness is something people have to live with and have to make long-term alterations in their life style. There could be wide fluctuations in the mood of patients with changes in their physical conditions and nature of disability. Pain and discomfort are other factors influencing affective state. Many of these affective reactions may be transitory or of a diffused kind, whereas, other reactions are specific to the appraisal of the symptoms. Broadly speaking, affective reactions could be of two types-general response to the situation, like fear, sadness, unpleasantness, anxiety etc., and those affects which are belief-dependent. The belief-related affects are often very specific reactions, based on causal and control appraisal of the situation. Such affective reactions are those of anger, depression, disappointment, pity, etc.

Studies have been done to establish linkages between affective reactions to an undesirable life condition, and causal and control related beliefs. Causal appraisal gives rise to a qualitative distinction among feelings. Weiner (1985) found that in the case of help-giving, lack of effort on the part of help-seeker aroused anger, whereas physical disability ensued the feeling of pity. Dalal & Tripathi (1987) in a study of help seeking behaviour found the linkages between control beliefs and affective reactions. Such attribution—affect linkages found in their two experimental studies were uncontrollable—sympathy, controllable-anger, dislike.

The onset of chronic illness and subsequent hospitalization result in more frequent feelings of anxiety, depression, suppressed anger and helplessness (Westerbrook & Viney, 1982). In an Indian study by Agrawal and Dalal (1993), the dominant affective reactions found in hospitalized patients were helplessness, depression and metaphysical rationalization. There were some gender differences—female patients showed greater anger and anxiety, whereas male patients more often engaged in disengagement and rationalization. It was also noted that anger was the least frequent reaction. In a study by Kohli (1992) on cancer patients, evidence for anger response was very low. There is greater degree of acceptance and rationalization in terms of the theory of *Karma*, where people look for justification in their own wrong-doing in the previous births. Higher attribution to metaphysical factors probably explains why Indian patients are low on anger reaction.

It seems that the feeling which is more often expressed to the loss of control is that of helplessness. People show acute helplessness when they feel loss of control in tragic situations. When all previously acquired behaviour skills fail to yield any desirable result and the patients start doubting their own ability to exercise any control then the feeling of helplessness overtakes. Abramson, Seligman Teasdale (1978) posited that the affective reaction will depend on causal attributions they make. If the cause is perceived as being permanent rather than temporary, then the feeling of helplessness will be long lasting. If the cause is perceived as influencing many situations rather than just one situation, then the feeling of helplessness is likely to generalize to other situations. Finally, if the cause is perceived as being internal rather than external, the person is likely to suffer a loss of self-esteem. Wortman and Brehm (1975) argued that whether a person would experience anger or helplessness depends on his or her causal attributions.

The feeling which is reported most frequently in the cases of chronic illnessess is that of depression. Depression is characterised by dejected mood, loss of desire to do things, general tiredness and inability to concentrate. The depressed person thinks that nothing can be done to change the undesirable life conditions.

Like anger and helplessness, the feeling of depression sets in at a later stage of the chronic illness. During the initial phase of the illness, the patients may be too pre-occupied with diagnosis and hospital procedure to feel depressed. The feeling surfaces at a later stage when the patient has tried many treatments unsuccessfully and now has to cope with a host of new problems, related to the adjusting to their day-to-day living. It is suggested that the emotional reaction of depression is beneficial in a sense that it is preparatory to the later adjustment that must be made as a consequence of illness. However, acute or prolonged depression is pathological.

Compliance with Treatment Regimen

In a chronic illness the treatment is long drawn, sometimes life-long, and its discontinuation at any stage may be hazardous. Secondly, in a chronic illness onus of adhering to the treatment largely depends on the patient himself or herself, once he or she is out of the critical phase. In diabetes and arthritis, for example, patients are expected to monitor their physical condition, follow the treatment regimen and take necessary precautions. Same is the case with heart patients, in whose case any neglect may be fatal at times. Patients' role in following the treatment regimen thus seems crucial in chronic illness.

Notwithstanding, universally, lack of compliance seems more a rule than exception. Sackett (1976) suggests that more than 50 per cent of the patients do not take prescribed medication in accordance with the instructions. Thus even in the situations where proper medicare is available, compliance is still a problem. The social characteristics of the patients such as age, gender and education were found to be poor predictors of compliance (Kasl, 1975), though a high correlation was found between characteristics of the treatment regimen and nature of patient-doctor relationship.

Rosenstock's (1974) health belief model, originally developed to predict preventive health behaviour, was later extended to account for compliance to the treatment regimen. In this, health belief model, the perception of threat to health is the most crucial factor. The perceived threat of the disease is determined by two considerations: perceived threat of the disease one is suffering from or could suffer from, and perceived vulnerability to the illness and its consequences. For example, a diabetic would first assess his condition as severe or mild and would think about its possible consequences for his life adjustments, before he perceives diabetes as a threat.

However, this perception of threat is not sufficient to engage in health-care behaviour. One important factor is the belief that a particular health-related activity will protect oneself from the threat. A second factor in the model which will determine health behaviour is the perceived cost and benefit of compliance. In order to comply, the patient must believe that the recommended regimen will be effective and the accrued benefits will offset cost, such as discomfort, side effects and other negative aspects. According to the health-belief model, to initiate or sustain any treatment regimen, the patient needs some cues to action, something that makes a patient aware of the potential consequences. Internal cues are very important in this context.

The health belief model is tested taking various chronic illnesses, and is found useful in predicting compliance. Where an illness is diagnosed and a course of treatment recommended, the patients' perception of the threat in terms of symptoms and future consequences becomes crucial. It is in relation to this threat that possible actions and their costs can be evaluated. Becker and Maiman (1975) and Kirscht (1983) reviewed the literature on patient compliance from the point of view of the health belief model. The model has been used in the studies of compliance to hypertensive regimen (Becker, *et al.*, 1977), tuberculosis (Hochbaum, 1958) and cardiac care (Johannsen, Hellmuth & Sorauf, 1966). There are now a number of studies which do not support the health belief model, particularly when the unhealthy behaviour is strongly habitual, like cigarette smoking (Weisenberg, Kegeles & Lund, 1980), or deeply rooted in the local culture.

Attempts have been made in the past to enhance compliance through systematic changes in health attitudes and beliefs. Tagliacozzo *et al.* (1974) examined role of information in compliance behaviour. To the experimental group a special nurse gave detailed instructions about various aspects of the disease, whereas the control group received regular medical care. There was no effect of the instructions. However, the factors found in that study having significant impact were : duration of illness, multiple illnesses, high anxiety, favourable attitude towards the clinic and the doctor, and perceived severity of illness. It appears that any information which is general and abstract does not result in compliance.

It was observed in many studies that those patients who show helplessness and depression, also show poor compliance. Some interventions using attributional concept have been tried to inculcate sense of self-efficacy and self-control. One such study was conducted by Chambliss and Murray (1979). In their study, the subjects who were inclined to give up smoking were given a placebo capsule to complement their efforts at self-control. The placebo was described as increasing, decreasing or having no effect on symptoms of withdrawal. In the second phase of the study, half of the subjects were told that the drug was inactive and that they had reduced their smoking through their own efforts, while the rest of the subjects were not debriefed at all. The debriefed group, and in particular those with internal locus of control, went on to reduce their smoking by significantly greater amount than the others. Colletti and Kopel (1979) also reported that the more the subjects attributed their improvement to their own efforts, the less they were smoking one year later. Sonney and Janoff (1982) gave their obese patients a choice between two weight loss programmes, one emphasizing self-control, another external control by the therapist. Both programmes were equally effective during the treatment period, but the self-control group maintained their progress significantly better at follow-up.

Managing Pain and Discomfort

In many chronic illnesses, such as arthritis, pain is the most disturbing consequence. Sometimes, treatment of the disease produces pain and discomfort, which by itself poses management problems. The chronic pain in many instances has greater debilating effects than the illness itself. Eventhough it may have a physiological basis, pain is basically a psychological experience. For example, pain can be minimal when attention is distracted but when attention is focussed on the pain, the pain experience is heightened. Pain tends to increase as the anxiety level of the person increases. Christopherson (1966) demonstrated that there are significant cultural differences in the magnitude of pain-responding to identical pain stimulation.

There is considerable research evidence showing that the degree of pain and level of distress that people experience largely depend on the labels and cognitions that are applied to the physical state. Nisbett and Schachter (1966) were among the first to show that when subjects attributed their fear arousal state to the side effects of a placebo pill, they rated electric shock less painful than the control group. In later work (Storms & Nisbett, 1970), reattribution technique was employed with therapeutic benefits. The subjects who were insomniacs were given placebos, described accompanying insomnia, like alertness, heart rate increase and feeling of increased body heat. They argued that the subjects taking pills would be able to attribute their arousal to the drug (external attribution), rather than to the self-generated emotional distress that intensified their insomnia. Their external attribution was expected to result in lowered emotionality and quicker onset of sleep. The subjects did in fact, report getting to sleep about 12 minutes sooner on the nights they took placebo pills than on the nights without the pills.

However, the findings in other studies are not so clear. Presumably, in some circumstances, people can tolerate pain better if they attribute their pain reactions to themselves, whereas in other circumstances, their pain tolerance is higher if they attribute their pain reactions to external causes. So far, there are few experimental or clinical investigations of pain, specifying the conditions under which one or the other reaction will occur. There are enough research possibilities in studying the effects of causal beliefs on the experience of pain.

Living with Chronic Illness

Once the diagnosis of chronic illness is accepted and patients have reconciled to the fact that they have to live with it, the spotlight shifts on efforts to integrate the illness with the patients' life. The concern is how and how quickly patients can be brought back to their usual life routine. In a large number of cases a major readjustment is required. Much would depend on the extent of physical impairment due to the illness. Physical problems engendered by the illness range widely. Breathlessness associated with asthma, metabolic changes in diabetic patients, motor coordination problems in spinal cord injury cases, impaired body-limbs movement associated with arthritis, are but a few examples of physical problems. There may be psychological problems such as loss of memory in epilepsy. The patients are required to put up with a large number of such impairments.

In chronic illnesses, physical rehabilitation is integral to the treatment procedure itself. According to Taylor (1986), physical rehabilitation of the chronically ill patients typically involves several goals: to help them use their body as much as possible, to sensitize patients about the physical change and reality, and to develop new management skills. Quite often patients are required to read bodily signals about the onset of the crisis, take precautionary measures, administer medicine, etc. Any comprehensive physical rehabilitation programme must pertain to all or most of these goals. The task is certainly challenging.

In the long term, an even more challanging task is that of psycho-social rehabilitation. Social support and patients' own internal resources are crucial factors in successful long term coping with the chronic disease. The psycho-social rehabilitation of the patient does not follow a predetermined course, rather there are many ups and downs and uncertainties which keep cropping from time to time. Much of the successful rehabilitation depends on patients' positive interaction with people in their socio-cultural milieu. Fortunately, most of the patients show impressive ability to cope with adverse life conditions. Many of the survival strivings are built-in the human nature which are activated whenever survival is endangered. Thus, very few need professional help to get rehabilitated (Taylor, 1983).

The phenomenon which facilitates the task of rehabilitation is, what Rosenbaum (1983) termed, 'learned resourcefulness'. Learned resourcefulness refers to an acquired repertoire of self-regulated internal responses, such as emotions, pain and cognitions (Rosenbaum, 1988; Rosenbaum & Ben-Ari, 1985). The conditions that activate the self-regulatory process are similar to those that are recognised as stress conditions. In the conditions of prolonged stress due to chronic illness, people gradually acquire a large response repertoire to cope successfully. In many instances, it is observed that the psychological adjustment or existence is even better than the one prior to the illness.

Against this background, the emphasis of any rehabilitation programme should be to provide the opportunity in which a patient can learn to become resourceful, i.e., acquire self-regulatory skills to live with the illness. Perhaps the important question is how one can learn to be resourceful. Meichenbaum (1977, 1985) developed a stress inoculation programme for this purpose. The major component of the stress inoculation programme are: (1) self-monitoring of maladaptive thoughts, images, feelings and behaviours, (2) training in cognitive and behavioural skills which enables them to cope effectively with the stress, and (3) emotion regulation. Meichenbaum argues that those who have acquired these skills develop a sense of learned resourcefulness. It is assumed that without any formal training, these behaviours are acquired in different degrees by most of the patients. These behavioural and cognitive skills facilitate the process of rehabilitation. Furthermore, it is suggested here that those who are able to help themselves (high resource persons) will be most helped by others. Those who are unable to help themselves are likely to deplete their social resources by their socially dependent behaviour (Monoroe & Steiner, 1986; Wortman & Lehman, 1985).

Consistent with this ideology, many self-help programmes have been developed in recent years. The basic philosophy behind self-help is that people who are suffering from similar illnesses can provide mutual support, understanding and information for successful adjustment. It is generally observed that patients tend to bring needed changes in their health habits through sharing experiences with others in the same plight. In a typical self-help programme, people with common illnesses are brought together and often with the help of a counselor they attempt to solve their problems collectively. Self-help groups emphasize face to face social interaction and assumes personal responsibility on the part of the members. These people come together for mutual assistance in satisfying a common need, i.e., overcoming a common handicap or life-disrupting problem, and bringing about desired social and personal changes (Katz & Bender, 1976). In these self-help groups the patients not only learn the skills to help themselves but also to help those who face similar crisis. Borne, Pruyn and Mey (1986) reviewed a large number of studies to examine the efficacy of self-help groups of cancer patients. They found positive results in almost all the studies reviewed, i.e., improvement in terms of general health perception and reduction in negative feelings.

The mutual support among fellow patients is a widely observed phenomenon. These patients come in contact with each other when they are in-patients in the same hospital or are visiting the same doctor. Kakar (1982) has described many social and religious institutions in India which are common meeting grounds for the patients and their relatives. Though their functioning is loosely structured and quite informal, they do serve the purpose. At the other extremity, as in the west, contact among fellow patients may be part of a highly structured intervention programme which is initiated in the hospital. There seems to be enough scope to develop various self-help type of interventions to alleviate the suffering of the chronic patients and to accelerate their rehabilitation.

REFERENCES

Abramson, L.Y., Seligman, M.E.P., & Teasdale, J.D. (1978). Learned helplessness in humans: Critique and reformulation. *Journal of Abnormal Psychology, 87*, 49-74.

Affleck, G., Allen, D.A., Tennen, H., McGrade, B.J., & Ratzan, S. (1985). Causal and control cognitions in present coping with a chronically ill child. *Journal of Social and Clinical Psychology, 3*, 369-379.

Agarwal, M., & Dalal, A.K. (1993). Causal beliefs and psychological recovery of myocardial infarction patients. *Journal of Social Psychology, 133*, 385-394.

Bandura, A. (1977). Self efficacy: Towards a unifying theory of behavior change. *Psychological Review, 84*, 191-215.

Bard, M., & Dyk, B.B. (1956). The psychodynamic significance of beliefs regarding the cause of serious illness. *Psychoanalytic Review, 43*, 146-162.

Bar-on, D. (1987). Causal attributions and the rehabilitation of myocardial infarction victims. *Journal of Social and Clinical Psychology, 5*, 114-122.

Becker, M.H., & Maiman, L.A. (1975). Socio-behavioral determinants of compliance with health and medical care recommendations. *Medical Care, 13*, 10-24.

Becker, M.H., Maiman, L.A., Kirscht, J.P., Haefner, D.P., & Drachman, B.H. (1977). The health belief model and dietary compliance: A field experiment. *Journal of Health and Social Behavior, 18*, 348-366.

Borne, H.W., Pruyn, J.F.A., & Mey, K.D. (1986). Self-help in cancer patients: A review of studies on the effects of contacts between fellow-patients. *Patient Education and Counseling, 8*, 367-385.

Brewin, C.R. (1984). Attributions for industrial accidents: Their relationship to rehabilitation outcome. *Journal of Social and Clinical Psychology, 2*, 156-164.

Brickman, P., Rabinowitz, V.C., Kariza. J., Coates, D., Cohn, E., & Kidder, L. (1982). Models of helping and coping. *American Psychologist, 37,* 368-384.

Bulman, J.R., & Wortman, C.B. (1977). Attribution of blame and coping in the "real world" : Severe accident victims react to their lot. *Journal of Personality and Social Psychology 35,* 351-363.

Chambliss, C., & Murray, E.J. (1979). Cognitive procedures for smoking reduction: Symptom versus efficacy attribution. *Cognitive Therapy and Research, 3,* 91-95.

Chandrasekhar, C.B., Isaac, M.K., Kapur, R.L., & Parthsarathi, R. (1981). Management of priority mental disorders in the community. *Indian Journal of Psychiatry, 23,* 174-178.

Chodoff, P., Friedman, S.B., & Hamburg, D.A. (1964). Stress, defenses and coping behavior : Observations in parents of children with malignant disease. *American Journal of Psychiatry, 120,* 743-749.

Christopherson, V. (1966). *Socio-cultural correlates of pain response* (Project No. 1390). Vocational Rehabilitation Administration, Washington, D.C.: Department of Health Education and Welfare.

Colletti, G., & Kopel, S.A. (1979). Maintaining behavior change. *Journal of Consulting and Clinical Psychology, 47,* 614-617.

Dalal, A.K., & Agrawal, R. (1987). Causal thinking and expectation of success in the achievement context. *Journal of General Psychology, 114,* 57-68.

Dalal, A.K. & Pande, M. (1988). Psychological recovery of the accident victims with temporary and permanent disability. *International Journal of Psychology, 23,* 25-40.

Dalal, A.K. & Singh, A.K. (1992). Causal beliefs and recovery from surgery. *Psychology and Health, 6,* 193-203.

Dalal, A.K. & Tripathi, M. (1987). When the help is denied: A study of attribution linked affective reactions. *International Journal of Psychology, 22,* 1-15.

de Charms, R. (1968). *Personal Causation: The Internal Affective Deteminants of Behavior.* New York: Academic Press.

Frankl, V. (1963). *Man's search for meaning.* New York: Washington Square Press.

Gerard, H.B. (1963). Emotional uncertainty and social comparison. *Journal of Abnormal and Social Psychology, 66,* 568-573.

Gokhale, B.G. (1961). *Indian Thought Throughout the Ages: A Study of Some Dominant Concepts.* Bombay: Asia Publishing House.

Herzlich, C. (1973). *Health and illness: A social psychological analysis*. New York: Academic Press.

Hochbaum, G. (1958). *Public participation in medical screening programs: A socio-psychological study*. Public Health Service Publication No. 572. Washington, D.C.: Super of Public Documents.

Janis, I.L. & Rodin, J. (1979). Attribution, control and decision-making: Social psychology and health care. In G.C. Stone. F, Cohen & N.E. Adler (Eds)., *Health Psychology*. San Francisco: Jassey-Bass.

Johannsen, W., Hellmuth, G., & Sorauf, T. (1966). On accepting medical recommendations. *Archives of Environmental Health, 12,* 63-69.

Jones, E.E., & Berglas, S. (1978). Control of attributions about the self through self-handicapping strategies: The appeal of alcohol and the role of under achievement. *Personality and Social Psychology Bulletin, 4,* 200-206.

Kanekar, S. (1988). Attribution of causal and moral responsibility: The case of a rape victim. In A.K. Dalal (Ed), *Attribution Theory and Research*. New Delhi: Wiley Eastern.

Kakar, S. (1982). *Shamans, mystics and doctors*. New Delhi: Oxford University Press.

Kasl, S.V. (1975). Issues in patient adherence to health care regimens. *Journal of Human Stress, 1,* 5-17.

Katz, A.H., & Bender, E.I. (Eds.) (1976). *The strength in us*. New York: Franklin Watts.

Kirscht, J.P. (1983). Preventive health behavior: A review of research and issues. *Health Psychology, 2,* 277-301.

Kohli, N. (1992). *Psycho-social adjustment in cervical cancer patients*. Unpublished report, University of Allahabad, Allahabad.

Kubler-Ross, E. (1969). *On Death and Dying*. New York.

Langer, E.J. (1975). The illusion of control. *Journal of Personality and Social Psychology, 32,* 311-328.

Lazarus, R.S. (1983). The costs and benefits of denial. In S. Bronsnitz (Ed.), *Denial of Stress*. New York: International University Press.

Lerner, M.J. (1975). Justice motive in social behavior. *Journal of Social Issues, 31,* 1-20.

Lerner, M.J. & Mathews, G. (1967). Reactions to other under conditions of indirect responsibility. *Journal of Personality and Social Psychology, 5,* 319-325.

Lipowski, Z.J. (1970). Physical illness, the individual, and the coping process. *Psychiatry in Medicine, 1,* 91-102.

Lowery, B.J. & Jacobson, B.S. (1984). Attributional analysis of chronic illness outcomes. *Nursing Research, 33,* 82-83.

Meichenbaum, D. (1977). *Cognitive Behavior Modification: An Integrative Approach.* New York: Plenum Press.

Meichenbaum, D. (1985). *Stress Inoculation Training.* New York: Pergamon Press.

Minturn, L., & Hitchcock, J.T. (1966). *The Rajputs of Khalapur India.* New York: John Wiley.

Monroe, S.M., & Steiner, S.C. (1986). Social support and pychopathology: Interrelations with pre-existing disorders stress and personality. *Journal of Abnormal Psychology, 95,* 29-39.

Mumma, C., & McCorkle, R. (1982). Causal attributions and life threatening disease. *International Journal of Psychiatry in Medicine, 12,* 312-198.

Nisbett, R.E., & Schachter, S. (1966). Cognitive manipulations of pain. *Journal of Experimental Social Psychology, 2,* 227-230.

Paranjpe, A.C. (1984). *Theoretical Psychology: The Meeting of East and West.* New York: Plenum Press.

Paranjpe, A.C. (1987). *The nature of suffering and its remedy: A perspective from the cultural tradition of India.* Unpublished manuscript, Simon Fraser University, Canada.

Parsons, T. (1972). Definitions of health and illness in the light of American values and social structure. In E.G. Jaco (Ed.), *Patients, Physicians, and Illness* (2nd ed.). New York: Free Press.

Radhakrishnan, S. (1926). *The Hindu view of life.* Bombay: Blakie.

Roberts. N., Smith, E., Bennett, S., Cape, J., Norton, R., & Kilburn, P. (1984). Health beliefs and rehabilitation after lumber disc surgery. *Journal of Psychosomatic Research, 28,* 139-144.

Rosenbaum, M. (1983). Learned resourcefulness as a behavioural repertoire for the self-regulation of internal events: Issues and speculations. In M. Rosenbaum, C.M. & Frnaks Jaffe (Eds.), *Perspectives on Behavior Theory in the Eighties* (pp. 54-73). New York: Springer.

Rosenbaum, M. (1988). Learned resourcefulness, stress and self-regulation. In S. Flesher and J. Reason (Eds.), *Handbook of Life Stress, Cognition and Health.* (pp. 483-496). New York: John Wiley & Sons.

Rosenbaum, M. & Ben-Ari, K. (1985). Learned helplessness and learned resourcefulness: Effects of non-contingent success and failure on individuals differing in self-control skills.

Journal of Personality and Social Psychology, 48, 198-215.

Rosenstock, I.M. (1974). Historical origins of the health model. *Health Education Monographs, 2,* 328-339.

Rothbaum, F., Weisz, J.R., & Snyder, S.S. (1982). Changing the world and changing the self: A two-process model of perceived control. *Journal of Personality and Social Psychology, 42,* 5-37.

Sackett, D.L. (1976). The magnitude of compliance and non-compliance. In D.L. Sackett and R.B. Haynes (Eds.), *Compliance with Therapeutic Regimens.* Baltimore: Johns Hopkins University Press.

Schussler, G., (1992). Coping strategies and individual meanings of illness. *Social Science and Medicine, 34,* 427-432.

Silver, R.K., & Wortman, C.B. (1980). Coping with undesirable life events. In J. Garber and M.E.P. Seligman (Eds.), *Human Helplessness: Theory and Applications.* New York: Academic Press.

Singh, A.K. (1987). *Role of causal and cosmic beliefs in the psychological recovery of tuberculosis patients.* Unpublished Master's dissertation, University of Allahabad, Allahabad, India.

Snyder, M.L., Stephan, W.G. & Rosenfield, D. (1978). Attributional egotism. In J.H. Harvey, W.J. Ickes, & R.F. Kidd (Eds.), *New directions in attribution research, Vol. 2.* Hillsdale, N.J.: Erlbaum.

Sonney, J.L. & Janoff, D.S. (1982). Attributions and the maintenances of behavior change. In C. Antaki & C.R. Brewin (Eds.), *Attributions and Psychological Change.* London: Academic Press.

Storms, M., & Nisbett R. (1970). Insomnia and the attributional process. *Journal of Personality and Social Psychology, 16,* 319-328.

Tagliacozzo, Luskin, D.B., Lashof, J.C. & Ima, K. (1974). Nursing intervention and patient behavior : An experimental study. *American Journal of Public Health, 64,* 596-603.

Taylor, S.E. (1983). Adjustment to threatening events: A theory of cognitive adaptation. *American Psychologist, 38,* 1161-1173.

Taylor, S.E. (1986). *Health Psychology.* New York: Randon House.

Taylor, S.E., Lichtman, R.R., & Wood, J.V. (1984). Attributions, beliefs about control and adjustment to breast cancer. *Journal of Personality and Social Psychology, 46,* 489-502.

Thompson, S.C. (1981). Will it hurt less if I can control it? A complex answer to a simple question. *Psychological Bulletin,*

90, 89-101.

Weiner, B. (1985). 'Spontaneous' causal thinking. *Psychological Bulletin, 97*, 74-84.

Weisenberg, M., Kegeles, S.S., & Lund, A.K. (1980). Children's health beliefs and acceptance of a dental preventive activity. *Journal of Health and Social Behavior, 21*, 59-74.

Westerbrook, M.T., & Viney, L.L. (1982). Psychological reactions to the onset of chronic illness. *Social Science and Medicine, 16*, 899-905.

White, R.W. (1959). Motivation reconsidered : The concept of competence. *Psychological Review, 66*, 297-333.

Wong, P.T.P., & Weiner, B. (1981). When people ask 'Why' questions and the heuristics of attributional research. *Journal of Personality and Social Psychology, 40*, 650-663.

Wortman, C.B. & Brehm, J.W. (1975). Responses to uncontrollable outcomes: An integration of reactance theory and the learned helplessness model. In L. Berkowitz (Ed.), *Advances in Experimental Social Psychology, Vol. 2*. New York: Academic Press.

Wortman, C.B. & Lehman, D.R. (1985). Reactions to victims of life crises: Support attempts that fail. In I.J. Sarason & B.R. Sarason (Eds.), *Social Support: Theory Research and Applications* (pp. 463-489). Dordrecht, The Netherland: Martinus Nijhoff.

7

Social Support, Stress and Psychological Well-Being

SAGAR SHARMA

The possible influence of social support and stress on well-being (health) and health behaviour has attracted the interest of psychologists, sociologists, anthropologists, and other public health professionals having different perspectives and orientations (Adler & Matthews, 1994; Beehr & McGrath, 1992; Cohen & Syme, 1985; Sarason, Sarason & Pierce, 1990; Veiel & Baumann, 1992). Unfortunatley, this multidisciplinary attempt has not resulted in a unified conceptualization of the meanings of stress and social support, their role in well-being, or even how to measure them. In fact, specific theories about the relation among stress, social support and well-being are rare and the empirical tests of hypotheses stemming from such theories are rather non-existent (Beehr & Bhagat, 1985; S. Fisher, 1989; Vaux, 1988).

Stress

The concept of stress is enshrouded by a thick veil of confusion and divergence of opinion (e.g., Pestonjee, 1987; Schuler, 1980; Sharma, 1988a). Stress has been used by researchers as a term for *stress-producing events and conditions* (SPECs; McGrath & Beehr, 1990) that are social psychological rather than physical in nature, and also as a strain variable (Ivancevich & Matteson, 1980). Stress has also been used to label an intervening process, either psychological or physiological, between a SPEC and well-being. Life stress presumably encompasses all SPECs in the past and present. Occupational stress includes SPECs in the work place i.e., relatively enduring or chronic stressors such as role conflict, role ambiguity, role overload, interpersonal conflict with a coworker, and frequently recurring daily hassles at work. All such situations, circumstances, events or conditions become SPECs for a given person if they produce serious adverse consequences to that individual's well-being/health and welfare. These consequences to the individual, sometimes referred to as strains, may be either physical or psychological (Beehr & McGrath, 1992).

Psychological Well-Being

Psychological well-being is a somewhat malleable concept which is to do with people's feelings about everyday life activities. Such feelings may range from negative mental states or psychological strains such as anxiety, depression, frustration, emotional exhaustion, unhappiness, dissatisfaction, to a state which has been identified as positive mental health (Jahoda, 1958; Warr, 1978). Scanning many studies on the perceived quality of life, Campbell (1980) distinguished three types of well-being: *affect, strain* and *satisfaction.* The concepts of psychological well-being and mental health, by and large, are used as interchangeable by majority of the researchers. It is widely recognized that the concept of mental health focuses on an ideal state emphasizing "positive well-being" of the WHO charter rather than on disease, statistical or conformity criteria. Negative components of psychological well-being are relatively easily assessed through self-reports of anxiety, depression, frustration, etc., but it is difficult to assess positive components of well-being. In this regard, Campbell, Converse and Rodgers (1976) wrote:

> "It may be necessary to distinguish between satisfaction which is associated with an experience of *rising expectations* and one which is associated

with *declining expectations*. An individual who has achieved an aspiration toward which he has been moving may be said to experience the *satisfaction of success*. Another person may have lowered his aspiration level to the point which he can achieve and he might be said to experience the *satisfaction of resignation*. The two individuals might be equally satisfied in the sense of fulfilled needs but the affective content associated with success and resignation may well differ. The difference may be less significant in experiences of dissatisfaction where affective content of disappointment and frustration might be expected to accompany any failure to achieve one's expectations." (p. 10).

Campbell *et al.* (1976) stated explicitly the view that a given level of satisfaction can go along with different affective states. Thus the study of psychological well-being/mental health might then be enhanced if the distinction between cognition and affect were more generally recognized and researched.

Stress and Well-Being Relationship

Over the last two decades, considerable evidence has accumulated suggesting that stressful life events are linked to low psychological well-being or ill health (e.g., Bhatti & Channabasavann 1985; Chandrika & Anantharaman, 1982; Cohen & Williamson, 1991; Kasl & Cooper, 1987; Gautam & Kamal, 1990; Kulhara & Prasad Rao, 1986; Ochaney & Sen, 1987; Pestonjee, 1992; I. Sharma & Ram, 1988; D.K. Sharma, Satija & Nathawat, 1985; Slack & Vaux, 1988; Snyder & Ford, 1987; S. Sharma, 1988a). Although the stress-illness relation is well-established, it is also obvious that not all individuals respond with health/well-being problems when exposed to major life changes. The magnitude of the stress-illness association is often low, with stress typically accounting for rarely more than 10 per cent of the variance in the illness indicators (Leventhal & Tomarken, 1987).

A number of literature reviews and models of occupational stress have also examined the relationship of occupation-specific stressors (job-related SPECs) with the indices of psychological strains like anxiety, depression, job dissatisfaction, burnout etc. (e.g., Brief, Schuler & Van Sell, 1980; S. Fisher, 1989; Ghadially & Kumar, 1989; Ivancevich & Matteson, 1980; Pestonjee, 1992; Prakash, 1990; S. Sharma & U. Sharma, 1983; 1984, 1987; U. Sharma & S. Sharma, 1989; A.K. Srivastava, 1982, 1983; A.K. Srivastava & H. Singh, 1988; S. Sharma, 1988a). Once again it is seen that the size of the correlations between job-related SPECs and psychological strains is rather on the lower side (C.D. Fisher & Gitleson, 1983; Jackson & Schuler, 1985; King & King, 1990). All this suggests that there is a large amount of variance still to be accounted for. It is likely that one or more moderator variables contribute to that unaccounted for variance. As a consequence, in recent years the primary research focus has shifted from main-effect models to more complex moderator models which assume that stressful experiences have a deleterious impact on well-being/health only under specific personal or situational conditions. Several moderators have been suggested such as coping style (Aldwin & Revenson, 1987; Long, 1990; A.K. Srivastava & H. Singh, 1988), optimism (Sheier & Carver, 1987), Type A Behaviour Pattern (Evans, Palsane & Carrere, 1987; Nakano, 1990) and Hardiness (Kobasa, Maddi & Puccetti, 1982; Nakano, 1990). Another important situational variable that has frequently been suggested as a moderator in stress and well-being research is social support. The remainder of this chapter will examine (i) the concept of social support, (ii) the current status of evidence on the role it plays in the relation between stress and well-being, and (iii) the major issues that need to be addressed in the study and application of social support. Lastly, the role of family as a support system in the Indian context will be discussed.

Social Support

It is apparent from the literature that the concept of social support, like the term 'stress', is a metaconstruct, or general rubric, to designate a loosely connected set of situations and activities (Beehr & McGrath. 1992; Vaux, 1988). Social support is usually defined as the existence and availability of people on whom we can rely, people who let us know that they care about, value and love us. Someone who believes that she or he belongs to a social network of communication and mutual obligation experiences social support (I. Sarason, Levine, Basham & B. Sarason, 1983). It is sometimes defined and measured in terms of the *structure* of a person's social relationships in general or of a particular type such as marriage, friendship, or organizational membership. In addition, social support is also conceptualized in terms of the *functional* content of the relationships, such as the degree to which the relationships involve flow of affect or emotional concern, instrumental or tangible aid, information and the like. Inspite of the diversity of approaches, some clear commonalities and differences in orientation, and a consensually valid set of types of social support have been delineated (Vaux, 1988). One apparent commonality is that social support is frequently considered to be a multidimensional construct. The examples of social support considered in the literature include emotional support, instrumental or tangible support and informational support. Social support can be provided by supportive people who stand in any of a variety of role relationships to the focal person. In an organization, the main sources of support are supervisors, coworkers, and people from outside the employing organization such as family and friends (see Beehr, King & King, 1990; Beehr & McGrath, 1992). Further, different types and functions of social support at different periods of time need to be emphasized since the meaning and significance of social support may vary throughout the life cycle. Thus from a life-course perspective, support needs and probability of specific types of support can vary as a function of an individual's temporal location in the life course.

A good social support measure should be (i) capable of distingushing between the structural and functional aspects of support, (ii) provide information about the quality of current relationship, that is whether or not support is perceived to be adequate, and (iii) it should assess *perceived* support in preference to *received* support, because received support may be confounded with level of stress (Power, Champion & Aris, 1988; Cohen & Wills, 1985). It may nevertheless be useful to measure level of support received during crisis. Most of these issues have been considered in the measures developed by I. Sarason *et al.* (1983), I. Sarason, B. Sarason, Shearin and Pierce (1987) and Power *et al.* (1988). Moos, Fenn and Billings (1988) have developed Life Stressors and Social Resources Inventory (LISRES), which provides an integrated assessment of an individual's life context. It taps aspects of life stressors and social resources in 8 domains: physical health, home/neighbourhood, financial, work, spouse/partner, children, extended family, and friends.

Social Support, Stress and Psychological Well-Being

There is growing evidence that social support is positively related to psychological well-being (e.g., Kasl & Cooper, 1987; Kumari & S. Sharma, 1990; Leiter, 1991; Sandler & Barrera, 1984; Sarason *et al.*, 1987; Schwarzer & Leppin, 1991; see also Cohen & Syme, 1985). During the last two decades, the predominant paradigm in the social support literature examines social support as an exogenous variable enhancing well-being/health irrespective of stress level (direct or main effect hypothesis) or protecting people from the pathogenic effects of stressful events (buffering hypothesis).

Direct Effects

This effect, for example, implies that if an individual's psychological strain is high due to life or occupational stress, the receipt of appropriate forms of social support might serve to reduce that psychological strain directly, without having any particular impact on situation determining SPEC. Non-experimental field studies show an inverse relationship between presence and magnitude of social support and psychological strains, but the relations do not always hold for all forms of social support, and the corrleations are not always strong (e.g., Beehr & McGrath, 1992; Jayaratne, Himle & Chess, 1988). Given that most are field studies, it is usually not appropriate to draw a strong causal inference. Moreover, many life events items are probably reflections of an underlying conflicted relationship (e.g., arguments with spouse, sexual difficulties). Consequently, main or direct effect ostensibly attributed to support may be a reflection of active conflict. Unnecessary confounding can be reduced by paying careful attention to the content and wording of the items of life events and support measures.

Buffering Effects

In contrast to direct effect model, the buffering hypothesis argues that support exerts its beneficial effect in the presence of stress. This has probably been the dominant hypothesis regarding stress, social support and well-being. The evidence regarding the buffering effect is 'mixed' (Beehr & McGrath, 1992; Cohen & Wills, 1985; Fuchs & Hahn, 1992; Landerman, George, Campbell, Richard & Blazer, 1989; Ganster, Fusilier, & Mayes, 1986). It is seen that expected effects might occur under some conditions and not others. The buffering effect may occur only when the kinds of available social support match the needs elicited by the stress a person is experiencing (Krause & Jay, 1991). The way interaction is conceptualized and estimated can also affect conclusions about the stress-buffering properties of social support (Landerman *et al.*, 1989). Cutrona (1990) has provided a model that specifies the type of social support that is most beneficial (i.e., most effective in preventing deleterious mental or physical consequences) following different kinds of stressful life events.

Issues in the Study and Application of Social Support

(a) It is yet not known what underlies the links of social support with well-being. An adequate (predictive) model of the relationship between social support and well-being must consider individual differences in need for social support as well as the social environmental contexts in which support is perceived, mobilized, given and taken. The efficacy of social support is also likely to be dependent on (i) who is providing the support, (ii) what kind of support is being provided, (iii) to whom is the support provided, (iv) for which problem is the support provided, and (v) when and for how long is the support provided (Kessler & McLeod, 1985).

(b) Significant advances in the understanding of support-health/well-being relationship will occur only if studies focus on the *process* by which support is linked to health/well-being. The multidimensional measurement of support functions is essential in determining the process or mechanism by which support affects health/well-being. While quantitiative strategies are useful in their own right, qualitative analysis of the data can offer information that is 'rich and deep' and suggest meaningful interpretation. Moreover, there is a need for examining causality in this domain using prospective-longitudinal designs since virtually all of the previous research has used non-experimental field methods (Beehr & McGrath, 1992). In a rare longitudinal attempt on a sample of 2034 employees of Dutch Companies, Marcelissen, Winnubst, Buunk and de Wolff (1988) concluded that the negative relationships between social support and psychological strains were more likely to be due to a reduction of social support being caused by more strain, rather than to the more traditional explanation that more social support causes a reduction in strain. Certainly such ideas have been ignored in past research.

(c) There has been considerably more research on the

consequences of receiving support than on the consequnces of providing it. The deleterious consequences for the provider may be substantial when provisions of sustained high levels of support are required but the recipient is unwilling or unable to reciprocate. The one-sided giving of support may not only become overburdening for the provider, it may also do a disservice to the recipient by fostering dependency and discouraging active efforts towards self-help. In fact, relatively little is known about whether there are good or aversive consequences to the person providing support.

(d) Although it seems obvious that personality characteristics would necessarily have an impact on the social support an individual experiences, few empirical studies have addressed this relationship. In a recent study, Connell and D'Augelli (1990) showed that individuals who perceive themselves as affiliative and as help seekers and help givers, receive more social supportive behaviours, and perceive that support is available to them. The perception that support is available shared a direct relationship with perceived health. They have also discussed the utility of including multiple measures of social support and personality characteristics related to receiving support in investigations of the relationship between social support and health/well-being.

(e) Although the effects of social support (considered as exogenous variable) on health/well-being are important, very little is known about its environmental determinants. G. Evans, Palsane, Lepore and Martin (1989) revealed that the adverse effects of residential crowding on psychological health/well-being are mediated by a breakdown of social support system. They view the weakening of social bonds as an unintended side-effect of a typical strategy for coping with overcrowding-social withdrawal. This study highlights the importance of examining social support as an endogenous variable as well in the stress and health process.

(f) Existing data are not sufficient to convince those forming health policy that social support interventions are effective models of health promotion. Not only is there a lack of intervention research that is adequate from a scientific perspective, but also a lack of evidence on the impact of social support interventions on variables critical to public policy decisions—impacts such as reduced incidence of disease, lower medical costs, and reduced mortality.

(g) Most of the social support research has been conducted in the western cultures. However, it has been empirically documented that despite a common autonomic nervous system, there are differences in the reported psycho-physiological reactions to SPECs in culturally different groups. Cultures determine an individual's vulnerability to stress, which is an outcome of different child rearing practices, change of role and provision or deprivation of social support. Cultures also differ in basic socio-cultural premises for coping with stress. These premises are transmitted and modelled in the course of socialization (see S. Sharma, 1985, 1988b). The provision of social support involves activities that entail complex patterns of interaction with other people, and these are likely to vary in crucial ways from one culture to another (see Beehr & McGrath, 1992). In non-western societies, for instance, there is more acceptance of dependence among intra-family and inter-family relationships (see Pederson, 1979; Tripathi, 1988). About the Indian society, Kakar (1982) comments that it is organized around the primacy of the thereapeutic in the sense that Indians, in comparison to the westerners, seem to emphasize protection and caring in their social (and political) relations more than the value of performance and equality. While social relationships in the West are based on intimacy through 'shared activity', in India they develop through mutual caring and mutual affinity. It is apparent that what constitutes an appropriate (social) supportive behaviour can vary in culturally distinct societies.

Moreover, it is now accepted that interventions aiming at prevention of disease and promotion of health/ well-being must be based on an understanding of the culture, traditions, beliefs and patterns of family interaction. Within every community there are indigenous resources that can be harnessed to promote health/well-being of the individual (see Holtzman, R.I. Evans, Kennedy & Iscoe, 1987; Kakar, 1982). Thus relevant investigations in this area across cultures might lead to better and more general insights into how social support works in relation to stress and well-being. Moreover, psychometric refinement of indicators of social support and well-being is necessary for conducting genuine cross-cultural research.

Family Structure as a Social Support System

Psychological attachment to family continues to be a major sociological phenomenon in the relationship-oriented Indian society. Various surveys put the incidence of joint family between 50 to 65 per cent, and the rest are characterized by extended or nuclear families— the latter are more prevalent in urban areas (Singh, 1986). The primacy of family or domestic happiness as a dominant concern still exists in rural and urban areas (Roy & R.K. Srivastava, 1986; Sinha, 1980). While some researchers concluded that a joint family provides greater amount of stress and gives rise to stress disorders (e.g., Sampurna, Ansari, Agrawal, & Udupa, 1979), others found that the persons belonging to nuclear families have significantly more psychiatric problems (e.g., Chaturvedi, 1983). Moreover, Carstairs and Kapur (1976), in an earlier study, did not find significant differences in mental disorders between people living in joint family and in nuclear family settings. Such an inconsistency in the findings is mainly due to considering nuclearity or jointness as a structural phenomenon. What should matter more is not the structural composition of the residential family group, but the nature and quality of social interactions and consequently the efficacy of social support emanating from it. The role of the Indian joint family for directly affecting the amount of stress or well-being experienced as well as in buffering the relation between daily hassles and health has also not been adequately explored. One important aspect of joint family and social support worthy of research is the relationship of wives in the in-law's family (G. Evans, Palsane, & D'Souza, 1983). The literature also suggests that the marital relationship is the single most important source of support.

Women in India have greater stresses in intrafamilial settings reflecting the predominance of their household role (G. Singh, Kaur, & Kaur, 1984). Wife battering, so alien to our image of non-violence and respect for womanhood is emerging as one of our least recognized and most appalling social problems. There is hardly any support system available to Indian women outside of marriage or the family. Most women (particularly the married ones) are not allowed to socialize independently and build solid friendships, and they are compelled to socialize in their husband's circles. Now increasingly urban women are in search of self-fulfilment, not through self-effacement, but outside home and hearth. As a consequence there is a spillover effect from work to family i.e. stresses at work settings are overwhelming family relationships so that the family's capacity for social support is being diminished and the daily impact of the demanding job situation becomes cumulative. This is also adversely affecting family routinization— the observable, repetitive behaviours that involve several family members, and that occur with predictable regularity in the ongoing life of the family. Such routines function as behavioural units providing structural integrity to family life and have important consequences for overall health/well-being of the family.

Rapid social change from industrialization, economic development and overcrowding is having profound effect on the structure and functioning of urban families and the psychological well-being of these persons. In many places, these changes are eroding traditional support systems and thus reducing the capacities of individuals (particularly women) and families to cope with distress, disease and disability. Accompanying changes in life cycles are bringing considerable changes in disease pattern including hypertension and other cardiovascular problems, and addictions. As a result of urban-based development, male-only migration from rural areas and the proportion of women left alone with little social and other resources or skills, is increasing in villages. Barring a few, existing Indian studies have not been concerned with the consequences faced by village-based families and we have little knowledge about the precise extent of suffering they undergo. However, there is much more evidence in the oral tradition and folk songs than in social scientific literature of the lower psychological well-being and daily hassles of the women of such families (see Jetley, 1987; Saxena, 1977). The sufferings in terms of unhappiness, loneliness, and other deprivations are also dependent on whether the family strucutre is patriarchal or matriarchal (Gulati, 1987). A thoughtful analysis of unique sense of maternal obligation of Indian women and her readiness for practically unlimited emotional investment in her children (particularly males) has been provided by Kakar (1978). He argued that such protection of children can act as a big social support system, but when in excess it might be resulting in violated men and women producing their own kind, thereby hampering their own well-being and the well-being of those under their care. Family can also serve as a source of stress due to role or value conflicts, problematic family structures, and interaction patterns.

A woman in India continues to be a *provider* of socio-emotional support rather than a receiver of such a support. Consequently marriage and family continue to be more supportive structures for men than women. The Indian men continue to be brought up and sustained by excessive sheltered universe of attachment which breeds greater dependence characteristics in their personality. Thus support needs tend to be higher for Indian men than women. It is expected that the denial of socio-emotional support to such men would have more serious health/well-being consequences as compared to Indian women-who seem to have developed internal psycho-social skills to cope with their peculiar life stresses. While a provision of socio-emotional support to an Indian women is an 'unexpected favour', the denial of such a support to Indian men is 'deprivation'. It implies that socio-emotional support functions that are effective buffers for Indian men might not be effective for Indian women and *vice-versa*. It must be emphasized that women are a key health source and provider of support. It is a paradox that while societies depend so heavily on them to provide health care and buffers against stress, their own health/well-being needs are frequently neglected.

While the family still continues to be a single source of social, emotional and economic support for most elderly people in India, Venkoba Rao (1987) concluded that it is the lack of family/social integration rather than social isolation that is the lot of gero-psychiatric groups. When the aged are not looked after by the kin, there is an increased need for alternate support systems such as Old Age Homes. However, the investigations have consistently shown that the aged (males & females) residing in Old Age Homes (institutionalized) have relatively lower psycholgoical and physical well-being than their counterparts living with families (e.g., Anantharaman, 1980; Chadha, Aggarwal & Mangla, 1990; Chandrika & Anantharaman, 1982; Gomathi, Sitharthan & Anantharaman, 1981; Reddy & Padmini, 1989; Vijayshree, 1989; Willigen, Chadha & Kedia, 1995). It is also seen that the social network size of the inmates of Old Age Homes is smaller than their family-based counterparts (e.g., Chadha *et al.*, 1990; Mangla & Chadha, 1991). Neither institutionalized care is efficacious nor liked by most Indians. Gangrade (1988), among others, highlight the need to strengthen family system and also to lessen economic burden on the aged. However, the fact remains that most of the aged in India continue to live with their families and supportive systems in terms of other social networks (friends, relatives) are still available. This should enthuse those who undertake the difficult task of organizing geriatric services. Moreover, there can be a half-way home (perhaps in the form of Age Care Centres) where the efficacy of such formal institutions can merge with the family/friendship ties of old age (see Mathur & Sen, 1989). In fact, the role of family and community remains an inter-related element in a well-balanced care of the well-being of all individuals.

Conclusions

Although research in India of the relationship of social support, stress and well-being is scant, a rapidly evolving literature in the West has established a link between social support and adaptation to stressful circumstances. While empirical evidence to date sheds some light on these relations, we still know virtually nothing about why this link exists. Multiplicity of available measurement strategies in the area makes the choice complex even for the researchers in the West. The problem becomes acute when these tools are utilized without modification in non western societies. To enhance our knowledge about how social support can and does affect stress-health/well-being relation, a theory guided research is required with its scope expanded to include a broader, cross-cultural base.

REFERENCES

Adler, N., & Matthews, K.K. (1994). Health and psychology : Why do some people get sick and some stay well? *Annual Review of Psychology, 45*, 229-259.

Adwin, C.M., & Revenson, T.A. (1987). Does coping help? A re-examination of the relation between coping and mental health. *Journal of Personality and Social Psychology, 53*, 337-348.

Anantharaman, R. N. (1980). A study of institutionalized and non-institutionalized older people. *Psychological Studies, 25*, 31-33.

Beehr, T.A., & Bhagat, R.S. (1985). Introduction to human stress and cognition in organizations. In T.A. Beehr & R.S. Bhagat (Eds.), *Human Stress and Cognition in Organizations : An*

Integrated Prespective (pp. 3-19). New York : Wiley.

Beehr, T.A., & Mc Grath, J.E. (1992). Social support, occupational stress and anxiety. *Anxiety, Stress and Coping*, *5*, 7-19.

Beehr, T.A., King, L.A., & King, D.W. (1990). Social support and occupational stress : Talking to supervisors. *Journal of Vocational Behavior*, *36*, 61-81.

Bhatti, R.S., & Channabasavanna, S.M. (1985). Study of neuroses : Life events and personality dimensions. *Indian Journal of Psychiatry*, *27*, 127-137.

Brief, A.P., Schuler, R.S., & Van Sell, M. (1980). *Managing Job Stress*. Boston : Little Brown and Company.

Campbell, A. (1980). *The Sense of Well-being in America*. New York : McGraw Hill.

Campbell, A., Converse, P.E., & Rodgers, W.L. (1976). *The Quality of American Life : Perceptions, Evaluations and Satisfactions*. New York : Russel Sage Foundation.

Carstairs, G.M., & Kapur, M.L. (1976). *The Great Universe of Kota : Stress. Change and Mental Disorders in an Indian Village*. Delhi : Hogarth Press.

Chaddha, N.K., Aggarwal, V., & Mangla, A.P. (1990). Social network and aging. *Spectra of Anthropological Progress*, *12*, 15-32.

Chandrika, P., & Anantharaman, R.N. (1982). Life changes and adjustment in old age. *Journal of Psychological Researches*, *26*, 137-141.

Chaturvedi, M.K. (1983). *Human Stress and Stressors : A Sociological Study*. New Delhi : Cosmo Publications.

Cochen, S., & Syme, S.L. (1985). *Social Support and Health*, New York : Academic Press.

Cohen, S., & Wills, T.A. (1985). Stress, social support and buffering hypothesis. *Psychological Bulletin*, *98*, 310-357.

Cohen, S., & Williamson, G.M. (1991). Stress and infectious disease in humans. *Psychological Bulletin*, *109*, 5-24.

Connell, C.M., & D' Augelli, A.R. (1990). The contribution of personality characteristics of the relationship between social support and perceived physical health. *Health Psychology*, *9*, 192-207.

Cutrona, C.E. (1990). Stress and social support : In search of optimal matching. *Journal of Social and Clinical Psychology*, *9*, 3-14.

Evans, G.W. Palsane, M.N., & D'Souza, R. (1983). Life stress and health in India. *Indian Psychologist*, *2*, 62-78.

Evans, G.W., Palsane, M.N. & Carrere, S. (1987). Type A behavior and occupational stress : A cross-cultural study of blue-collar workers. *Journal of Personality and Social Psychology*, *52*, 1002-1007.

Evans, G.W., Palsane, M.N., Lepore, S.J., & Martin, T. (1989). Residential density and psychological health : The mediating effects of social support. *Journal of Personality and Social Psychology*, *57*, 994-999.

Fisher, C.D., & Gitleson, R. (1983). A meta-analysis of the correlates of role conflict and ambiguity. *Journal of Applied Psychology*, *68*, 320-333.

Fisher, S. (1989). Stress, control, worry prescriptions and the implications for health at work : A psychological model. In S.L. Sauter, J.J. Hurrell, & C.L. Cooper (Eds.), *Job control and Worker Health* (pp. 205-236). Chichester : Wiley.

Fuchs, R., & Hahn, A. (1992). Physical exercise and anxiety as moderators of the stress-illness relationship. *Anxiety, Stress and Coping*, *5*, 139-149.

Gangrade, K.D. (1988). Social network and the aged in India. In A.B. Bose & K.D. Gangrade (Eds.), *Aging in India : Problems and Potentialities*. New Delhi : Abhinav.

Ganster, D.C., Fusilier, M.R., & Mayes, B.T. (1986). Role of social support in the experience of stress at work. *Journal of Applied Psychology*, *71*, 102-110.

Gautam, S., & Kamal, P. (1990). A study of impact of stressful life events in neurotic patients. *Indian Journal of Psychiatry*, *32*, 356-361.

Ghadially, R., & Kumar, P. (1989). Stress, strain and coping styles of female professionals. *Indian Journal of Applied Psychology*, *26*, 1-8.

Gomathi, S., Sitharthan, T., & Anantharaman, R.N. (1981). A study of the institutionalized and non-institutionalized older people. *Journal of Psychological Researches*, *25*, 125-128.

Gulati, L. (1987). Coping with male migration. *Economic and Political Weekly*, *22*, 41-46.

Holtzman, W.H., Evans, R.I., Kennedy, S., & Iscoe, I. (1987). Psychology and health: Contributions of psychology to the improvement of health and health care. *Bulletin of the World Health Organization*, *65*, 913-935.

Ivancevich, J.M., & Matteson,M.T. (1980). *Stress at Work: A Managerial Perspective*. Glenview, IL: Scott, Foresman and Company.

Jackson, S.E., & Schuler, R.S. (1985). A meta-analysis and conceptual critique of research on role ambiguity and role conflict in work settings. *Journal of Applied Psychology*, *36*, 16-78.

Jahoda, M. (1958). *Current Concepts of Positive Mental Health.*

New York: Basic Books.

Jayaratne, S., Himle, D., & Chess, W.I. (1988). Dealing with work stress and strain: Is the perception of support more important than its use? *Journal of Applied Behavioral Science, 24*. 199-202.

Jetley, S. (1987). Impact of male migration on rural females. *Economic and Political Weekly*, 22, 47-53.

Kakar, S. (1978). *The Inner World: A Psychoanalytic study of Childhood and Society in India*. Delhi: Oxford University Press.

Kakar, S. (1982). *Shamans, Mystics and Doctors: A Psychological study into India and its Healing Traditions*. Delhi : Oxford University Press.

Kasl, S.V., & Cooper, C.L. (Eds.). (1987). *Stress and Health: Issues in Research Methodology*. Chichester : Wiley.

Kessler, R.C., & McLeod, J.D. (1985). Social support and mental health in community samples. In S. Cohen & S.L. Syme (Eds.), *Social Support and Health* (pp. 219-240). New York: Academic Press.

King, L.A., & King, D.W. (1990). Role conflict and role ambiguity: A critical assessment of construct validity. *Psychological Bulletin, 107*, 48-64.

Kobasa, S.C., Maddi, S.R., & Puccetti, M.C. (1982). Personality and exercise as buffers in the stress-illness relationship. *Journal of Behavioral Medicine, 5*, 391-404.

Krause, N., & Jay, G. (1991). Stress, social support and negative interaction in later life. *Research on Aging, 13*, 333-363.

Kulhara, P., & Prasad Rao, G. (1986). Life events in obsessive compulsive neurosis. *Indian Journal of Psychiatry, 28*, 221-224.

Kumari, K., & Sharma, S. (1990). Social support, organizational role stress and well-being: A study of medicos. *Psychological Studies, 35*, 163-169.

Landerman, R., George, L.K., Campbell, R.T., Richard, T., & Blazer, D.G. (1989). Alternative models of stress buffering hypothesis. *American Journal of Community Psychology, 17*, 625-642.

Leiter, M.P. (1991). Coping patterns as predictors of burnout: The function of control and escape patterns. *Journal of Occupational Behavior, 12*, 123-144.

Leventhal, H., & Tomarken, A. (1987). Stress and illness: Perspectives from health psychology. In S.V. Kasl & C.L. Cooper (Eds.). *Stress and Health: Issues in Research Methodology* (pp. 27-55). Chichester : Wiley.

Long, B.C. (1990). Relation between coping strategies, sex-typed traits, and environmental characteristics: A comparison of male and female managers. *Journal of Counselling Psychology, 37*, 185-194.

Mangla, A.P., & Chadha, N.K. (1991). Social network approach to old age: An empirical study. *Eastern Anthropologist, 44*, 356-369.

Marcelissen, F.M., Winnubst, J.A., Buunk, B., & de Wolff, C.J. (1988). Social support and occupational stress: A causal analysis. *Social Science and Medicine, 26*, 365-373.

Mathur, D., & Sen, A. (1989). Depression in the elderly and some of its psychosocial concomitants: A study of the efficacy of Aged Care Centres. *Indian Journal of Community Guidance Service, 6*, 27-39.

Moos, R.H., Fenn, C.B., & Billings, A.G. (1988). Life stressors and social resources: An integrated assessment approach. *Social Science and Medicine, 27*, 999-1002.

Nakano, K. (1990). Hardiness, Type A Behaviour and physical symdroms in a Japanese sample. *Journal of Nervous and Mental Diseases, 178*, 52-56.

Ochaney,M., & Sen, (1987). Some psychological aspects of depression in senescence: An empirical study. *Mind, 13*, 1-6.

Pederson, P. (1979). Non-Western psychology: The search for alternatives. In A.J. Marshella, R.G. Tharp & T.J. Cibordwski (Eds.). *Perspectives on Cross-Cultural Psychology*. New York: Academic Press.

Pestonjee, D.M. (1987). Executive stress: Should it be avoided? *Vikalpa, 12*, 23-29.

Pestonjee, D.M. (1992). *Stress and Coping: The Indian Experience*. New Delhi : Sage.

Power, M.J., Champion, L.A., & Aris, S.J. (1988). The development of a measure of social support: The Significant Others Scale (SOS). *The British Journal of Clinical Psychology, 27*, 349-358.

Prakash, G.P. (1990). Occupational stress, strain and coping in university faculty members. *Indian Journal of Psychology, 65*, 37-43.

Reddy, V., & Padmini, N.C. (1989). A study of problems of institutionalized and non-institutionalized elderly men and women. *Journal of Psychological Researches, 33*, 7-9.

Roy, R., & Srivastava, R.K. (1986). *Dialogues on Development*. New Delhi : Sage.

Sandler, I.N., & Barrera, M. (1984). Toward a multimethod approach to assessing the effects of social support. *American*

Journal of Community Psychology, 12, 37-52.

Sampurna, T.V., Ansari, A., Agarwal, P., & Udupa, K.N. (1979). The role of social factors in certain stress disorders. *Indian Journal of Social Work, 40,* 73-77.

Sarason, G., Sarason, B.R., & Pierce, G.R. (Eds.) (1990). *Social Support : An Interactional View.* New York : Wiley.

Sarason, I.G., Levine, H.M., Basham, R.B., & Sarason, B.R. (1983). Assessing social support: The social support questionnaire. *Journal of Personality and Social Psychology, 44,* 127-139.

Sarason, I.G., Sarason, B.R., Shearin, E.N., & Pierce, G.R. (1984). A brief measure of social support: Practical and theoretical implications. *Journal of Social and Personal Relationships, 4,* 497-510.

Saxena, D.P. (1977). *Urban Migration in India: Causes and Consequences.* Bombay: Popular Prakashan.

Scheier, M.F., & Carver, C.S. (1987). Dispositional optimism and physical well-being: The influence of generalized outcome expectancies on health. *Journal of Personality, 55,* 169-210.

Schuler, R.S. (1980). Definition and conceptualization of stress in organizations. *Organizational Behavior and Human Performance, 25,* 189-202.

Schwarzer, R., & Leppin, A. (1991). Social support and health: A theoretical and empirical overview: *Journal of Social and Personal Relationships, 8,* 99-127.

Sharma, D.K., Satija, D.C., & Nathawat, S.S. (1985). Psychological determinants of depression in old age. *Indian Journal of Psychiatry, 27,* 83-90.

Sharma, I., & Ram, D. (1988). Life events in anxiety neurosis. *Indian Journal of Psychiatry, 30,* 61-67.

Sharma, S. (1985). Well-being and organizational stress: A case for cross-cultural study of correlates and moderators. *Social Science International, 1,* 20-32.

Sharma, S. (1988a). Stress and anxiety. In J. Pandey (Ed.). *Psychology in India: The State-of-The-Art, Vol. 1* (pp. 191-248). New Delhi: Sage.

Sharma, S. (1988b). Psychological well-being and social support in the Indian context. *Guru Nanak Journal of Sociology, 9,* 17-23.

Sharma, S., & Sharma, U. (1983). Relationship of organizational role efficacy with anxiety and job satisfaction at two job levels. *Indian Journal of Clinical Psychology, 10,* 319-323.

Sharma, S., & Sharma, U. (1984). Organizational role stress, anxiety and job satisfaction. *Personality Study and Group Behavior, 4,* 1-7.

Sharma, S., & Sharma, U. (1987). Organizational stress and well-being. *Personality Study and Group Behavior, 7*, 9-18.

Sharma, U., & Sharma, S. (1989). Organizational role stress and anxiety: A comparative study of bureaucrats and technocrats. *Indian Journal of Industrial Relations, 24*, 281-288.

Singh, G., Kaur, D., & Kaur, H. (1984). Presumptive stressful life events scale (PSLES): A new stressful life events scale for use in India. *Indian Journal of Psychiatry, 26*, 107-114.

Singh, Y. (1986). *Modernization of Indian Tradition: A Systematic Study of Social Change*. Jaipur: Rawat Publications.

Sinha, J.B.P. (1980). *Nurturant Task Leader.* New Delhi: Concept.

Slack, D., & Vaux, A. (1988). Undesirable events and depression: The role of event appraisals and social support. *Journal of Soical and Clinical Psychology, 7*, 290-296.

Snyder, C.R., & Ford, C.E. (Eds.) (1987). *Coping with Life Events; Clinical and Social Psychological Perspective.* New York: Plenum Press.

Srivastava, A.K. (1982). A study of the effects of occupational stress and job involvement on job anxiety. *Perspectives in Psychological Researches, 5*, 12-15.

Srivastava, A.K. (1983). Role-based stress and mental health of white collar employees. *Indian Journal of Clinial Psychology, 10*, 343-347.

Srivastava, A.K., & Singh, H.S. (1988). Modifying effects of coping strategies on the relation of organizational role stress and mental health. *Psychological Reports, 62*, 1007-1009.

Tripathi, R.C. (1986). Aligning development to values in India. In D. Sinha & H.S.R. Kao (Eds.). *Social Values and Development: Asian Perspectives* (pp. 315-333). New Delhi: Sage.

Vaux, A. (1988). *Social Support: Theory, Research, and Interventions*. New York: Praeger Publishers.

Veiel, H.O.F. & Baumann, U. (Eds.) (1992). *The Meaning and Measurement of Support*. New York : Hemisphere Press.

Venkoba Rao, A. (1987). Family jointness and social integration among the elderly. *Indian Journal of Social Psychiatry, 3*, 81-103.

Vijayashree, J.B. (1989). Life satisfaction and its correlates amongst the aged. Master's Dissertation, University of Delhi (Mimeographed).

Warr, P.B. (1978). A study of psychological well-being. *British Journal of Psychology, 69*, 111-121.

Willigen, J.V., Chadha, N.K. & Kedia, S. (1995). Personal networks and sacred texts : Social aging in Delhi, India. *Journal of Cross-Cultural Gerontology, 10*, 175-198.

8

Coping with Life Stresses

KOHINOOR CHAKRAVARTY and **GIRISHWAR MISRA**

This chapter has twin goals. First, to examine the concept of coping and second, to empirically examine the pattern of coping with life stresses. It is argued that coping strategies have culture specific features. In Indian setting confronting the problem situation and changing the environment are often combined with self regulation.

The Concept of Coping : An Overview

A close perusal of literature reveals that 'coping' has been viewed in diverse ways. Dewe, Guest and Williams (1979) consider coping as an attempt to remove the feeling of discomfort. White (1974) defined coping as the process which involves efforts towards solution of problems. It occurs when a person faces a threatening or dynamic change or problem that defies known or usual ways of behaviour and might give rise to anxiety, guilt, grief and shame, and again forms the necessity for adaptation.

McGrath (1970) has viewed coping as the covert and overt behaviour by which the organism actively prevents, removes or circumvents stress inducing circumstances. Schregardus (1976) proposed two major styles of coping namely *repression* and *sensitization*. He also found that patterns of defensive style were related to the perception and experiences of stress and to subsequent patterns of coping and adjustment.

Pearlin and Schooler (1978) have suggested that "coping responses are the behaviors, cognitions and perceptions in which people engage when actually contending with their life problems. Coping responses represent some of the things that people do, their concrete efforts to deal with the life strains they encounter in their different roles" (p. 5). Responses that are directed at modification of the stressful situations are the most direct ways to cope with strain because they tend to eliminate the source of stress itself. Pearlin and Schooler (1978) found that this is not a commonly used mode of coping. Before the onset of action which is directed at the modification of stressful environment the person must recognize the problem. The action intended to modify a situation may at times lead to other unwanted outcomes. Thus at times a person is rendered helpless in dealing with action oriented coping. According to them coping refers to behaviour that protects people from being psychologically harmed by problematic experiences. They have identified three protective functions of coping behaviour i.e. by eliminating or modifying the conditions that give rise to the problematic situation, by perceiving the meaning of experience in such a manner that it neutralizes its problematic character and by keeping the emotional consequences under control.

Irving (1977) has presented a descriptive typology of distinctive patterns of coping that included *vigilance*, *hypervigilance* and *defensive avoidance*. On the other hand, Robbins (1978) has identified seven patterns of coping viz, *seeking social support*, *dysfunctional behaviour*, *narcotizing anxiety*, *problem solving*, *reliance on professionals; bearing with discomfort*, and *escape*. In recent years attention has been given to coping with stressful events of day-to-day life. Broadly, three major approaches to measurement of coping can be identified i.e., coping in terms of ego processes (Hann, 1977; Valliant, 1977), coping as traits and coping as situation specific response.

According to Silver and Wortman (1980) coping refers to any and all responses made by an individual who encounters a potentially harmful situation. In addition to overt behaviour psychologists have included cognitions, emotional reactions (e.g. anger, depression) and psychological responses (e.g. nausea, insomnia etc.) also as types of coping mechanisms. However, most theorists restrict the term coping to efforts made by an individual in problem solving, in order to master, control or overcome threatening situations.

The controversy regarding treatment of coping as a trait or situation specific effort is yet unresolved. The complexity of coping cannot be captured through unidimensional measure. Lazarus and Folkman (1984) assert that coping is a shifting process where a person must at certain stages and certain times rely more on one form of coping (e.g. defensive strategies) and at other times on another form of coping (e.g. problem solving) as and when the status of the situation changes. Trait measures assume that people are behaviourally and cognitively consistent in their coping behaviour across situations. Cohen and Lazarus (1973) assert that trait measures are poor predictors of coping. Situation oriented research focuses on how people endeavour to cope with specific stressful situations (Visotsky *et al.*, 1961; Weisman & Worden, 1976).

A critical and important distinction between the trait oriented and the process-oriented approaches lies in the importance attached to the psychological and the environmental context in which coping takes place. The trait approach assumes that coping is mainly a property of the person and variation in stressful situations is of not much significance. In contrast, process oriented approach assumes that coping is a response to the psychological and environmental demand of specific stressful encounters.

The most comprehensive approach to coping has been developed by Lazarus and his associates over a number of years (1966, Delongis, 1983; Folkman, 1984; Kanner & Folkman, 1980). It utilizes the transactional framework in which person and environment are seen in terms of a continuous ongoing relationship of actions which are reciprocal in nature. These psychologists have argued that appraisal and coping processes mediate this transactional relationship.

Appraisal is considered as the cognitive process through which an event is evaluated as to whether the event is relevant to his/her well being and in what ways. Coping responses are made after the appraisal of the stress episode. Also, appraisal and coping continuously affect and influence each other throughout a given encounter. Coping, as Folkman and Lazarus (1980) have defined, is the cognitive and behavioural effort made to master, tolerate or reduce external demands and conflicts. Coping, according to them, serves two main purposes, the management, change or modification of the source of the stress (*problem-focused coping*) and the alteration and control of stressful emotions (*emotion-focused coping*). These forms of coping were found in more than ninety-five per cent of the stressful encounters reported by middle aged men and women and college students (Folkman & Lazarus, 1980). Also, the episodes involving people at work generated more problem focused coping in comparison to the episodes which involved family members. The context of the episode (e.g., work, family, health related) also influenced the use and outcome of coping mechanism employed. For instance, work was found to be related to higher levels of problem focused coping, whereas health was related to emotion focused coping.

The study of coping with stress has also received attention of researchers in the field of organisational behaviour. In these studies, however, coping strategies are viewed as attempts of an individual to respond to the feeling of discomfort with the aim of its reduction (Dewe, Guest & Williams, 1979). Some attempts have been made to identify coping strategies among industrial workers. Kohn *et al.* (1964) identified four types of coping strategies viz. work addiction, cynicism, idealization of other's and dependent behaviour, and contrived conflict. Singh and Sinha (1986) have reported seven dimensions of coping viz. cheerful and optimistic work orientation, yogic recourse, rash reactions, temporary relaxation and quick decision, anger-expression to subordinates and superiors, anger expression to family members, drug addiction and smoking, and independent problem solving. They noted that the first two strategies were inversely related to strain.

Lazarus and Folkman (1984) have noted that coping is "a person's constantly changing cognitive and behavioural efforts to manage specific external and/or internal demands that are appraised as taxing or exceeding the resources of the person" (p. 141). This definition implicates that coping is a process involving thoughts and behaviours in a specific context. Also, coping is a function of continuous appraisals and reappraisals of the shifting person-environment relationship.

The empirical study of coping with stresses has drawn the attention of Indian researchers only recently. These studies may be briefly examined here. In a study of examination stress Caplan, Naidu and Tripathi (1984) examined the relationship of coping and defense with affective outcomes. Working within the framework of person-enviornment (P-E) fit model, they found that defense-like measures were associated only with poor objective fit. The measures of coping-like responses were associated with current subjective fit. These effects, however, were weak. The effects of coping and defense, as indicators of being ill were generally stronger. The defenses were associated positively with the negative affects and somatic complaints whereas the coping—like measures were associated positively with positive affect. They also noted that defenses moderated the relationship between fit and being ill. They found that prayer, unlike withdrawal, appears to buffer the effects of poor-fit on being ill. The measure of coping used in this study included diagnosis and mobilization and the measure of defense included resignation, aggression, withdrawal, prayer, and cognitive change. Due to methodological limitations, this study as authors have observed is "likely to yield conservative estimates of the effects of situation specific coping and defense on poor fit and ill being" (Caplan, *et al.*, 1984, P. 284).

Sinha and Misra (1983) have studied the coping strategies of underprivileged university entrants. They noted that the disadvantaged students used conformity, feeling of inadequacy, withdrawal and ignoring the situation as coping strategies more than the advantaged students. They also noted that there were some ecological differences in the use of coping strategies. It was found that the urban students adopted affirmation and evidenced successful acceptance in the university stream to significantly greater extent than their rural counterparts. The rural-urban group did not differ significantly from other groups in most of the strategies except feeling of inadequacy and withdrawal which were in greater magnitude than the urban group. Conformity or changing with the situation was employed by rural students more than the urban students.

Misra and Ganguly (1984) have investigated coping with stresses resulting from cultural transition among a group of African students studying in India. They found that the students with high psycho-social competence used more problem focused coping and less amount of wishful thinking and self-blame than their low competent counterparts. In addition, they showed greater amount of positive affect, positive self-perception and less amount of somatic complaints and negative affect than low competence students. The relationship of coping strategies with health measures also differed for the two groups.

Singh and Pandey (1985) examined coping with problems in economic, family, personal and social aspects of life in a sample of university students. Using an open ended measure they identified five dimensions of coping namely appraisal-focused coping, emotion-focused coping, problem-focused coping, secondary coping and collective coping. The use of coping dimensions varied with nature of problems faced by the individual.

Another important study of coping has been reported by Singh (1990) in relation to the stresses of executives. This study employed a measure of coping strategies involving four factors, namely, active problem solving, non-directional work approach, constructive deferred problem solving, and information seeking. He found that the high level executives experienced lesser stress and strain, utilized better coping strategies, and enjoyed more positive outcomes. Also, a combination of coping strategies forming a condition of passive coping strategy was related to high stress condition.

Coping with Life Stresses : An Empirical Analysis

The present investigation adopted an unconventional approach to the study of stress phenomenon. Following an intensive strategy, an attempt was made to unravel the nature and extent of stressful experiences encountered in work and family domains, and to examine the ways in which people cope with them.

In order to measure coping strategies a variety of approaches have been put forward and several measures have been developed. A close perusal of studies revealed that the coping efforts to manage stressful experiences were characterized by multiplicity and indicated certain cultural differences. This led to development of a new measure of coping. For this purpose existing measures (Billings and Moos, 1984; Folkman & Lazarus, 1980; Latack, 1986; Lazarus & Folkman, 1984; McCrae, 1984; Parke, 1987; Stone & Neal, 1984) were screened and many new items were prepared. These items had to be rated on 5-point scales ranging from "never" (1) to "mostly (5) and a pool of 63 items was created. They included a wide range of cognitive and behavioural strategies people use to manage the internal/external demands in specific stressful experiences encountered as a part of everyday life. There were 12 factors in the measure as listed in Table 8.3. (See Ganguly, 1988 for details).

In view of the fact that the goal of study was to explore the stressful experiences in family and work domains, it was considered desirable to draw the sample from one organisation so that the objective characteristics of work setting may be controlled. With this purpose, a sample of 120 adult males was drawn from a large organisation located in Bhopal in central India.

The organisation manufactures hydro, thermal, nuclear and marine turbines, industrial machines, large AC/DC motors, traction motors, switchgears, transformers, rectifiers, capacitors, battery powered vehicles, power packs, generators, and various types of tools and guages. The sample of the study was drawn from its water turbine manufacturing (WTM) division. It is one of the major divisions of this factory and has a manpower of about 1200 employees. From this division forty participants were selected from each of the three cadres, i.e. manager, supervisor, and artisan. The demographic features of the sample are summarized in Table 8.1.

TABLE 8.1 : Characteristics of the sample (N = 120)

Characteristics	Range	M	SD
Age (years)	23-57	44.20	7.33
Qualification*	1-3	1.70	0.69
Tenure	2-30	21.50	6.98
Nature of Job**	1-2	1.38	0.48
Promotion	0-7	3.40	1.41
Family size	1-10	5.07	1.76
Number of children	0-7	2.57	1.20

* See Table 8.2
** See Table 8.2

Background variables. The descriptive statistics concerning background variables for the three groups of participants appear in Table 8.2. It was found that managers, supervisors and artisans differed significantly with respect to all the variables except number of children. It was noted that the age and tenure of service was greater in the case of supervisors, followed by managers and artisans, respectively. The size of family was negatively related to the hierarchical position. The artisans had families with largest size followed by supervisors and managers, respectively. The number of promotions received was greater in the case of managers followed by supervisors and artisans. Finally, the managers were more involved in table work than artisans.

TABLE 8.3 : Comparison of Artisans, Supervisors and Managers on Demographic Characteristics

Variables	Artisans		Supervisors		Managers		F
	M	SD	M	SD	M	SD	(2,117)
Age (in years)	41.55	7.22	46.8	6.35	44.55	7.48	5.61**
Nature of Job	1.13	0.33	1.55	0.50	1.45	0.50	9.85**
Family size	5.58	1.88	5.15	1.97	4.60	1.28	3.17**
Number of Children	2.60	1.17	2.70	1.28	2.45	1.06	0.45
Number of Promotions	2.55	1.08	3.80	1.22	3.85	1.56	12.78**
Tenure (in years)	18.73	6.88	24.30	5.69	21.80	7.18	7.12**

$p < .01$

Note = Nature of Job was coded as follows:
Table work = 2
Shop floor = 1

* Coded as follows:
diploma and below = 1, graduate =2,
post graduate or professional degree =3

** Coded as follows : work shop =1, Table work =2.

Group Differences in the Use of Coping Strategies

The mean scores for the coping strategies used by artisans, supervisors and managers appear in Table 8.3. The analysis of variance showed that artisans and supervisors used greater amount of rational effort than managers. In contrast, supervisors and managers used avoidance more than the artisans. Social manipulation was used more by artisans and supervisors than managers. The appraisal focused coping was used more by the supervisors than the other two groups. On other scales the differences were statistically not significant though there was differential use of coping strategies among the three groups. For instance, religion was used more by artisans and supervisors than managers while emotional discharge and affective regulation showed a different trend. The use of logical analysis and tension reduction was greater among supervisors and managers than artisans.

TABLE 8.3 : Mean Scores on Coping Scales

Variables	Artisans		Supervisors		Managers		F
	M	SD	M	SD	M	SD	(2,117)
Rational effort	24.26	3.16	23.89	3.20	22.07	3.00	9.34*
Avoidance	8.23	4.32	10.77	3.36	10.05	3.82	4.64*
Religion	10.33	3.44	10.42	3.42	8.90	2.83	2.76
Social manipulation	9.98	2.86	8.87	2.96	6.65	2.23	15.72*
Fatalistic	5.88	3.31	6.40	2.26	5.70	2.61	0.70
Problem sovling	17.85	3.86	17.72	2.89	16.68	3.27	1.47
Emotion discharge	11.25	3.61	11.75	3.08	12.25	3.40	0.89
Affective regulation	11.90	4.07	11.77	3.33	13.48	3.64	2.63
Appraisal focused coping	14.58	4.21	17.60	4.24	15.05	5.06	5.17*
Situation redefinition	10.25	3.07	10.15	2.69	10.15	1.76	0.02
Logical analysis	9.98	2.79	10.60	2.71	10.33	2.73	0.52
Tension reduction	11.38	3.33	12.32	3.42	12.48	3.35	1.25

* $p < .01$

Prediction of Coping-Strategies

In this analysis, three broad categories of coping strategies i.e., *active behavioural coping, active cognitive coping* and *avoidance coping* were used instead of 12 categories. This classification was based on the work of Billigs and Moos (1984) and Holahan and Moos (1987). Thus the scores on these variables constituted criterion variables. The predictors included 12 measures referring to background variables (age, tenure, family size), stresses (job stress, family stress, work family spill, family-work spill), involvement (work involvement, family involvement), perceived control (perceived control, control appraisal) and support. These measures were identical with those used in the preceding analysis. However, the measure of perceived control was a new one derived on the basis of sum of scores on the measures of perceived control, self control and control over environment. This was done because of the fact that all these variables were strongly positively related to each other.

In the regression analysis, global coping measures were treated as dependent variables. The hierarchical regression analyses were carried out to evaluate the contribution of different variables in predicting the three coping strategies. The resatts are summarized as followed.

Active Behavioural Coping

This coping strategy was predicted by different configurations of measures in the three groups of participants. In the case of managers 10 variables explained 33.34 per cent of the total variance. The measure of perceived control explained maximum amount of variance followed by support, control appraisal and family-to-work spill. The overall multiple correlation was .57. The group of supervisors displayed a different pattern. In this group 11 measures explained 45.7 per cent of the total variance. Work involvement was the best predictor followed by control appraisal, family to work spill and tenure. The overall multiple correlation was .67. The group of artisans manifested a different trend. In this group 11 measures explained 20.5 per cent of the total variance. Out of this, tenure emerged as the most important predictor followed by age, family-work spill, and family size. The overall multiple correlation was .45.

Active Cognitive Coping.

Among managers this strategy was explained by a set of 12 variables accounting for 28.7 per cent of the total variance. It was found that work involvement explained maximum amount of variance followed by age, perceived control and tenure. Other variables explained less that 1 per cent of the total variance. The overall multiple correlation was .53. In case of supervisors 12 variables together explained 31 per cent of the total variance. Out of this, tenure emerged as most important variable. This was followed by job stress, work involvement, family stress, family-to-work spill, family size and work to family spill. Support explained 2 per cemt of variance while other variables explained less than 1 per cent of variance. The overall multiple correlation was .55. The artisan group showed a different pattern characterized by a different set of measures explaining 25 per cent of the total variance. Out of this, age and family stress explained maximum amount of variance. Work involvement, job stress, control, work-to-family spill, and support also contributed to some extent. The overall multiple correlation was .50.

Avoidance Coping

In the case of managers this strategy was explained by a set of 10 measures. They explained 41 per cent of the total variance. Out of this 26 per cent variance was accounted by perceived control which was negatively related to avoidance strategy. Other variables accounting for about 2 per cent of the variance were family involvement, job stress, age and tenure. The overall multiple correlation was .64. The group of supervisors indicated that 59 per cent of the variance was explained by 11 measures. Out of these, work-to-family spill accounted for 24 per cent of the variance, followed by perceived control, job stress, control appraisal, support, work involvement, family size, age and family involvement. The overall multiple correlation was .76. The pattern of results in the case of artisans showed that 12 measures accounted for 28 per cent of the total variance. Out of this, family stress explained 19 per cent of the variance followed by family involvement, work involvement and family size. The rest of the variables explained less than 1 percent of the variance. The overall multiple correlation was .53.

Discussion

The results indicated that the use of coping strategies was partly related to hierarchical position. The managers and supervisors used avoidance—like coping strategy which focused on regulation of interpersonal distance. This is congruent with the roles assigned to them. They are in a position to supervise people for attaining organisational goals. Distancing is a mechanism for incumbents of higher positions to influence their subordinates. This is particularly true in the Indian bureaucratic system where ingratiation is desired (Pandey, 1980).

The use of social manipulation by supervisors and artisans is a significant finding. The results indicated that supervisors and artisans used rational effort and social manipulation more frequently. On the other hand, emotional discharge and affective regulation were used more frequently by managers. Religion and fatalistic coping were used more by the artisans followed by supervisors and managers. Logical analysis and tension reduction were also used more by supervisors and managers than artisans. It appears that supervisors share some of the coping strategies with artisans as well as managers. The managers and artisans, however, as expected were different in the use of coping strategies.

Within-group analysis revealed different priority orders of the coping strategies for the three groups of participants. Porblem solving, affective regulation, appraisal focused coping, and emotional discharge were the prominent strategies for all the groups. The core of all these strategies was characterised by emotional function. The problem solving strategy consisted of items aimed at managing stressful experiences through diverse efforts. This strategy is neither purely self-directed nor purely environment-directed. It involves both and defies the dichotomy of primary and secondary control. This strategy is flexible and reflects a mixed pattern of goal directed behaviour. It seems to be a culturally loaded strategy and reflects the diversity and complexity of influences characterising the stresses experienced in Indian socio-cultural context. The use of affective regulation and emotional discharge also indicates the emotional emphasis in coping process. The configuration of relatively more prevalent strategies suggests greater emphasis on the use of non-confrontive form of coping.

In fact, the problem-focused strategy did not clearly emerge from the data. A category closer to this was identified which was termed as rational effort. This strategy occupied a relatively lower position in the priority order. Thus, the pattern of coping could not be neatly categorised as emotion-focused which implies avoidance like strategies.

The significance of social manipulation along with fatalistic coping and religion are culturally relevant coping strategies. Pandey (1980, 1981) has indicated that ingratiation is a positively valued and expected behaviour in Indian society. He has attributed it to the large scale acceptance of feudal and hierarchical structure in Indian society. The studies of Tripathi (1981) also indicate frequent use of manipulation as one of the prevalent modes of social influence in Indian socio-cultural setting. The present results showed that this strategy was associated with other strategies irrespective of the fact whether they are problem focused or emotion focused. Social manipulation was positively associated with the strategies like affective regulation, emotional discharge and tension reduction. The strategies termed as rational effort, situation redefinition, problem solving, logical analysis and appraisal focused coping, with minor variations, went together. It was also observed that emotion discharge and tension reduction were not independent but related to other strategies.

Concluding Comments

It appears that the use of mixed form of coping in which problem focused and emotion focused coping strategies is the dominant mode. This situation might be due to the "encompassing system (prevailing in India) where logically opposites peacefully co-exist..... and where actions do not necessarily follow thoughts and emotions, nor they confront with each other. Instead they are *balanced* and *accommodated*. Such a composite frame", as J.B.P. Sinha (1982) has characterised, "is seemingly irrational and inconsistent. It is often slow in adaptation and generally inefficient from the purely rational point of view. And, yet, it manifests a resilience which has more than counterbalanced its inner contradictions, and it follows a logic which is rooted in the Indian intra-psychic affective-cognitive structures which reflect the configuration of the Indian social-institutions, the Hindu religio-philosophcial thinking, and the present socio-economic realities" (p. 14-15).

The linkage between effort and goals, as J.B.P. Sinha (1982), has indicated "is believed to be dependent on the interaction of some superior order power or supernatural forces to which a person tends to be devotionally committed" (p. 16). This partly explains the close ties between religion and fatalistic coping and other problem-focused coping strategies. Commenting on the strong need for power, J.B.P. Sinha (1982) has conjectured some interesting culture specific strategies. He argues that "a superior with power and status might feel a need to brag and to make his power and influence more visible and legitimate. Overt and exaggerated self-appreciation is accompanied with strong demands for loyalty and compliance from the dependents" (p. 17).

The findings implicate that individuals from higher socio-economic groups tend to utilize more adaptive forms of coping than the low socio-economic status individuals. This trend is consonant with the findings reported by Haan (1977), Pearlin and Schooler (1978) and Billings and Moos (1981). However, the role of type of stressful event and psychological and social resources cannot be ignored. It appears that the experience of control and support lead to the use of active behavioural coping and active cognitive coping; while lack of these resources results in adopting avoidance strategies. Finally, it is also important to note that, at least for the relatively higher income group people, type of stress is not significant while useing active behavioural coping strategy, and partly active cognitive coping strategy. The avoidance strategy, on the other hand, was importantly related to the type of stress.

Some caution should be exercised in interpreting the

present findings. Although the present results suggest important associations between some important stress-related variables, they do not indicate causal effects. Similar to most survey type studies on stress, this study involved correlational data collected at a single point in time. Some prospective research, however, (e.g. Kobasa *et al.* 1982) has indicated that hardiness significantly predicted physical and psychological symptoms upto two years. Eaton (1978) and Theorill (1976) have shown the predictive linkage of support and health. Johnson and Sarason (1978) reported an associaton between stress and anxiety and depression in people with extreme control but not in internals. In a longitudinal study Holahan and Moos (1986) noted "that feelings of self-confidence, an easy-going disposition, a disinclination to use avoidance coping and the availability of family support operate jointly to protect individuals from negative psycho-social consequences of life stress" (p. 392).

It may be concluded that conceptualization of coping requires a more comprehensive framework incorporating individual as well as situational variables. Lazarus and Folkman (1984) have provided an outline of transactional model of stress in which the person and environment transaction involves, "a mutually reciprocal, bi-directional relationship" (p. 325). The present results indicate that coping strategies are flexible and their use is related to dispositional variables, type of stress and the context.

REFERENCES

Abramson, L., Seligman, M.E.P., & Teasdale, J. (1978). Learned helplessness in humans : Critique and reformulation. *Journal of Abnormal Psychology, 87*, 49-74.

Billings, A.G., & Moos, R.H. (1981). The role of coping responses and social resources in attenuating the stress of life events. *Journal of Behavioral Medicine, 4*, 157-189.

Caplan, R.D., Naidu, R.K., & Tripathi, R.C. (1984). Coping and defence: Constellations Vs. Components. *Journal of Health and Social Behavior, 25*, 303-320.

Cohen, E., & Lazarus, R.S. (1973). Active coping processes, coping disposition, and recovery from surgery.

Psychosomatic Medicine, 35, 375-389.

Dewe, P., Guest, D., & Williams, R. (1979). Methods of coping with work related stress. In C. Mackay, & T. Cox (Eds.), *Response to stress: Occupational Aspects*. London: IPC Science and Technology Press.

Folkman, S., & Lazarus, R.S. (1980). An analysis of coping in a middle-aged community sample. *Journal of Health and Social Behavior, 21*, 219-239.

Folkman, S. (1984). Personal control, stress and coping processes: A theoretical analysis. *Journal of Personality and Social Psychology, 46*, 839-852.

Ganguly, K. (1988). *Role of Perceived Control in Coping with Stress*. Unpublished doctoral disertation, Bhopal University, Bhopal.

Hann, N. (1977). *Coping and Defending*. New York: Academic Press.

Irving, J. (1977). *Decision Making: A Psychological Analysis of Conflict, Choice and Commitment*. New York: Free Press.

Latack, J.C. (1986). Coping with job stress: Measures and future directions for scale development. *Journal of Applied Psychology, 71*, 377-385.

Lazarus, R.S. (1966). *Psychological Stress and the Coping Process*. New York: McGraw-Hill.

Lazarus, R.S., & Folkman, S. (1984). Coping and adapation. In W.D. Gentry (Ed.). *The Handbook of Behavioral Medicine*. New York: Guilford.

McGrae, R.R. (1984). Situational determinants of coping responses: Loss, threat, and challenge. *Journal of Personality and Social Psychology, 46*, 919-928.

Mc Grath, J.E. (1970). *Social and Psychological Factors in Stress*. New York: Holt, Reinehart and Winston.

Misra, G., & Ganguli, K. (1984). *Competence and coping: The case of African students studying in india*. Paper Presented at 20th Annual convention of Indian Academy of Applied Psychology held at IIT, New Delhi.

Parkes, K.R. (1984). Locus of control, cognitive appraisal and coping in stressful situations. *Journal of Personality and Social Psychology, 46*, 655-668.

Pandey, J. (1980). Ingratiation as expected and manipulative behaviour in Indian society. *Social Change, 10*, 15-17.

Pandey, J. (1981). Ingratiation as a social behaviour. In J.Pandey (Ed.) *Perspectives on Experimental Social Psychology in India*. New Delhi : Concept.

Pearlin, L.T., & Schooler, C. (1978). The structure of coping.

Journal of Health and Social Behavior, 19, 2-21.

Schregardus, D.J. (1976). A study of defensive style and its interaction with perception and experience of stress, *Dissertation Abstracts International* 400.

Singh, A.K., & Pandey, J. (1985). Dimensions of coping with socio-economic problems. *Social Change, 15*, 51-54.

Singh, S. (1990). *Organizational Stress and Executive Behaviour* New Delhi : Shri Ram Centre for Industrial Relations.

Singh, S., & A.K. Sinha (1986). Relationship of coping strategies with Job related strain. *Advances in Psychology, 1*, 8-15.

Silver, R.L., & Wortman, C.B. (1980). Copoing with undesirable life events. In J. Garbes M.E.I. Seligman (Eds.). *Human Helplessness*. New York: Academic Press.

Sinha, D. & Misra, G. (1984). *Coping strategies of underprivileged disadvantaged university entrants*. Unpublished results, University of Allahabad.

Sinha, J.B.P. (1982). The Hindu (Indian) identity. *Dynamic Psychiatry, 15*, 148-160.

Sinha, J.B.P. (1982). The spirit and frame. *Seminar.* Special issue on National Character.

Stone, A.A., & Neale, J.M. (1984). New measure of daily coping: Development and preliminary results. *Journal of Personality and Social Psychology, 46*, 892-906.

Tripathi, R.C. (1981). Machiavellianism and social manipulation. In J. Pandey (Ed.). *Perspectives on Experimental Social Psychology in India*. New Delhi: Concept Publishing Company.

Valliant, G.E. (1977). *Adaptation to Life*. Boston: Little Brown.

Visotsky, H.M., Hamburg, D.A., Gross, M.E., & Lebovits, B.Z., (1961). Coping behavior under extreme stress. *Archives of General Psychiatry, 5*, 423-448.

Weisman, A.D., & Worden, J.W. (1976). The existential plight in cancer: Significance of the first 100 days. *International Journal of Psychiatry in Medicine. 7*, 1-15.

White, R.W. (1974). Strategies of adaption: An attempt at systematic description. In G.V. Coelho. D.A. Humberg, & J.E. Adams (Eds.), *Coping and Adaptation*. New York: Basic Books Inc.

9

Induced Stress and Human Cognition

CHANDRA BHAL DWIVEDI

In our day-to-day common parlance as well as in scientific deliberations in many disciplines we very often use the term "stress," yet offering a precise definition of this term poses an enormously difficult problem mainly because there is lack of agreement about its exact meaning. In general the term stress has acquired a negative and aversive connotation. It is considered as a state and experience that is unpleasant and needs to be avoided. Realizing this difficulty, Lazarus (1966) has defined stress by the responses of people to different kinds of stressors, i.e., by the sources of stress which reside in an external or internal aversive event as well as in the disposition or sensitivity of the individual to perceive aversiveness. In other words, while studying the effects of stress we invariably investigate complexly mediated response states which are substantially influenced by existing levels and ranges of vulnerability to stress and the dependent variable from which stress could be inferred are levels and types of strain. The strain is the effect of stressors on various response systems of the person; stressors and strain feedback together define the load on the whole adaptive system of an organism (Hamilton, 1982). Mandler (1982) has contended that most psychologically stressful situations are the result of interruption and stressors are the interrupters.

In experimental studies usually induced effects of stress have been studied largely because in normal working conditions one comes across only milder stressful conditions such as bursts of loud noise, fatigue, sleeplessness, prolonged experiential deprivation, and so on. Some times a noxious stimulus such as mild electric shock has also been used to induce an anticipatory stress. The use of stress in this context tends to refer to the conditions themselves, effects of which can then be analyzed. The studies to be discussed in this chapter have relied on the use of arousal or activation as the major theoretical construct which refers to the suggested non-specific changes in brain activity that results from stimulation (Duffy, 1957; Hebb, 1955; Malmo, 1959). The concept of arousal has proved a useful one in accounting for the effects on behaviour brought about by general changes in environmental conditions. In this respect, conditions defined as 'stressful' have the connotation of those which increase arousal. Nevertheless, in some cases, such as sleep deprivation, arousal may be reduced by this form of stress (Hockey, 1979).

The use of arousal in stress research is largely based on a complex relationship between arousal, task difficulty, and efficiency. This relationsip was first demonstrated by Yerkes and Dodson (1908) in an experimental study of the effects of electric shock on discrimination learning in mice. The subjects were trained to choose the brighter of the two boxes, and received an electric shock for failing to make the discrimination. As the intensity of the shock was increased, faster acquisition for the easiest brightness discrimination was observed, but as the brightness discrimination was made more difficult the optimum level of shock was progressively reduced. This interaction between difficulty of discrimination and level of shock is known as the Yerkes-Dodson law. This law can be expressed, in modern terms, as two separate postulates (Hockey, 1979) :

(a) For any task there is an optimal level of arousal such that performance is related to arousal in the form of an inverted U.
(b) The optimum level of arousal is a decreasing monotonic function of the difficulty of the task.

There is considerable experimental support for these postulates. In 1940, Freeman confirmed an inverted U-shaped relationship between arousal and cognitive efficiency. On the other hand, Easterbrook (1959) proposed a cue utilization hypothesis and thereby supported the inverted U-shaped relationship between performance, efficiency, cognitive competence, and arousal. Easterbrook suggested that "the number of cues utilized in any situation tends to become smaller with increase in emotion" (p. 197). Several experiments have confirmed the generality of this law in human stress research.

This paper integrates the findings of experiments that have tried to relate stress and human performance. In this context, the emphasis is on experiments undertaken by Indian researchers though reference to others will also figure occasionally. The experiments to be discussed belong chiefly to the areas of sustained attention, human learning, and memory.

Sustained Attention and Skilled Performance

Early work on stress and work efficiency concentrated on practical needs arising out of industrial problems and their explanations in terms of arousal or activation were taken up much later. Even in these studies, however, stress was regarded as an unwanted source of trouble which only impaired the efficiency of work. The vigilance tasks employed in these studies required the subjects to detect and report occasional critical signals. Mackworth (1950) showed that this kind of task was subject to a fairly pronounced decrement in efficiency with continuous time at work as well as by such other contingent environmental factors as heat, and poor illumination. A wide range of environmental variables such as loss of sleep, increases in temperature, and diurnal rhythm have been employed in vigilance experiments. The general picture that has emerged from this work shows that performance is improved by mildly stressful conditions that are thought to increase arousal, but performance is impaired by factors such as sleep loss or fatigue which presumably reduce arousal. In the following section the effects of electric shock and white noise on performance are discussed.

Effects of Electric Shock on Vigilance

The effect of electric shock on the clarity of perception has been demonstrated by a few studies on perceptual vigilance (Dulany, 1957; Pustell, 1957). Singh (1975), and Dwivedi and Singh (1977, 1978) attempted to study the role of an accessory shock stimulus in varying the level of performance of subjects in reporting pairs of tachistoscopically presented words. The study was conducted on (eighty postgraduate psychology students, forty males and forty females), young adults aged 19 to 22 years. The average age of the sample was 20.5 years. The design was a 2 (supra-threshold, i.e., 500 msec, and sub-threshold, i.e. 200 msec durations of presentation) x 2 (high and low levels of electric shock) x 2 (males and females) factorial. The stimuli were twenty pairs of seven-syllable English words. Each pair was so selected that the two members had the same letters recombined to form two meaningful words. Harper (1973) had reported the ambiguity level of stimuli affects the vigilance behaviour. Therefore, an attempt was made to ascertain whether the stimuli were unambiguous.

The stimulus words were presented singly through a camera-shutter tachistoscope and simultaneously appropriate level of electric shock was also administered in the forefinger of subjects through a hand-withdrawal apparatus. Following the proceduce of Harper (1973), half of the subjects received shock on an even number of stimulus presentation while the other half received it on random trials. Altogether the subjects received only ten shocks and no subject received electric shock on more than three consecutive trials. The correct reproduction was used as an index of vigilance. Each correctly reproduced verbal pair was awarded one credit, and a half credit was allowed for a partially correct reproduction (i.e., correct recall of either member of a verbal pair).

The results showed that the male subjects evinced

higher vigilance performance with high intensity of electric shock (40 volts) while their female counterparts performed better with low intensity of electric shock (20 volts). The mean vigilance score for the shock-related as well as non-shocked trials (see Figure 9.1) showed that the intensity of shock interacted significantly with sex (F = 10.17, df = 1.72, p < .01). The obtained sex difference in perceptual vigilance can be seen as reflecting the differences in affective arousal among the male and female subjects (t = 2.45, p < .02 and t = 3.14, p < .01, respectively for male and female subjects given long exposure and high shock or non-shock on trials). The subjects could not develop an expectation for the onset of shock because the shock presentation was either random or evenly spaced.

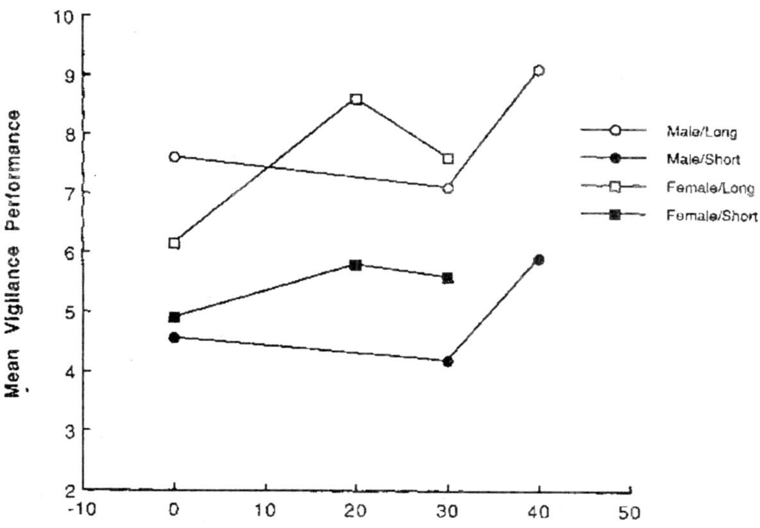

FIG. 9.1 : Mean correct responses for varying amounts of shocks for males and females. (Reproduced from Dwivedi & Singh, 1978).

The temporal uncertainty regarding shock was also analyzed. For this purpose, all subjects were asked whether they were certain about the occurrence of shock throughout the experiment, and if they actually were certain, what was the range of their such anticipation? Following Price (1966), certainty was defined as anticipating shock on alternate trials, whereas uncertainty was conceived of as anticipating the same after more than two trials. The number of subjects falling under certainty group was higher for shock induced group than for no-shock group (t = 13.0, $p < .001$). Further, the vigilance score obtained by the subjects of certainty group was also significantly higher (X^2 = 10.83, $p < .001$). These results show that certainty was a matter of experimental manipulation of shock and the subjects of certainty group could guess such manipulation of shock which was administered on even number of stimuli only. Contrarily, the subjects of uncertainty group could not apply this anticipation technique as they were left with too little opportunity to be certain about the occurrence of shock. These findings extended the theory that females are more easily brought to an optimum level of arousal than are males contingent upon which was their differential receptivity of the stimuli.

An inverted U-shaped curve was obtained for the females (see Figure 9.1) while males showed its reverse trend. As the effects of shock did not generalize to non-shock, arousal was being manipulated. The phasic alertness as introduced by a warning signal was not found to involve changes in basic receptivity (see Posner, 1975).

Dwivedi, I.L. Singh, and N.B. Singh (1978) attempted to study the differential effect of anxiety and inducement of shock on perceptual vigilance. Besides administering either a high or a low intensity of electric shock to subjects along with the presentation of a paired stimulus word followed by the recording of their vigilance performance, the subjects were asked to rate on 7-point scales how relaxed-anxious; comfortable-uncomfortable; undistrubed-annoyed; pleasantness-unpleasantness toward shock; pleasantness-unpleasantness toward experimental tasks;

and the perceived level of anxiety toward shock did they feel during the experimental sessions. The scale values (1 = least and 7 = most) were totalled to obtain the score of perceived level of anxiety. And for the purpose of obtaining the level of manifest anxiety, the Sinha Manifest Anxiety Scale (Sinha, 1968) was administered. The inter-correlations between the obtained scores on the test of manifest anxiety and other dependent measures of perceived level of anxiety were computed.

Figure 9.2 shows that under long exposure the anxiety toward shock as well as the level of manifest anxiety were accelerated and the rate of this acceleration was proportionate to the intensity of electric shock. Under long exposure females generally obtained higher indices of correlation (see for example, the correlation between self-reported anxiety and pleasantness-unpleasantness toward experimenal tasks, $r = .92$, $p < .001$ for females and $r = .31$ for males). Nevertheless, similar trend was not seen for short exposure. The high intensity of shock was a more potent and powerful inducer of anxiety and the intercorrelations (see Fig. 9.2) demonstrated that three out of five significant correlations between self-reported anxiety and pleasantness-unpleasantness toward experimental tasks were obtained for high-shock induced group. As the uncertainty was also manipulated by presenting shock either randomly or on even number of trials, the subjects could not develop any expectancy about the occurrence of shock. Only moderate correlations were obtained between vigilance scores and the variable of self-reported anxiety which was aroused by the periodicity and different intensities of electric shock in this experiment.

As the experiment of Dwivedi *et al.* (1978) reported only low positive correlations between vigilance scores and anxiety, I.L. Singh, Dwivedi, and Sinha (1979) attempted to test it further with a larger sample of subjects. They employed a 2 (high, i.e., 60 volts, and low, i.e., 30 volts electric shocks) x 2 (high, i.e., 90 dbA, and low, i.e., 60 dbA white noises) factorial design and conducted the study on 480 undergraduates. Twenty 5-lettered paired nouns were tachistoscopically displayed with simultaneous

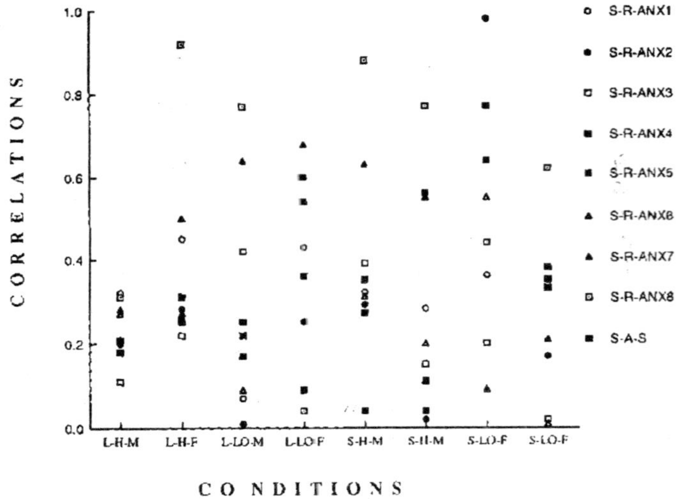

FIG. 9.2 : Intercorrelations between various self-reported measures of anxiety, vigilance scores and Sinha Anxiety Scale. (Reproduced from Dwivedi, *et al.*, 1978).

inducements of appropriate levels of electric shock and white noise as per the scheme of the experiment. There were two conditions, namely threatening and non-threatening, which denoted the attachment or non-attachment of electric shocks and the recognition of ten pairs in threatening condition was used as an index of vigilance. The Sinha Manifest Anxiety Scale (Sinha, 1968) was used to measure the level of anxiety.

High intensity of shock evoked more vigilance (Mean = 7.42, SD = 1.69) than did the low intensity of shock (Mean = 5.58, SD = 1.99). The main effect of shock was highly significant ($F = 90.41$, $df = 1{,}476$, $p < .001$). Similarly, noise main effect was also significant ($F = 24.19$, $df = 1{,}476$, $p < .001$), though their interaction between vigilance and anxiety was very low ($r = .07$ for high shock inducement and $r = .007$ for low shock inducements, respectively) but positive which supported the findings of Dwivedi *et al.*, (1978). However, such a low index of correlation called for a further probing in as much as the phasic arousal appeared to be almost depleted in this experiment. In their next experiment, the researchers used one hundred and sixty male undergraduates and employed a 2 (long, i.e., of 200 msec, and short, i.e. of 40 msec durations of exposure) x 2 (certainty and uncertainty expectations) x 2 (high, i.e., of 60 volts, and low, i.e., of 30 volts shock intensities) x 2 (high, i.e., of 90 dbA, and low, i.e., of 65 dbA levels of white noise inducements) factorial experimental design.

The stimuli were twenty pairs of 5-lettered words which were displayed by a camera-shutter tachistoscope for the required durations of exposure and shock as well as noise inducements were also operative. Immediately after the exposure of paired words, which was presented one at a time, their recognitions were obtained separately for threatening and non-threatening situations. The correct recognitions under a threatening situation were used as an index of vigilance. The results showed significant main effects for durations of exposure ($F = 20.88$, $df = 1,144$, $p < .01$), expectation ($F = 241.53$, $df = 1,144$, $p < .001$), shock ($F = 44.77$, $df = 1,144$, $p < .001$), and white noise ($F = 22.48$, $df = 1,144$, $p < .01$). Interactions between expectation x noise ($F = 4.09$, $df = 1,144$, $p < .05$), and expectation x shock ($F = 7.08$, $df = 1,144$, $p < .01$) were also significant. Most of the inter-group comparisons were significant on Newman-Keuls multiple range test. The effectiveness of cognitive appraisal in elicting vigilance behaviour was thus corroborated.

These findings notwithstanding, the effects of individual difference variables on vigilance behaviour remained quite controverted and in their next experiment Dwivedi, I. L. Singh, and R. S. Singh (1981) addressed this issue. The subjects in this experiment were forty males and forty females, aged 19 to 22 years, who participated in a 2 (long and short durations of exposure) x 2 (high and low intensities of electric shock) x 2 (certainty and uncertainty manipulations of expectation) x 2 (male and female sexes) factorial between subjects design.

The results are shown in Fig. 9.3. The long duration of exposure made the subjects more vigilant (Mean = 8.07,

S.D. = 1.08) whereas high intensity of shock induced in them a coping behavour which also enhanced their vigilance performance (Mean = 7.02, SD = 1.58).

A more pronounced arousal function was found in certainty manipulation than was in uncertainty manipulation and this was clearly visible in females than in males. An unequivocal support for inverted U-shaped curve was found for females, who were optimally aroused by low shock inputs. However, there was a mixed trend for males for whom an increasing function over respective shock levels was visible in three out of four conditions. The sole exception was the long exposure with uncertainty manipulation where low and high intensities of shock showed a straight line function (see Fig. 9.3). The main effect for duration of exposure was statistically reliable (F = 59.16, df = 1,64, $p < .01$) besides the interactions between shock x sex (F = 11.96, df = 1,64, $p < .01$) and between exposure x sex x certainty (F = 10.06, df = 1,64, $p < .01$) which were also significant.

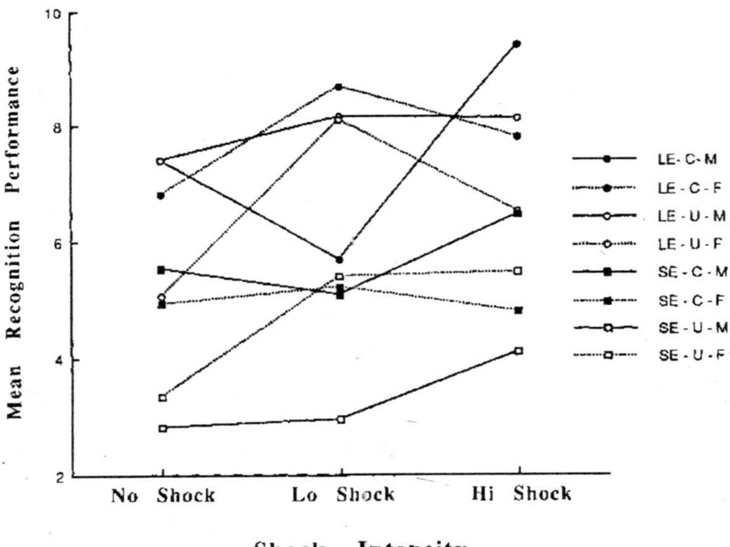

FIG. 9.3 : Average vigilance responses of males and females for different exposure and certainty conditions. (Reproduced from Dwivedi, *et al.*, 1981).

The cue value of shock inputs was found to vary in terms of sex of the subjects which supported the findings of Posner *et al.*, (1973).

I.L. Singh (1984) reasoned that anticipated and unanticipated stressful situations invoke different coping activities in an organism and as such the joint effects of anticipation and shock inducement required more rigorous study. In a carefully designed experiment he employed four hundred eighty male undergraduates, aged 16 to 20 years (mean age = 18 years), and followed a 2 (anticipated and unanticipated mode of presentation of shocks) x 2 (high, i.e., of 60 volts, and low, i.e., of 30 volts shock intensities) factorial design with 120 subjects in each cell. Stimuli were twenty paired 5-letter meaningful words which were displayed through a camera-shutter tachistoscope with a simultaneous inducement of electric shock with or without anticipating instructions for shock. Vigilance was defined as a tendency to anticipate a threatening stimulus over a series of trials with unavoidable shock inducements. There was significant main effect of anticipation ($F = 57.46$, $df = 1,476$, $p < .001$), and shock ($F = 94.44$, $df = 1,476$, $p < .001$), though their interaction was not significant. The trend of results further confirmed that only phasic and not tonic arousal was operative in this experiment.

Effects of Noise

The vigilance tasks have proved sensitive to changes in a wide range of environmental variables, such as loss of sleep, increase in temperature, diurnal rhythm, and noise. The effects of noise are quite complex, and usually impairment has been found with tasks involving more than one signal source, or a high signal rate, while vigilance has been often found enhanced in the case of simpler tasks. Poulton (1976) has argued that all stressors which increase arousal should improve performance. However, impairment in performance in the case of noise occurs because noise prevents subjects from making use of intrinsic auditory cues present in the tasks. Poulton

(1978) further pointed out that noise was most effective in masking speech in the three octaves centered on 1, 2 and 3 KHz and about 85 per cent of the intelligibility of speech comes from these three octaves. According to Poulton if speech in these three octaves was masked by loud noise, we would not be able to listen to the consonants without which we would fail to distinguish one word from the other. Besides this, noise also isolates a person from his normal auditory environment and it distracts him from what he is doing.

Koelega and Brinkman (1986) reviewed the literature on the effects of noise on visual performance and found that there was no agreement in results. They found that even within a single study, performance might at any given time be seen to be decreased, increased, or unaffected depending on a number of variables (Lysaght, Warm, Dember, & Loeb, 1984) and sometimes depending on very specific features of experimental conditions (Jones, Smith, & Broadbent, 1979). The studies to be discussed in this section portrays the findings which are of mixed variety.

One of the most important factors in discussing noise effects stems from the type of noise input, i.e., whether the noise is continuously presented or intermittently administered. There are widespread effects from an intense interrupted noise, however this also disappears as subjects develop an adaptation towards it. Even with this adaptation there does occur some strain in the subjects either in the form of some latent physiological changes or in apparent deterioration in performance or both.

Chatterjee and Krishnamurthy (1972) studied the differential effects of noise on the skill of typewriting. After a preliminary test the subjects were categorised into high scorer and low scorer groups on the basis of their performance score which was calculated by the number of words correctly typed excluding the omitted and repeated words. The experimental task involved ten minutes typing job from a predetermined prose passage in different conditions of ambient noise input. The noise input was either continuous or intermittent and was presented through magnetic tape played on a tape recorder. The pattern of performance showed that intermittent noise had a more deteriorating effect on task. In contrast to the high skilled subjects, the low skilled group was uniformly affected by both kinds of noise. The job of typing becomes mechanical after some time and therefore one develops adaptation to it. Another reason for not finding any effect of noise lies probably in the relatively easy task that a skilled typist was given to perform. For any highly skilled typist the task of typing for ten minutes is nothing but an amusement whether done under a noisy background or otherwise.

Purohit (1976) attempted a study involving auditory noise, pay-off, and signal probability as factors. He varied the signal probability at five levels, pay-off at three levels, and noise at two levels and employed a 5 x 3 x 2 factorial design with ten subjects in each of the thirty cells. The signal probability as well as pay-off significantly affected the detection performance but noise did not do so. The mean hits under two noise conditions did not show any difference which could be taken as an indicator of mixed effect of noise input.

Chatterjee (1984) conducted three experiments. In the first experiment he studied the physiological strain as affected by environmental factors such as heat. Construction workers engaged in building industry formed the experimental group while the control group comprised such subjects whose nature of job was of sedentary type. Their body temperature for different periods of the day was recorded. The two groups showed differences in body temperature. In his second study effects of noise on a skilled job were analysed, but the results did not show any effect of noise. In the third experiment, Chatterjee studied the task load and psychological strain. Five short sentences graded in difficulty were transmitted, one after the other, to the subjects through earphones. The intensity of transmission was gradually increased and the threshold of hearing was recorded in decibels. In the second stage similar procedure was followed with five different sentences which were identical in nature but differed in contents. The subjects were also simultaneously asked to do simple arithmetic problems of multiplying two digits by two digits. The subjects were asked to do both tasks as effectively as possible. The results showed that the strain caused by the loading of the arithmetic problems had an adverse effect on the threshold of intelligibility of sentences at all levels of difficulty. The induced stress by the secondary task increased the load on the subjects. The attentive selectivity was therefore not obtained.

B.V. Singh (1978) studied the auditory and visual vigilance detection as affected by induced expectancies and white noise inputs. In a 2 (chance and skill expectations) x 2 (high, i.e., 90 dbA and low, i.e., 65 dbA intensities of white noise) x 2 (visual and auditory modalities) factorial experiment with ten subjects in each cell, he presented twenty signals which were even numbers of four digits interspersed with five hundred eighty non-signals (also of four digits but odd numbers). The subjects' task was to detect the signals which were presented both auditorily as well as visually. White noise presentation was continuous throughout the experiment. High intensity of noise was found to impair vigilance more than that of low intensity of noise. Auditory vigilance was more severely affected presumably because noise masked the inner speech of the subjects which was evident in greater magnitude in auditory modality than in visual modality.

I.L. Singh (1978) and I.L. Singh, Dwivedi, and Sinha (1979, 1980) conducted several experiments to study the effects of noise on vigilance performance. they found better vigilance with high intensity of noise inputs. One of the possible reasons for this effect could be that they employed electric shock as well as noise and it might have been that the two sources of stress cancelled out each other and shock being a more potent and noxious source of stimulation occupied the driving seat (see Hockey, 1979). There appeared a crossover interaction between expectation and noise ($F = 4.09$, $df = 1{,}144$, $p < .05$).

Dwivedi and R.S. Singh (1993) studied arousal differences in the processing of congruent and incongruent stimuli. Following the technique of Osgood (1971) facial expressions were generated for visual as well as kinesthetic modalities. A similar method was also adopted for constructing the sentences. In their first experiment the processing of congruent and incongruent paired facial expressions were examined under two types of noise input. The facial expressions were generated by the use of different eye brow types, eye types, and mouth types. Two types of loading, positive and negative, on the pleasantness dimension were used. The congruent positive facial expressions pair had identical mouth features with one difference in either the brows or eyes. The congruent negative facial expressions had negative loadings on the pleasantness dimension and they also had identical mouth features. Two types of incongruent paired stimuli, viz., less incongruent, and more incongruent, were also used. In less incongruent type, mouth features were different but brows and eyes were identical, while in more incongruent type there were different mouth features as well as different brows and eyes.

The design was a 2 (high, i.e., 90 dbC, and low, i.e., 65 dbC levels of white noise) x 2 (wityh cue and without cue statements) x 4 (congruent positive, congruent negative, less incongruent, and more incongruent types of paired facial expressions) mixed factorial with repeated measures on the last factor. The errors in processing were used as the dependent measure. Subjects were one hundred twenty male high school students, aged 13 to 16 years (mean age = 14 years 8 months). There were thirty subjects in each of the four between subjects factors from whom congruent and incongruent processings were obtained. Twelve pairs of each type of facial expressions were prepared besides which similar number of positive and negative sentences were also constructed. The subjects were asked to imagine that each pair of presented faces represented two different persons reacting to the same situation. The faces showed either positive or negative feelings and the subjects were required to respond *and* or *but* to conjoin the faces depending upon whether they thought the respective expressions were congruent or incongruent. When cue statements were also attached the subjects were told to imagine that each pair showed something being said along with a simultaneous display of facial expressions of the speaker. The manner of responding remained the same. The paired stimuli were displayed by a camera-shutter tachistoscope for 1.5 seconds and simultaneously the white noise of required intensity was also presented. The response given by the subjects was noted verbatim without any comments.

And or *but* responses which differed from what were expected in terms of predetermined affective meanings of the respective conjoint faces were defined as errors. Total number of errors for faces without cue attachments could range from 0 to 3 whereas with cue statement attachments it could range from 0 to 6. Mean errors presented in Figure 9.4 show that errors were higher for incongruent polarity.

The mean errors for more incongruent condition were higher. This trend was even more pronounced with high noise presentation for more incongruent polarity (Mean = 2.55). However, with low noise presentation the errors were less (Mean = 1.15). The main effect of noise was highly

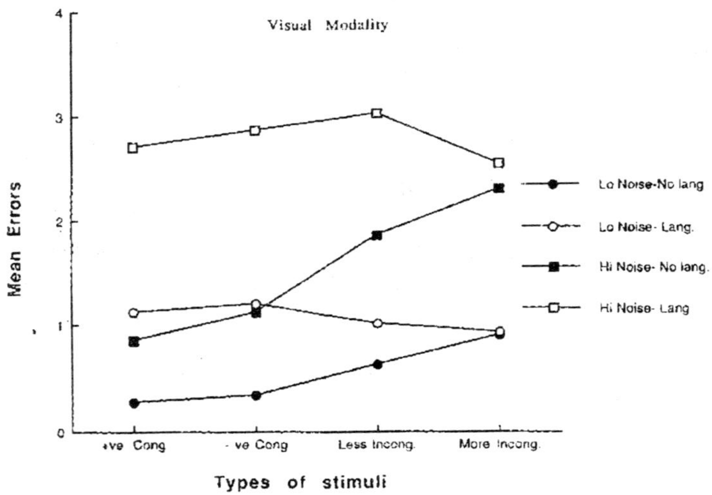

FIG. 9.4 : Mean errors for congruent and incongruent stimuli in visual mode of presentation. (Reproduced from Dwivedi & R.S. Singh, 1993.)

significant (F = 159.41, df = 1,116, p < .001). The attachment of cue statements adversely affected the processing of facial expressions. Mean errors for different polarities without cues were much less than with cues (F = 81.30, df = 1,116, p < .001). The interaction between noise and cue attachments was also significant (F = 24.87, df = 1,116, p < .001). There was a gradient in mean errors with congruent positive condition showing the least mean errors while more incongruent showed most mean errors. The polarity main effect was also significant (F = 15.89, df = 3,348, p < .001). The interaction between noise x polarity (F = 24.872, df = 3,348, p < .001), cue statements x polarity (F = 13.963, df = 3,348, p < .001), and noise x cue statement x polarity (F = 9.938, df = 3,348, p < .001) were significant.

The second experiment used twelve wooden grooves which were based on original paired stimuli of first experiment. Another group of one hundred twenty high schools students, aged 14 to 17 years (Mean = 15 years 6 months), were used as subjects in this experiment. The design and other details were same as in the first experiment. The mean errors (see Figure 9.5) for more incongruent polarity were highest while the mean errors for congruent positive polarity were the lowest.

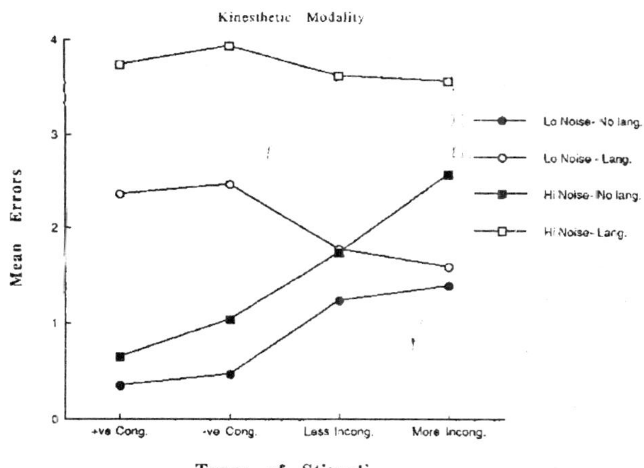

FIG. 9.5 : Mean errors for congruent and incongruent stimuli in Kinesthetic mode of presentation. (Reproduced from Dwivedi & R.S. Singh, 1993).

The polarity main effect was significant ($F = 4.90$, $df = 3,348$, $p < .05$) and interaction between noise x polarity ($F = 19.75$, $df = 3,348$, $p < .001$) was also significant. The detrimental effects of noise and cue statements were found both of which reflect the arousal variation and resultant differences in cognitive performance. There is a universal human tendency to use evaluatively positive stimuli more frequently than evaluatively negative ones and the findings of these two experiments suggest that there are less detection errors in positive stimuli than in negative stimuli. Noise was found to increase the error component presumably because there is more inhibition of inner speech in high noise input condition than is there in low noise input.

Noise thus appears to interact with individual difference characteristics. Smith (1984) has suggested that when subjects carry out a task which could be performed in several different ways, noise inducement supposedly leads to the adoption of certain strategies in preference to others. Once a subject has adopted one mode of responding, the inducement of noise may make it very hard for the subject to modify his pattern of responses. The studies discussed in this section showed that moderate intensity of noise influenced the attentional selectivity even when the task involved the responding or detecting the sensory stimuli.

Short-term and Long-term Memory

As compared to the sustained attention experiments which employed several sources of arousal, the literature which has been produced regarding arousal effects in memory is concerned mainly with noise input. The reasons for this difference becomes immediately clear when one considers the length of experimental session and the levels of attendant stress. In memory experiments, tests are usually very brief and mostly one session alone gives the desired dependent measure. If the long-term memory is also to be measured, the stimulus material at input is not presented again and the subject is required to recall, reproduce, or recognise the earlier presented material. The comparison with sustained-attention experiments can be attempted merely because noise as a source of arousal has been used in both of them.

The major theoretical proposition regarding arousal effects in retention has been that of Walker (1958) who contended that high arousal would result in the setting up of a strong perseverative trace leading to a greater long-term retention. He further proposed that there does occur a greater temporary inhibition against recall (which he named as the 'action decrement') during the process of consolidation. Several studies have supported this theory.

One of the early experiments which could be called as the trend setter for further researches, was conducted by Kleinsmith and Kaplan (1963). They presented subjects with an eight-item paired-associate task, with emotional words, of varying degree, such as rape or exam, as the stimuli and digits as the responses. Arousal was inferred from the GSR responses to the presentation of each of the words during the task. Each subject's data were sorted into the three items associated with the highest GSR and the three with the lowest GSR, thus ignoring the middle two items. Their results indicated a cross-over interaction between autonomic arousal level and time of testing the recall. They demonstrated that low arousal items were best retrieved in immediate tests (2 minutes) then they became progressively less accessible. On the other hand, high arousal items were found to be less available in immediate tests; however they were better recalled at longer delays. High arousal associates showed an improvement in recall performance as a function of time, which has been discussed as a reminiscence effect by many (see Hockey, 1979).

This phenomenon has since been demonstrated in a variety of experimental conditions including arousal manipulated by learning material (Walker & Tarte, 1963), film content (Levonian, 1967), delayed auditory feedback (King, 1963; King & Dodge, 1965; King & Wolf, 1965) and noise (Berlyne, Borsa, Craw, Gelman, & Mandell, 1965; Berlyne, Borsa, Hamacher, & Koenig, 1966; M.W. Eysenck,

1975, 1976; McLean, 1969; Smith, 1982, 1984, 1985; Smith, Jones, & Broadbent, 1981). It needs to be kept in mind that although the degree to which long-term retention was enhanced by each of the aforesaid methods varied from differential forgetting to strong reminiscence, there did emerge a striking feature pointing out an interaction between arousal and time of recall which was common in almost all experiments.

However, some experiments reported a facilitatory effect of noise on long-term recall but no effect on recall in an immediate test (e.g., Berlyne *et al.*, 1966; Farley, 1969; Haveman & Farley, 1969). In view of this controversy N.B. Singh (1978) studied the effects of induced arousal and meaningfulness on short-term and long-term recall. He reasoned that one of the probable reasons for not finding any effects of noise could be that these studies did not control the factor of meaningfulness. Besides this, he also manipulated orientational instructions. The subjects were one hundred twenty postgraduate students. Their age ranged from 22 to 24 years (Mean = 23 yrs. 2 months). The design was a 2 (high and low levels of meaningfulness) x 2 (high, i.e., 90 dbA and low, i.e., 65 dbA levels of white noise inducements) x 2 (intentional and non-intentional instructions) between subjects factorial. There were 15 subjects in each of the eight cells of this experiment from whom both the short-term and long-term recalls were obtained. The stimuli consisted of 15 disyllabic paired-associates, which were presented through a memory drum at the rate of 2 seconds per paired-associate. The immediate and 24 hours delayed responses were obtained. Noise impaired both immediate as well as delayed recall responses which contradicted the findings of the action decrement theory.

Dwivedi, N.B. Singh, and I.L. Singh (1982) studied the differential role of meaningfulness, white noise, and intentionality of recall. The noise presentation was intermittent. They manipulated the intentional-non intentional treatment by instructing the subjects prior to initiating the experiment that they would be required to recall the paired associates later. The non-intentional group was not given any such instruction. The subjects were one hundred twenty postgraduate students aged 20 to 24 years (Mean = 22 years). Two separate lists of fifteen 5-letter paired-associates, having low and high levels of meaningfulness as ascertained by S. Singh (1971) were used. The number of trials for displaying high and low level of meaningful paired-associates was determined in a preliminary study on 20 subjects. In this study five and eight trials were found optimum for high and low meaningful paired associates. The paired-associates were displayed at the rate of two seconds per pair through a memory drum. The pre-recorded cassettes of white noise were used for noise input.

The design was a 3 (no, low, i.e., 60 dbA, and high, i.e., 90 dbA levels of white noise inducements) x 2 (low and high levels of meaningfulness) x 2 (intentional and non-intentional instructions for recall) factorial. There were ten subjects in each of the twelve cells of this study from whom immediate and delayed recalls were obtained. The obtained recall scores were transformed by the Bartlett's square root formula. The mean scores (see Figure 9.6) show higher means for no-noise treatment in both the

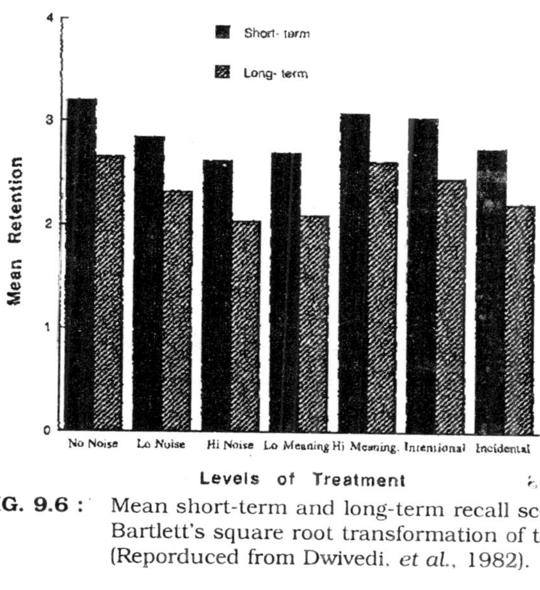

FIG. 9.6 : Mean short-term and long-term recall scores after Bartlett's square root transformation of the data. (Reporduced from Dwivedi, *et al.*, 1982).

short-term as well as the long-term recalls as compared to either types of noise inducement. This difference was significant (F = 45.82, df = 2,108, p < .001). High meaningful materials were more easily recalled than that of low meaningful ones. Similarly intentional instructions evoked more short-term and long-term recalls than neutral or non-intentional instructions.

The deleterious effect of white noise was found to be related with its intensity which failed to support the action decrement theory proposed by Walker (1958). There was found a gradient in recall for both the durations of retention with no noise evincing highest recall followed by low and high noise inducements. These results extended the theory that better long-term recall for high arousal items, as found by many researchers, could be a function of subjective arousal along with the noise presentations.

Mishra (1982) examined the effects of noise and modes of presentation on levels of processing of verbal and pictorial materials. He conducted four experiments. In his first experiment, 240 male high school students served as subjects in a 2 x 2 x 2 x 6 factorial design with repeated measures on the last factor. The masked and unmasked presentation of high (85 dbC) and low (60 dbC) intensities of noise, visual and auditory modes of presentation and six types of acquisition task were the levels of different factors. Both the short-term and long-term retentions were obtained. The to-be-remembered stimuli were thirty 3-lettered Hindi words with frequency count below 1 in a million on Tripathi's (1974) norms. The six acquisition modes comprised of six words which were presented in sentence frames. Memory drum and cassette tape recorder were used for visual and auditory presentations, respectively. Noise was also presented by a cassette tape recorder. The short-term and long-term retentions were obtained by standard recognition, rhyming recognition, and cued recall methods. The results showed significantly higher short-term retention with low noise whereas in the long-term high noise showed higher retention. Visual modality and unmasked presentation yielded higher retention. The second experiment replicated the findings of the first experiment. The subjects were 160 male students of classes X and XI, aged 15 to 18 years. In this experiment 32 non-meaningful CVC trigrams were also used besides an equal number of meaningful ones as in Experiment 1. The results showed a shift in processing besides supporting the findings of Experiment 1. In this study Spielberger's state-trait anxiety test was also used. Extreme group analysis showed that high A-trait and high A-state subjects yielded less retention.

Pictorial superiority was studied in the third experiment in which 160 subjects (90 boys and 80 girls) of classes VII and VIII, aged 12 to 15 years participated. Forty paired associated pictures were drawn on 5 x 7 inch cards in Chinese ink. The names of those objects were also written on similar cards. The stimulus member of the paired associate picture was displayed first and the subject was asked to guess the response member. After subject had guessed the actual card was shown and the error in responding was noted. This procedure was continued till subjects correctly anticipated all response members up to three errorless trials. The results showed that low noise incurred less error and higher long-term recognition than high noise. The girls recognised more than boys which showed the presence of imagery in them. In the fourth experiment sentence processing was studied. Determined-stem and undetermined-stem sentences were used and forward and backward recalls were noted. Sentence completion showed higher recall than that of reading only treatment and similarly determined sentences were recalled better. These experiments thus demonstrated that low noise is more effective in both short-term as well as long-term recall.

N.B. Singh (1982) also conducted a series of four experiments to study the effects of noise on episodic memory of verbal and pictorial materials. In his first experiment, 120 male high school students, aged 13 to 17 years, were used in a 2 x 2 x 3 factorial experiment with repeated measures on the last factor. Low (60 dbC) and high (90 dbC) intensities of white noise, 5-seconds and 10-seconds lengths of interval, and relevant, irrelevant and no-treatment categories were levels of the factors. Short-term processing, latency and recall were obtained. Twenty-four 3-lettered Hindi triads were used as stimuli, six of which were for practice purposes and eighteen were used in final study. Three methods of priming were used by the types of cue statement, viz., relevant, irrelevant, and no sentence. The triads were displayed one by one by a camera-shutter tachistoscope for 2.5 seconds along with noise. Immediately after displaying the triads one by one, a four digit number was presented and the subject was asked to count backward by threes. The priming was done after 5- or 10- seconds interval and the backward counting continued with a fresh digit. After 15 seconds the subjects were asked to recall all the three items in the same order as presented.

The results showed that high intensity of noise was far more detrimental for retention and the latency of this group was higher as compared to that of low noise. Ten-seconds interval hampered the retention more than its five seconds counterpart. In his second study, N.B. Singh used pictorial contextual stimuli to test the effects of priming. The subjects were 160 male high school students. The design was a 2 x 2 x 4 factorial in which the last factor differed from Experiment 1 because herein four types of priming were used which were none, common, unusual and bizarre. Fifteen easily recognisable objects appeared in the settings according to the priming types. The low noise moderately aroused the subjects which facilitated their recall performance. There was a clear superiority of priming at 5-seconds which also pointed toward a transient arousal. In his third experiment N.B. Singh studied the bilingual superiority on 160 Intermediate students, (80 boys and 80 girls), aged 15 to 19 years. The stimulus materials were twelve 4-lettered Hindi and twelve 6-lettered English words belonging to four categories. The words were presented in both language scripts and the short-term and long-term recall and recognition were obtained. The facilitative role of low noise in short-term recall and recognition were obtained but high noise was found to facilitate long-term recall and recognition with inhibited short-term retention performance.

In the fourth experiment inferential reasoning was studied on 160 male students of classes XI and XII, aged 15 to 19 years. Four stories were used in story and story-controlled conditions. Twelve acquisition sentences were constructed for measuring the retention of story contents. Four complex ideas each with three interrelated propositions were used for framing twelve complex idea sentences and four inference sentences. The stories were presented in both visual and auditory modalities. The acquisition of stories, detection of complex ideas, and generation of inferential reasoning were all significantly enhanced with low noise inducement. The visual modality was found significantly better in processing and retention of stories. Thus in all four experiments low noise was found better in retaining the to-be-remembered materials and in most cases this effect was seen in the long-term as well.

Dwivedi, Mishra, and Chaturvedi (1986) studied orientation, arousal and intentionality of processing differences in retention. In a reanalysis of the findings of Dwivedi, Singh, and Singh (1982) it occurred to them that may be the difficult task used in that study was not very difficult and this could have confounded the findings. Accordingly they devised a semantic and an acoustic task which could be used with the two lists of paired-associates in this experiment. They used high school students, aged 13 to 18 years (Mean = 15 yrs 8 mos) and followed a 2 (high, i.e., 90 dbC and low, i.e., 65 dbC levels of white noise) x 2 (intentional and incidental processing types) x 2 (semantic and acoustic orientations) factorial experimental design. The stimulus materials were 15 three-letter paired-associates, frequencies of the words were below 1 in a million as ascertained by Tripathi (1974). The words had sufficiently high associative strength among pairs. Both the orienting task lists comprised of three categories (namely, object, person, and place in semantic orientation while sounds of A, AA, or I, as in Hindi words in acoustic orientation). The difficulty level of both lists was equated in a preliminary experiment. The paired words were displayed by a camera-shutter tachistoscope while a tape recorder was used for presenting the required intensity of white noise. The paired words were presented for one second with an interval of six seconds between two pairs. Immediately after presentation of the last pair, the subjects were given a recall sheet in which one member of each pair (either a TBR or a LC) was given and the subjects were asked to recall the other member. Five minutes time was allowed for recall test. Delayed recall was also obtained in a similar manner after 24 hours but subjects were not informed beforehand about it.

Each correct recall was awarded one score. The results (see Figure 9.7) showed that the mean recall of moderate noise-intentional instruction-semantic orientation subjects was higher than their counterparts. The main effects for short-term recall were significant beyond .001 level. But none of the interactions was found significant which

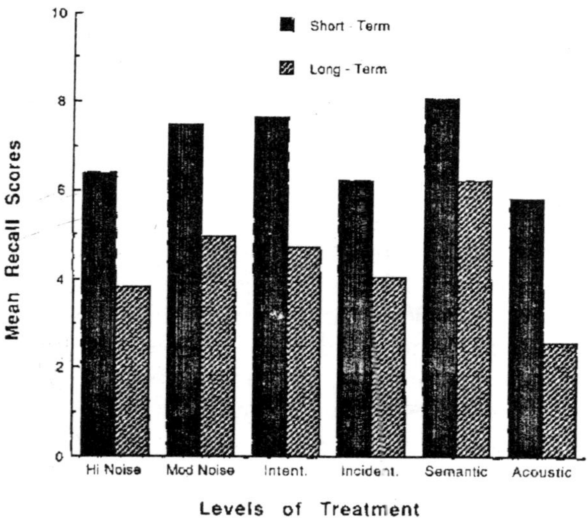

FIG. 9.7 : Average short-term recall scores for various treatment levels. (Reproduced from Dwivedi *et al.*, 1986).

supported most researches. The long-term recall data showed these significant main effects besides the significant interactions between noise x orientation (F = 5.71, df = 1,72, p < .01), and intentionality x orientation (F = 16.51, df = 1,72, p < .001). Significantly higher retention in both durations by moderate noise inducements contradicted most of the arousal studies and failed to support action decrement theory. It appears that due to intentionality instructions moderate noise induced the required level of arousal while the high noise made the subjects more aroused which inhibited their short-term and long-term retentions. These results lent partial support to the contentions of Christie (1974) who has suggested that due to some sort of habituation the subjects at long-term are less aroused than they are at short-term.

Employing a somewhat different methodology, Dwivedi (1990) attempted to study reward-induced arousal differences in retention. Relying on the premise that inappropriate use of extrinsic rewards had an unintended deleterious effect on performance, he designed an experiment in which extreme scorers on a test of intrinsic motivation either received an extrinsic reward or nothing for their performance. In this manner he employed the trait aspect of intrinsic motivation and tested the overjustification hypothesis (Lepper, Greene & Nisbett, 1973). Experiments on the over justification hypothesis have extended the theory that the presentation of extrinsic rewards induces more than an optimum level of arousal in high intrinsically oriented subjects which in turn hampers their later performance. On the other hand, the presentation of rewards to low intrinsically oriented subjects induces an optimum level of arousal in them which enhances their later performance. A large group of subjects was administered a test of intrinsic motivational orientation (Haywood, 1968) nearly one week prior to the experiment. The high and low scorers on intrinsic motivational orientation were identified and they were then randomly assigned to reward and no-reward groups.

The subjects were sixty class VIII boys, aged 12-14 yr. (Mean = 13 yr. 2 months) who were the extreme scorers on Haywood's choice motivator scale (1968) administered one week prior to the actual experiment. The design was a 2 (high intrinsic motivational orientation and low intrinsic motivational orientations) x 2 (reward and no-reward incentive types) factorial with 15 subjects in each cell. Both the short-term and the long-term retentions were obtained from them. As the expected reward-inducement procedure was adopted in this experiment, the instructions for the rewarded and non-rewarded subjects were different.

The subjects working in the reward groups irrespective of their high or low motivational orientations, were asked to read attentively the to-be-remembered story (which was a Hindi version of Bartlett's story the 'war of ghosts') for ten minutes. They were told that they would be required to answer some questions based on the story read earlier and only the subjects with correct answers would be given a reward. They were further told that more than one subject could win a reward and therefore, they should also try to win by answering a maximum number of questions correctly. After presenting the story for ten minutes, a sheet containing the questions was given to the subjects and they were asked to answer them. This phase also continued for ten minutes during which subjects had to answer ten questions each having two parts. After a subject had completed answering, his answer sheet was collected and he was given the reward as promised which was in kind, worth 5 rupees. The no-reward group subjects, on the other hand, received similar instructions excepting that they were not informed of any possibility of a reward outcome. An unexpected long-term retention test was taken after 24 hours. The procedure for this was same as that of the short-term test.

The low intrinsic-rewarded subjects (see Figure 9.8) showed higher short-term (Mean = 17.97, S.D. = 1.13) and long-term (Mean = 17.80, S.D. = 1,82) retentions than their no-reward inducement counterparts. On the other hand, the high instrinsic no-reward subjects showed higher short-term (Mean = 16.80, S.D. = 1.03) and long-term (Mean = 16..83, S.D. = 1,47) retentions than that of their reward induced counterparts. Figure 9.8 clearly shows a significant interaction between intrinsic motivational orientation and incentive type. These results thus supported reward-induced shifts in motivational orientations as well as in retentions. The high intrinsically oriented non-rewarded subjects evidenced higher short-term and long-term retentions while low intrinsically oriented rewarded subjects retained more than non-rewarded ones. These results supported the overjustification hypothesis insofar as the intrinsic interest of high intrinsically oriented subjects was decreased by inducing them to engage in the retention activity as an explicit means to the extrinsic reward.

Dwivedi (1992) examined the induced instructional effects in paired-associate recall, along with continuous free-field noise presentation of a moderate level. His main goal was to determine whether an immediate recall test would eliminate instructional effects in delayed recall as had been reported by Masson and McDaniel (1981). To test it he used two groups of instructional subjects. One group was warned that there would be a delayed recall test after the immediate recall test had been taken, while

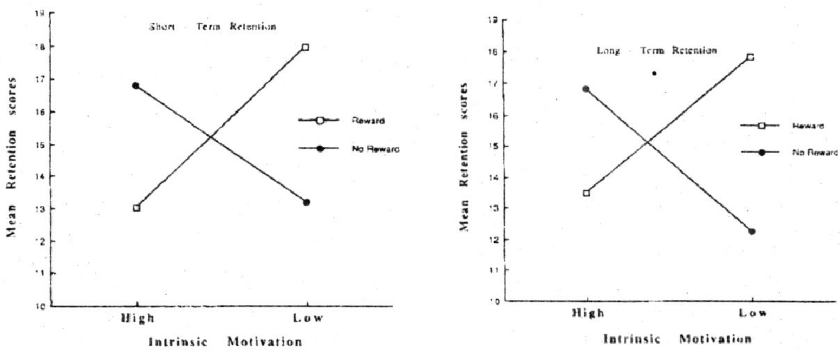

FIG. 9.8 : Mean retention scores as a function of arousal differences due to reward-inducements. (Reproduced from Dwivedi, 1990).

the other group simply took a delayed recall test. The subjects in this study were 160 male high school students, aged 13 to 18 years (Mean = 15 years 6 months). The design was a 2 (85 dbC, moderate and 65 dbC low levels of noise) x 2 (semantic and acoustic orienting tasks) x 4 (intentional with and without short-term recall, and incidental with and without short-term recall test) factorial. There were ten subjects in each of the 16 cells of this experiment. Half the subjects took both a short-term and a long-term recall test, while the other half took only a long-term recall test. Thus all subjects were tested for long-term recall.

The subjects were awarded one point for each target item correctly recalled by them. Items recalled partially or incorrectly were excluded from an analysis of mean scores showed that short-term retentions were better with 65 dbC noise than they were with 85 dbC noise input. Contrary to expectations, the associates presented in 65 dbC were recalled more often (Mean = 8.45 for intentional and Mean = 5.66 for incidental conditions in semantic orientation) than were those presented in 85 dbC noise input. A comparison of the delayed recall performance of the subjects who took an immediate recall test indicated a differential pattern. The delayed recall of those subjects who took only a delayed recall test improved when noise input was 85 dbC.

However, pattern was reversed when the noise input was 65 dbC where the subjects who took both an immediate and a delayed recall test scored better (see Figure 9.9). This showed that partial elimination of the instructional effect was a product of noise input and intentionality which was evident by a significant interaction between noise and intentionality.

The percentage of items the subjects recalled on the immediate test that they also recalled on the delayed test changed over time. For 85 dbC noise input intentional instructions improved subjects' long-term recall performance. This finding supported the theory that organisational processes are revamped by instructions for intent to learn. Nevertheless, this was visible only with

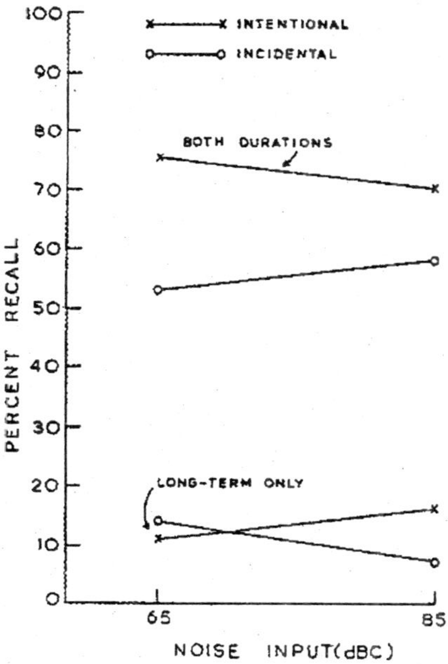

FIG. 9.9 : Mean percentage of change in recall over time for semantic orientation. (Reproduced from Dwivedi, 1992).

semantic orientation, and not with acoustc orientation where incidental instructions enhanced recall over two noise inputs.

Concluding Comments

This review of studies on cognition thus provides evidence for the traditional view that arousal is a unitary, non-specific process. However, the way in which arousal was manipulated in each study must be taken into account for a clear understanding of the induced stress phenomenon. Apart from this, such an effort would also enable us to explain whether the changes in performance are due to natural variations or the effect of stimulus materials or whether they occur as a result of some environmental manipulations. The impairment in vigilance as well as in immediate memory with nigh arousal has been frequently reported in the literature which naturally entails some changes in the phasic states of an organism. However, as was discussed in this review this effect is also still far from clear.

REFERENCES

Berlyne, D.E., Borsa, D.M., Craw, M.A., Gelman, R.S., & Mandel, E.E. (1965). Effects of stimulus complexity and induced arousal on paired-associate learning. *Journal of Verbal Learning and Verbal Behavior, 4*, 291-299.

Berlyne, D.E., Borsa, D.M., Hamacher, J.H., & Koening, I.D.V. (1966). Paired-associate learning and the timing of arousal. *Journal of Experimental Psychology, 72*, 1-6.

Chatterjee, A. (1984). Differential nature of stress-strain relationships and arousal. Unpublished manuscript.

Chatterjee, A., & Krishnamurthy, V. (1972). Differential effect of noise as an environmental stress. *Behaviorometric, 2*, 1-8.

Christie, M.J. (1974). Individual differences in the psycho-physiological stress response. Paper presented at the meeting of the British Psychological Society Conference, social section, University of York.

Duffy, E. (1957). The psychological significance of the concept of 'arousal' or 'activation'. *Psychological Review 64*, 265-275.

Dulany, E., Jr. (1957). Avoidance learning of perceptual defense and vigilance. *Journal of Abnormal and Social Psychology, 55*, 333-338.

Dwivedi, C.B. (1990). Reward-induced arousal differences in retention. *Personality and Individual Differences, 11*, 685-691.

Dwivedi, C.B. (1992). Induced arousal and orienting tasks as determinants of intentional recall. *Journal of General Psychology, 119*, 265-277.

Dwivedi, C.B., Mishra, R.K., & Chaturvedi, U. (1986). Orientation, arousal, and intentionality of processing differences in retention. *Psychological Studies, 32*, 103-107.

Dwivedi, C.B., & Singh, I.L. (1977). Induced perceptual vigilance behaviour and the reduction of uncertainty. *Psychologia, 20*, 163-171.

Dwivedi, C.B., & Singh, I.L. (1978). Effects of shock inputs on perceptual vigilance. *Perceptual and Motor-Skills. 47*, 1207-1212.

Dwivedi, C.B., Singh, I.L., & Singh.N.B. (1978). A study of differential role of anxiety and the stress inducing shock on perceptual vigilance. *Indian Journal of Psychology, 53*, 51-55.

Dwivedi, C.B., Singh, I.L, & Singh, R.S. (1981). Vigilance and arousal differences in males and females. *Psychologia, 24*, 51-53.

Dwivedi, C.B., Singh, N.B., & Singh, I.L. (1982). Differential role of meaningfulness, white noise and intentionality of recall. *Psychological Studies, 27*, 8-11.

Dwivedi, C.B., & Singh, R.S. (1993). Arousal differences in processing of congruent and incongruent stimuli. Unpublished manuscript.

Easterbrook, J.A. (1959). The effect of emotion on cue utilization and the organization of behavior. *Psychological Review, 66*, 183-201.

Eysenck, M.W. (1975). Effects of noise, activation level, and response dominance in retrieval from semantic memory. *Journal of Experimental Psychology: Human Learning and Memory, 104*, 143-148.

Eysenck, M.W. (1976). Arousal, leaning and memory. *Psychological Bulletin, 83*, 389-404.

Farley, F. (1969). *Memory storage in free learning as a function of arousal and time with homogeneous and heterogeneous lists*. (No. 87). Wisconsin University center in Cognitive Learning, Technical Reports.

Freeman, G.L. (1940). The relationship between performance level and bodily activity level. *Journal of Experimental Psychology, 26*, 602-608.

Hamilton, V. (1979). 'Personality' and stress. In V. Hamilton & D.M. Warburton (Eds.) *Human Stress and Cognition: An Information Processing Approach*. New York: Wiley.

Hamilton. V. (1982). Cognition and stress: An information processing model. In L. Goldberger & S. Breznitz (Eds.), *Handbook of stress*. New York:Macmillan.

Harper, R.G. (1973). Perceptual vigilance and reduction of uncertainty. *Perceptual and Motor Skills. 37*, 951-955.

Haveman, J.E., & Farely, F.H. (1969). *Arousal and Retention in Paired-associate, Serial and Free Learning*. (No. 91). Wisconsin University Center for Cognitive Learning, Technical Reports.

Haywood, H.C. (1968). Motivational orientation of over-achieving and under-achieving elementary school children. *American*

Journal of Mental Deficiency, *72*, 662-667.

Hebb, D.O. (1955). Drives and the C.N.S. (conceptual nervous system). *Psychological Review*, *62*, 243-254.

Hockey. R. (1979). Stress and the cognitive components of skilled performance. In D.M. Warburton & V. Hamilton (Eds.) *Human Stress and Cognition: An Information Processing Approach*. New York: Wiley.

Jones, D.M., Smith, A.P., & Broadbent, D.E. (1979). Effects of moderate intensity noise on the Bakan vigilance task. *Journal of Applied Psychology*, *64*, 627-634.

King, D.J. (1963). Immediate memory of connected meaningful material practiced under delayed auditory feedback. *Psychological Reports*, *13*, 91-96.

King, D.J., & Dodge, A.M. (1965). The influence of oral recall on immediate and delayed memory for meaningful material practiced under delayed auditory feedback. *Journal of Psychology*, *59*, 141-147.

King, D.J., & Wolf, S. (1965). The influence of delayed audiotory feedback on immediate and delayed memory. *Journal of Psychology*, *59*, 131-139.

Kleinsmith, L.J., & Kaplan, S. (1963). Paired associate learning as a function of arousal and interpolated interval. *Journal of Experimental Psychology*, *65*, 190-193.

Koelega, H.S., & Brinkman, J.A. (1986). Noise and vigilance: An evaluative review. *Human Factors*, *28*, 465-481.

Lazarus, R.S. (1966). *Psychological Stress and the Coping Process*. New York: McGraw-Hill.

Lepper, M.R., Greene, D., & Nisbett, R.E. (1973). Undermining children's intrinsic interest with extrinsic rewards: A test of the 'Overjustification' hypothesis. *Journal of Personality and Social Psychology*, *28*, 129-137.

Levonian, E. (1967). Retention of information in relation to arousal during continuously presented material. *American Educational Research Journal*, *4*, 103-116.

Lysaght, R.J., Warm, J.S., Dember, W.N., & Loeb, M. (1984). Effects of noise and information-processing demand on vigilance performance in men and women. In A. Mital (Ed.) *Trends in Ergonomics/Human Factors*. Amsterdam: North-Holland.

Mackworth, N.H. (1950). *Researches on the Measurement of Human Performance*. London: His Majesty's Stationery Office.

Malmo, R.B. (1959). Activation: A neuropsychological dimension. *Psychological Review*, *66*, 367-386.

Mandler, G. (1982). Stress and thought processes. In L.

Goldberger & S. Breznitz (Eds.), *Handbook of Stress.* New York: Macmillan.

Masson, M.E.J., & McDaniel, M.A. (1981). The role of organizational processes in long-term retention. *Journal of Experimental Psychology; Human Learning and Memory, 7,* 100-110.

McLean, P.D. (1969). Induced arousal and time of recall as determinants of paired-associate recall. *British Journal of Psychology, 60,* 57-62.

Mishra, R.K. (1982). *Effects of noise and modes of presentation on levels of processing of verbal land pictorial materials.* Unpublished doctoral dissertation, Banaras Hindu Universtiy, Varanasi.

Osgood, C.E. (1971). Exploration in semantic space: A personal diary. *Journal of Social Issues, 27,* 5-64.

Posner, M.I. (1975). Psychobiology of attention. In C. Blakemore & M. Gazzaniga (Eds.) *Handbook of Psychobiology.* New York: Academic Press.

Posner, M.I., Klein, R., Summers, J., & Buggie, S. (1973). On the selection of signals. *Memory and Cognition, 1,* 2-12.

Poulton, E.C. (1976). Continuous noise interferes with work by masking auditory feedback and inner speech. *Applied Ergonomics.*

Poulton, E.C. (1978). Blue collar stressors. In C.L. Cooper & R. Payne, (Eds.) *Stress at Work.* New York: John Wiley.

Price, R.H. (1966). Signal detection method in personality and perception. *Psychological Bulletin. 66,* 55-62.

Purohit, A.K. (1976). Effects of auditory noise, pay off and signal probability on visual detection. *Indian Journal of Psychology, 51,* 255-261.

Pustell, T.F. (1957). The experimental induction of perceptual vigilance and defense. *Journal of Personality, 25,* 425-436.

Singh, B.V. (1978). *Effects of induced expectancies, different intensities of white noise and individual differences on detection of auditory and visual vigilance tasks.* Unpublished Master's thesis, Banaras Hindu University, Varanasi.

Singh, I.L. (1975). *An experimental study of induced perceptual vigilance in males and females using two durations of presentation and intensities of electric shock.* Unpublished master's Dissertation, Banaras Hindu University, Varanasi.

Singh, I.L. (1978). *Visual vigilance performances as affected by induced shock, durations of presentation, irrelevant auditory stimulation, expectancy and anxiety.* Unpublished doctoral dissertation, Banaras Hindu Univerity, Varanasi.

Singh, I.L. (1984). Anticipatory stress and vigilance. *Perceptual and Motor Skills, 58,* 574.

Singh, I.L., Dwivedi, C.B., & Sinha, M.M. (1979). Effects of anxiety on vigilance. *Perceptual and Motor Skills, 49,* 142.

Singh, I.L., Dwivedi, C.B., & Sinha, M.M. (1980), Phasic arousal and vigilance. *Perceptual and Motor Skills, 50,* 798.

Singh, N.B. (1978). *Effects of induced arousal intensities of white noise, levels of meaningfulness and individual differences on short-term recall.* Unpublished Master's dissertation, Banaras Hindu University, Varanasi.

Singh, N.B., (1982). *Effects of noise on episodic memory for varyingly presented verbal and pictorial stimuli.* Unpublished doctoral dissertation, Banaras Hindu University, Varanasi.

Singh, S. (1971). *A study on paired-associate learning of differentially meaningful verbal materials.* Unpublished doctoral dissertation, Banaras Hindu University, Varanasi.

Sinha, D. (1968). *W.A. Self-analysis Form.* Varanasi: Rupa Psychological Corporation.

Smith, A.P. (1982). The effects of noise and task prioirty on recall of order and location. *Acta Psychologica, 51,* 245-255.

Smith, A.P. (1984). The effects of noise on strategies of human performance. In G. Rossi (Ed.) *Proceedings of the Fourth International Congress on Noise as a Public Health Problem.* Milan: Centro Ricerche e Studi Amplifon.

Smith, A.P. (1985). Noise, biased probability and serial reaction. *British Journal of Psychology, 76,* 89-95.

Smith, A.P., Jones, D.M., & Broadbent, D.E. (1981). The effects of noise on recall of categorised lists. *British Journal of Psychology, 72,* 299-316.

Tripathi, L.B. (1974). *Calibration of verbal materials in Hindi for research purposes.* Unpublished ICSSR research project. Gorakhpur University, Gorakhpur.

Walker, E.L., (1958). Action decrement and its relation to learning. *Psychological Review, 65,* 129-142.

Walker, E.L. & Tarte, R.D. (1963). Memory storage as a function of arousal and time with homogeneous and heterogeneous lists. *Journal of Verbal Learning and Verbal Behavior, 2,* 113-119.

Yerkes, R.M., & Dodson, J.D. (1908). The relation of strength of stimulus to rapidity of habit formation. *Journal of Comparative and Neurological Psychology, 18,* 459-482.

10

Temporal Tuning, Stress and Quality of Life

G.C. GUPTA

Any theory of human performance, and in particular any theory that deals with the interaction between man and a structured task environment, must incorporate the fact that the man is aware of it or is at least, using the relations of simultaneity, order, temporal locus and duration when coping with the requirements of this sort of environment. It has been reasonably well-established that circadian rhythms, of approximately 24 hours duration, exist in respect of human performance on a wide range of tasks, may be it is an on-line assembly task, an eight hours regular clerical job, auditory vigilance task, letter cancellation, or simple arithmetic task. Thus the simple tasks such as those involving immediate processing are better performed as the day progresses. In contrast, the performance of difficult tasks such as those imposing substantial demand on memory might be expected to be disrupted by the high arousal associated with the end of the working day.

The temporal tuning that underlies this sort of coping mechanism, if unduly disturbed, may cause stress to the performing individual, albeit a temporary one. Human organism is highly adaptable, and if this sort of stressful performance is repeated rather too often, the human will adapt, even though at certain psychophysiological cost.

Biological Rhythms

Although we find that people are subject to several important biological rhythms, they have no innate clocks of a great enough sophistication to help them cope automatically with all the intricacies of temporal structure of human life. The number of different options available to the organism for establishing a time base for its performance in a particular timed task is apparently very large and choices appear to be highly opportunistic. Amongst the peripheral mechanisms, heart rate plays a prominent role. The relation between the regularity of cardiac activity and mental effort has been thoroughly established. It has been found that many simple motor responses occur in phase with the cardiac cycle. It remains unclear, however, whether this is in fact due to a specific pacemaker function of the peaks in the cardiac response.

The status as "internal clock" of all physiological and behavioural mechanisms remains somewhat ambiguous. Many authors agree that humans will select whatever mechanism will suit their needs (e.g., Macar, 1985). Multiple time bases are continuously constructed in response to the particular requirements of situation and replaced by others when they become useless (Richelle & Lejeune, 1980).

Evidently we have reached the limits of a psycho-biological explanation of human time experience in terms of "clocks".

Temporal Tuning

The human organism appears to be a very subtle system that is capable of tuning itself to the sequential or temporal requirements of the outer world. By natural selection and through learning it is able to filter the relevant events in its environment and to respond to them in a very precise way. Skilled movements in athletes and musicians for instance, are timed within a few milliseconds. Thus a professional tennis-player or a fencing champion is able to pick up all the required information needed for countering within less than 80 ms after the opponent has made the first move. Musicians will deliberately speed up, or slow down their performance rate in tiny steps of 2 or 3 per cent, which under circumstances may be equivalent to not more than 4 or 5 ms. Think of the survival value for a prey animal to initiate its flight within a tenth of a second after the attack of its predator— and what about the survival chances of a predator that would always be more than a tenth of a second late. As I shall argue later in more detail, tuning (or temporal regulation as it has also been called) is a basic property of organisms to avoid unnecessary risks of stress, injury or even death. In the most literal sense the physiological and psychological processes that are responsible for coping with the temporal requirements of a situation are attempts to bring the organism into harmony with the surrounding world.

There are essentially two major areas of required "tuning" to the temporal environment. There are, first of all, the various biological rhythms that determine many of the processes in the organism. Apart from the circadian rhythm which is clearly observable in all living systems, there are other less evident or less well studied rhythms ranging from years and months to perhaps 90 or 45 minutes. The organismic and behavioural changes that follow these rhythms are likely to be the output of one or more rather fixed— but thus far unlocalized-structures, perhaps at the level of cells or even at the level of genes. They are usually synchronized by environmental cues (Zeitgeber), and even when left to themselves under so called "free running" conditions they will remain more or less stable (even though they may become desynchronized, each running at a somewhat different rate).

The second category of tuning processes is entirely different. Unlike the biological rhythms these processes have no particular repeating cycle of their own. They aid the organism in coping with the instantaneous, irregular and some times quite unique temporal requirements of its present circumstances. As we shall see, no regular clock-like structure can answer to the needs of the temporal complexities of reality, certainly not in humans. It will, therefore, be necessary to assume that other mechanisms of a more general and not intrinsically periodical nature can serve to extract the regularities from the prevailing situation and to translate this information into harmonious and well tuned behavioural responses.

Quality of Life and Temporal Tuning

The present paper attempts to review what we know about such general processes, and focuses largely on the structurally stable biological rhythms in so far as they exert an influence on the availability and the precision of the general temporal processes. For example, since the circadian rhythm manifests itself in the way human memory operates, throughout the day, and since memory processes play an important role when we are dealing with temporal information it is likely that the two will interact. Certainly this interaction has important consequences for the quality of life. In shift work and travel across time zones, for instance, the interaction is temporarily altered, which causes considerable distress in many (but not all) people.

From the strict temporal stance taken in the preceding section promoting quality of life means taking care of the adequate interfacing of human beings with the temporal structure of their environment — both the physical and the social. The word interfacing is derived from engineering and suggests the functional adaptation of the organism to its task (Simon, 1969). The great flexibility of the human organism ensures an extremely wide range of situations to which adaptation is possible; only in extreme circumstances will the performance of motivated people break down (Ursin, Baade, & Levine, 1978).

Yet adaptability comes at a cost: it may suppress errors in the short run, but creates irritation, panic, and in the long run psychosomatic disorders, withdrawal symptoms and depression. In general, the absence of adequate temporal interfacing—tuning is what we called it—may induce stress. A practical analysis of this problem, and of a possible way out, is given by Mackenzie (1972) in a typical western way.

It is good to consider which factors are especially critical in creating temporally induced stress or, in other words, which factors prevent adequate tuning. On the basis of such considerations it may be possible to change the temporal environment or, for particular tasks at least, select people who are least susceptible to the ill effects of a hostile temporal environment. As Rutenfranz and Colquhoun (1979) argue, "in recent years we have learned not to accept work tasks merely for what they are, to be performed more or less adequately by the people doing them; instead we more and more frequently start from the assumption that task performance can be improved by means of redesign or rescheduling. In this connection, man is no longer regarded as an isolated factor, but is seen as a part of a system, the man-machine system" (p. 173).

This appears to be one of the basic policies when improving the quality of life: while developing industries, and while designing jobs for the workers in these industries we have to take into account the temporal structure of these jobs. Life to a large extent being structured around work, job usually puts heavy constraints on the way people can use their time, deeply affecting the spatio-temporal accessibility of their environment (Hagerstrand, 1975). The industrialized countries have, in the past, made very serious errors in the way they have structured time, and the developing countries should be careful to avoid those errors. In *Zeit* and *Kultur*, Wendorff (1980) offers similar considerations in a much wider cultural perspective. In general, it can be said that in the past spatial relations have dominated the structure of individual as well as social behaviour. Temporal relations have been taken into explicit consideration only much more recently (Burns, 1979).

Stress and Temporal Tuning

Stress, due to lack of temporal interfacing or tuning, can result from two separate factors. The first is an inadequate temporal structure of the task to be performed, the second derives from the inadequate embedding of a task in the waxing and waning of the biological rhythms.

A task can be badly structured temporally in several ways that are related to the temporal mechanisms and strategies discussed in the earlier sections of this paper. Time pressure, unpredictability, aborted expectations, incompatible simultaneous information (lack of correlation), and other structural aspects of a task are likely to prevent adequate sequencing and timing even by experienced subjects. Those who play a musical instrument in a somewhat advanced amateur ensemble know the stress that results from the initial attempts at mastering a new piece, as well as the delicate balance on the edge of disaster even when performance has reached an acceptable level. The remarkable thing is that it is not primarily playing out of tune or a wrong note every now and then, but rather the timing (synchronization) that is most important: when to do something frequently is more problematic than what to do (Michon, 1966).

The recent developments in the analysis of human information processing appear to offer an opportunity to temporally structure tasks much better than before. There are several lines of research that could contribute to such an effort; such as the recently developed insights in motor programming (timing and sequencing of complex movements), the hierarchical vs. the associative organization of behaviour, the distinction between throughout tasks and memory tasks, and the role of time constraints in information processing (Schaffer, 1980).

The effects of these factors on the arousal system, i.e. the amount of stress potentially generated, are by and large of the short lasting (phasic) kind. While they may disrupt performance and also may make the performer feel very uncomfortable, their influence will normally not long outlast the period during which the task is performed.

This, however, is true only when recovery is possible and if the required level of task performance is such that the difference with the actual performance level does not by itself sustain a high level of stress (anxiety). The fear of losing one's job multiplies the stress caused by the poor temporal structure of one's task.

Temporally induced stress might in principle also result from the inadequacy of the timing mechanisms a person has available. Temporal somatic "diseases" in this sense should be considered exceedingly rare cases. If, for example, the limbic system of an individual incapacitates the timing of task elements, we will observe gross behavioural disturbances any way, of which inadequate timing may be one of the least tragic. Similarly, if some form of collateral behaviour is made impossible, a different one will soon take over. It appears that coping with temporal requirements of the environment is adaptive to the extreme, and that nature has taken every possible step to secure a very high potential level of correspondence between the real world and the internal representation of that world in the organism. Fraser (1975; 1978) has elaborated on the intricate networks that constitute this correspondence.

In summary, from the point of view chosen for this paper, serious disruptions of temporal adaptation (regulation) of complex behaviour are not easily to be expected. When one mechanism gives up, another is likely to take over — possibly after a period of training. The biological rhythmicities to which the human organism is subjected can create serious stress that may be totally disruptive for the quality of life. For the greater part the discussion of these influences is beyond the scope of the present paper but a few aspects may be emphasized.

Temporal Tuning and Stress : Repurcussions for Behaviour

The performance on many tasks is noticeably affected by the time of day over the day shifts of 15-20 may be observed. To what extent such shifts are the results of the circadian rhythm only, or of fatigue, or — even more subtly — of the proactive or retroactive loads imposed on our working memory is only beginning to emerge. Disentanglement of such factors requires much more sophisticated psychological experiments involving desynchronization of various rhythmic components than have been the rule up to about 1975.

Two major conclusions, however, can be drawn from what is known today. One is that temporal shifts in the pattern of activity can be overcome by most people rather smoothly if sufficient time for (re-) adaptation is allowed but only if social acceptance of such shifts is high. In both cases the stress created by the desyn-chronization can be coped with and need not build up to intolerable levels. It also seems possible to spot those people who would not tolerate desychronization stress and to protect them by not exposing them to a hostile temporal environment. The second conclusion, although still somewhat speculative, is related to the basic tenet of chronotoxicology (Reinberg, 1976). The sensitivity of the human organism for poisonous substances varies widely in the course of the day. Careful tracing of this sensitivity can help the chemo-therapeutic administration of highly toxic substances. Similarly, tracing the sensitivity (specific arousal levels) for various types of information processing, may help to structure jobs and tasks in such a way that the requirements of a task correspond maximally with the varying state of processing capacity of the subject. Undoubtedly there is abundant individual experience as well as folklore, indicating that some tasks can be done better at some times than others. Little systematic thought has been given to this promising possibility, however.

Yet careful consideration seems warranted. The most explicit, albeit somewhat speculative example of what this approach might offer in the way of general policy advice on time and the quality of life is given by Folkard (1980). The finding that STM tasks are better performed in the morning hours and LTM tasks better later in the day would seem to indicate "that the only advantage to be gained from confining the teaching of academic subjects to the morning will be the superior immediate retention of unimportant information. Afternoon presentation would appear to result in superior delayed retention of both important and unimportant information. The current practice of teaching most academic material in the morning may be ill-founded" (Folkard, 1980, p. 96). Perhaps this will also make us reconsider our conventional schedules for speakers at conferences and symposia.

In conclusion, it appears that already at the present level our knowledge about the physiological and psychological aspects of coping with a temporal environment can indeed be instrumental in improving the quality of life. The two major areas of impact are (a) optimization of the structure of jobs and tasks, taking into account what we know about the possibilities and limitations of man as an adaptive information processing system, and (b) optimization of the layout in time of these tasks, taking into account various exogenous and endogenous rhythms (not necessarily only the circadian rhythms). In this way we may contribute to a better tuning (interfacing) of the human beings with the temporal requirements of their environment and, by reducing the stress resulting from being out of tune, contribute to the quality of life.

REFERENCES

Burns, L.D. (1979). *Transportation, Temporal, and Spatial Components of Accessibility.* Lexington, Mass : Lexington Books.

Folkard, S. (1980). Circadian rhythms and human memory. In F.M. Brown & R.C. Graeber (eds.), *Rhythmic Aspects of Behavior.* Hillsdale, N.J.: Erlbaum.

Fraser, J.T. (1975). *Of Time, Passion and Knowledge.* New York: Braziller.

Fraser, J.T. (1978). *Time as Conflict.* Basel: Birkh-aeuser.

Hagerstrand, T. (1975). Space, time and human condition. In A. Karlquist, L. Lunquist & F. Snickars (eds.) *Dynamic Allocation of Urban Space.* Lexington, Mass: Health.

Mackenzie, R.A. (1972). *The Time Trap: Managing Your Way Out.* New York: American Management Association.

Macar, F. (1985). Time, psychophysics and related models. In

J.A. Michon & J.L. Jackson (Eds.). *Time, Mind, and Behavior.* Heidelberg, Springer Verlag.

Michon, J.A. (1966). Tapping regularity as a measure of perceptual motor load. *Ergonomics, 9,* 401-412.

Reinberg, A. (1976). Advances in human chronopharmacology. *Chronobiologia, 3,* 151-166.

Richelle, M., & Lejeune, H. (1980). *Time in animal behavior.* Oxford: Pergamon.

Rutenfranz, J.S., & Colquhoun, W.P. (1979). Circadian rhythms in human performance. *Scandinavian Journal of Work Environment and Health, 5,* 167-177.

Schaffer, L.H. (1980). Rhythm and timing in skill. *Psychological Review, 89,* 109-122.

Simon, H.A. (1969). *The Sciences of the Artificial.* Cambridge, Mass: MIT Press.

Ursin, S., Baade, E., & Levine, S. (eds.) (1978). *Psychobiology of Stress: A Study of Coping Men.* New York: Academic Press.

Wendorff, R. (1980). *Zeit and Kultur.* Opladen, Westdeutscher: Verlag.

11

Job and Well-Being : The Experiences of Employed Women

GAURI THAKAR and **GIRISHWAR MISRA**

Recent years have increasingly brought a great change in the life of Indian women influencing their attitudes, values, inspirations, feelings, as well as participation in various walks of life. In particular, the forces of urbanisation, education and employment, have provided women with new avenues to express and assert themselves. They have come out of the four walls of their homes in search of economic gain as well as fulfilment of their personal hopes and desires as human beings. By gaining employment outside homes they are seeking different identities (see Kumar, 1986 for a review of relevant issues). Since the inner experiences of women are inextricably embedded in the socio-economic and cultural matrix (Kakar, 1978), it is likely that their role of wage earner will bring a change in the quality of life. In the traditional India every women is born into a well defined community of women within her particular family. The existence of this discrete sphere of femininity and domesticity gives women a tangible opportunity to be productive and lively, to experience autonomy and to exercise power. This world is free from patriarchal values of the outside world and other women are shields for these girls against male world (Nandy & Kakar, 1980).

In the modern period social reforms, legal provisions and feminist activities have been trying to influence and change the status of women. It is however, to be noted that there is still a wide gap between their legal, political, economic rights and privileges and 'actual' rights and privileges that they enjoy and utilise.

In this context, transformation in the pattern of women's role has received some research attention. Concern for survival and economic need are found to be one of the main reasons for taking up gainful employment. In addition, non-economic factors have also been reported to be important for female's participation. It is further noted that though employment gives women more opportunities and choices in many important respects, for most, a right to work does not necessarily mean a better status because, (1) doing jobs increases their physical burden, and (2) it may intensify their family responsibilities, now being expected to finance sibling's education, marriage and the like (Pushpa Sundar, 1981).

However, as employment of women particularly from the middle class is a new phenomenon, no fixed pattern or redefinition of role of women in terms of the changed context has yet been achieved. Neither working wives, nor their husbands or other relatives, nor society in general is clear about their role. Women's role and position at present are, therefore, not clearly defined and thus the situation leads to role conflict (Chakraborty, 1977). Family's greater demand on women takes a higher tall on women's mental health in the dual-earaer family as compared to males (Barnett, Breman, Raudenbush, Plack & Marshall, 1995).

So, now the question arises, as what does work mean to an Indian woman? How does it affect her life? The economic independence of women is commonly advocated as a solution to many problems considered under the rubric of women's issue, and employment of women outside home is widely regarded as a key to sexual equality, autonomy and self-fulfilment. If this is so, then can Indian women's experience of work hold a parallel to that of its western counterpart where paid work is considered essential to women's bid for liberation? The compelling observation is, that work for the majority of Indian women becomes an avenue of exploitation, and discrimination by the employer, a source of conflict with the spouse and other members of the family and an inducer of doubt and guilt about one's role as a wife/ mother. Due to emphasis on the financial-gain from employment, issues of self enrichment, fulfilment and satisfaction of emancipation is largely supressed.

The relationship of multiple role involvement with stress and psychological well being has become an important issue for debate amongst researchers. As Long and Porter (1984) pointed out, the psychological consequences of role accumulation depend not only on the total number of roles occupied but on the nature of particular roles, because roles differ in social values attached and in the patterning of priveleges and obligations associated with them, (Vandewater, Ostrove & Stewart, 1997).

Consequences of Women's Employment

The present status of research suggests twofold consequences of employment for women as it yields rewards as well as costs. It is by and large agreed upon by the researchers that stress has become omnipresent in today's life. The main question here is whether employment causes any change in the content and quality of stressor for women, and also, to understand what are the other outcomes of employment and which processes mediate them.

The studies on stress deal mainly with three sources. Sudden, powerful and the unusual single life events making-up the category of *cataclysmic* stressors (e.g., flood, war etc.). Life events are changes affecting a fewer number of persons or single individuals (e.g., bereavement, illness of a serious nature etc.). Whereas, these categories emphasize extraordinary changes of one or the other kind, there are other forms of environmental stressors which are referred to as *daily hassles*. Some daily hassles may occur rarely or occasionally while others may be chronic or repetitive. These ongoing stresses are specially important in determining social functioning, health and morale (Lazarus & Cohen, 1977). The present paper focuses on the daily hassles of working women. These include troubles of ordinary day-to-day life, which might be related to work, family and social environment. Hassles can be defined as the irritating, frustrating, distressing demands that to some degree characterize everyday transactions with the environment (Kanner, Coyne, Schaefer & Lazarus, 1981), dealing with children or parents (Levine & Scotch, 1970) and problems in bringing up children.

The transactional approach views stress as a process determined by various factors. As Lazarus and Folkman (1984) argue stress is a "particular relationship between the person and the environment, that is appraised by the person as taxing or exceeding his or her resources and endangering his or her well being" (p. 19). Hobfoll (1988) has pointed out that psychological stress is a reaction to environment in which there is (a) the threat of a net loss of resources, (b) the net loss of resources or (c) lack of resource gain following the investment of resources. The model also tells that when not confronted with stress, people strive to develop resource surpluses so as to offset the possibility of future loss. When people develop resource surpluses, they are likely to experience positive well being (*eustress*).

Women's Roles in Indian Societal Context

The embeddedness of the feminine role in the socio-cultural context crystallizes woman's connections to others in the context of a multitude of familial relationships. Unlike western women, Indian women's identity is situated in the web of institutions of family, caste, class and community. It is this rootedness, that has made it impossible for even Indian feminists to seriously challenge or question family as the single most oppressive institution. Radicalization and innovativeness in the life style have not yet become part of the Indian women's consciousness (Ghadiyally, 1988). Regarding working women's role Mehta (1975) points out that "the hope of many women was to try and create a new model that would combine the eastern virtues of modesty, discipline and commitment to marriage with self-reliance, efficiency and work ethics of the western women" (p. 166).

The ethos surrounding womanhood moderates the objective power that the economic status has extended to them and limits their ability to bargain about the ground rule governing a hierarchic marital and family structure. Consequently, the social context in which most working wives function in India seldom allows them to redefine and remodel their marital roles: they are essentially home makers with added responsibilities (Ramu, 1989). The Indian thought on the status of women reveals that socio-cultural values hold considerable importance in women's inner-world, and the psychological processes occurring in the Indian cultural context determine the status of today's Indian women in many telling ways.

Women's Employment and a Complex Outcome Sequence : An Empirical Analysis

As women's employment occurs in the midst of socio-cultural matrix, it evolves into a complex process of antecedent and mediating variables yielding positive (well-being) and negative outcomes (stress).

Family holds a special meaning in Indian context. Urbanization, first broke the traditional joint family into nuclear families. Employment of women puts further demands for change in the family structure. Working women face different problems and receive diverse treatments in the two types of families. Work-home interface is an issue worth studying, for spillover in both the directions is possible. Looking at the key place that home and family occupies in the lives of Indian women, type of family was included as an important antecedent variable.

The nature of role one is expected to play changes with advancing age. Women's role in particular undergoes significant changes with the passage of time, in family and work spheres. For example changing health status may cause additional change in appraisal of social roles and work and may thereby change the nature of outcome.

Income, occupational complexity, availability of resources all are intimately related with employment status. So, status at job appears to be another significant variable contributing to the experience of stress.

Mediating Variables

Despite extensive research on stress, the studies do not yield definite answer to what are the conditions which moderate the experience and consequences of stress (Dohrenwend & Dohrenwend, 1978). Nevertheless, identifying them is important because it furthers the theoretical understanding of the process by which people adapt to stressors.

Coping

Coping is viewed as an important resource that may help individuals maintain psychosocial adaptation during a stressful episode. Lazarus and Folkman (1984) define coping as constantly changing cognitive and behavioural effort to manage specific external and/or internal demands that are appraised as taking or exceeding the resources of the person. They utilize a transactional framework in which person and environment are seen in terms of continuous ongoing relationship which is reciprocal in nature; and appraisal and coping processes mediate this transactional relationship.

As for employed women, work environment is added on to their traditional home environment, their transactions become more varied. Does it also mean that they have a more efficient repertoire of strategies to cope with the stresses of their lives? On the other hand, with role conflict and work overload, do they become disadvantaged when compared to their non-working counterparts? Employment's effect on coping thus can be important in determining the former's meaning in women's lives.

Social Support

Recent studies in the field of community psychology and health behaviour indicate that stress is significantly moderated by social support. Social support is an especially germane topic to the study of coping among women. Aneshensel (1986) argues that both working women and the housewives experience stressors due to the role versus reward character of their lives. In both the cases, women who receive affiliation for who they are and what they do, experienced less psychological strain, than women who did not receive support. The role of support in moderating stress is multifaceted. It may be linked with person-environment transactions, differing in the kind of support as well as personal appraisal of the same.

Employment Outcome

Depending on the importance of mediating processes women's employment may result in diverse outcomes like daily hassles, organizational stress on one hand and uplift and life satisfaction on the other. Researchers (Baruch & Barnett, 1986; Thakar & Misra, 1995) have found that it is the quality of women's experience in performing her social roles that constitutes the key for understanding the status of their psychological well-being.

The present study examines the daily hassles that working women encounter and also tries to identify the variation in their stressful experiences as related to roles that they inact. Positive outcomes of employment are also examined. The mediating processes of coping, social support and family orientation are also analysed for their mediational role in employment-outcome relationship. On examining the literature related to women, stress and employment it was found that employment had complex effect on the lives of Indian women. On one hand the multiple role involvement is found to increased well being (Baruch & Barnett, 1986) while on the other hand it also increases daily hassles and conflict (Chakraborty, 1977). It was expected that—

1. employed women would experience more daily hassles than unemployed women,
2. employed women experience greater well being than the unemployed women.
3. experiences of well being and stress would vary for the women differing on level of job.

It may be noted that the traditional social norms still influence and constitute the Indian women's psyche. The traditional role division, however, has evolved over time. The role of employment entails complex paradoxes for women. Social support, family orientation, coping and well being all must be viewed within the societal and personal context of their lives.

The detailed analysis of data is available elsewhere (Thakar, 1994). Here an attempt is made to focus on the contrast in the experiences of employed and unemployed women, and to explicate the positive and negative outcomes of employment for them. Effort also has been made to explain the difference in stressful experience due to difference in job status (role quality). The sample of the present study consisted of 250, educated, married (196 working and 54 non-working) mothers. The employed women were working with different government organisations located in Bhopal, in central India. Out of these, 182 came from nuclear families, and 68 came from joint families. Table 11.1 shows the chief background features of the sample.

The age of participants ranged from 20 years to 57 years, with a mean age of 35.20 years. For the total sample, the education was found to average on slightly higher than graduation level, while the average family size was 4.74. The average income for the total sample was Rs. 6500.89 per month.

Measurement of Variables

Daily Hassles

On the basis of semi-structured interviews the items for

TABLE 11.1 : Background Characteristics of the sample (N = 250)

Characteristics	Range	M	SD
Age (years)	20-57	35-20	17.79
Education	1-5	2.85	.91
Employment Status	1-4	2.90	.96
Monthly Income total (in Rs.)	2700-14500	6500.89	440.60
Duration of present job (years)	1-32	28.07	7.84
Number of family members	3-22	4.74	12.49

Codes are :
as follows : * 1 = H.Sc., 2 = upto graduation
3 = upto post graduation, 4 = technical,
5 = Any other
** Class I = 1, Class II = 2, Class III = 3
Unemployed = 4

daily hassles scale were generated in an earlier study by Thakar and Misra (1988). A set of 33 items were prepared. The hassels were rated on 6 point scales describing incidence of each hassle ranging from 'never' (1), through 'sometimes' (3) to 'always' (6). A factor analysis of the measure yielded 9 factors, which dealt with several domains of women's life (e.g., daily hassles due to feeling of confinement, children related daily hassles, daily hassles due to interruptions in daily life). The content of the items generated revealed that apart from hassles related to family domain, employed women had stressful experiences, arising due to work. These events were pertaining to the work place as well as home. A separate 8 item scale, related to the daily hassles experienced particularly by employed women was also prepared (Thakar & Misra, 1988).

Uplift

This scale contained 16 items to measure the frequency of uplifting events happening in daily life. Varimax rotated factor analysis yielded four factors, i.e., uplift due to interaction, uplift due to efficient management of household, uplift due to positive physical state and uplift due to considerate spouse. The items were rated on 6 point scales.

Mental Health

Mental Health Questionnaire, (MHQ) developed by Wig, Dwarka Prashad and S.K. Verma (1983) was used in this study. It contained 51 items dealing with inadequacy, depression, anxiety, sensitivity, anger and tension. Scoring was bipolar in nature and more the score better was the mental health.

Social Support

A 10 item scale was constructed to determine the extent of social support received from various sources like husband, children and friends. To this end, 5-point scales were used.

Family Orientation

An 8 item scale was used to assess participant's commitment towards family. The items had to be rated on a 4-point rating scale ranging from "not at all" (1) to "very much" (4).

Coping Strategies

A measure of coping developed by Ganguly (1988) was used. It has 37 items representing 12 factors. The items had to be rated on 5 point rating scales from "never used" (1) through "used sometimes" (3) to "very often" (5). The items of the scale described various strategies which may be used for coping with stress. The factors included logical analysis, tension reduction, active avoidance, introversion, religion, inflicting guilt on self and others, self criticism, social manipulation, affective regulation, avoidance, problem solving and acceptance.

Organizational Stress and Job Satisfaction

Organizational Stress Questionnaire (OSQ) and Job Satisfaction Scale developed by S. Singh (1990) were used. OSQ dealt with the stress experienced at the work place. It had 10 factors and 33 items. Each item was rated on a five point scale ranging from "true" to "almost no extent" (1), through "to some extent" (3) to "true to a very great extent" (5).

The Job Satisfaction Scale measured the satisfaction derived from the job. This had 20 items, which were to be scored on 5 point scales ranging from "very dissatisfied" (1), "neutral" (3) to "very satisfied" (5). Thus overall job satisfaction could range from 20 to 100.

Each participant was contacted and after clarifying the purpose of the study, appointment with each was fixed. Each participant was interviewed individually, using the schedule. Although the time required for completing the schedule was long, most of the participants seemed pleased to note that researcher was interested in studying women and their lives' experiences.

The analysis revealed that employment status did make a significant difference in adaptive outcomes. As seen in Table 11.2, the employed women reported significantly larger number of daily hassles as well as uplifts than their unemployed counterparts. On the other hand, unemployed women reported higher levels of depression and anxiety than employed women. While coping strategies were used similarly by the two groups, it was seen that employed women received significantly greater social support than their unemployed counterparts.

Daily Hassles

A factorial ANOVA with four levels of job (Class I/Class II/Class III/ Unemployed) and three age groups (young/middle/old) yielded significant age x job level interaction for total daily hassles, $F (6,238) = 2.68$, $p <.001$. It was

TABLE 11.2 : Means and SDs on daily hassles scale for the groups of employed women (n = 196) and unemployed women (n =54)

Variables	Employed		Unemployed		
	M	SD	M	SD	t
Total Hassles	95.09	24.08	87.56	23.57	2.07*
Hassles due to feeling of confinement	13.57	5.40	13.51	4.91	.08
Hassles due to too many expectations	12.09	4.64	10.36	4.07	2.68*
Children Related Hassles	10.81	4.18	9.50	4.00	2.11*
Hassles due to Interruptions in daily life	22.35	6.52	22.89	7.37	.49
Hassles due to feeling of helplessness	11.35	4.27	11.35	4.56	.02
Worries about family members	8.42	3.41	9.46	3.87	1.79
Environment related hassles	5.66	2.59	5.25	2.66	1.01
Financial hassles	5.98	2.3[illegible]	5.90	2.38	.22
Hassles due to Social interactions	8.29	3.03	8.00	2.90	.64
Coping Strategies					
Logical Analysis	24.83	4.79	24.64	4.30	.28
Tension Reduction	16.04	4.19	16.00	4.41	.06
Active Avoidance	9.34	3.31	9.73	3.52	.73
Introversion	8.68	2.74	8.05	2.84	1.45
Religion	9.32	2.99	9.46	3.07	.30
Inflicting guilt on self and others	4.89	1.96	4.33	2.04	2.92*
Self Criticism	2.58	1.24	2.52	1.27	0.31
Social Manipulation	6.27	1.96	6.07	2.06	0.64
Affective Regulation	8.67	2.74	8.55	2.75	0.28
Avoidance	5.11	2.04	5.00	2.02	0.35
Problem Solving	9.77	2.34	9.92	2.71	0.37
Acceptance	2.86	1.21	2.81	1.93	0.18
Uplift					
Uplift (Total)	67.70	11.79	64.20	10.53	2.11*
Uplift due to Interaction	19.45	4.80	18.84	4.56	0.99

Uplift due to efficient management of household	25.98	5.01	23.32	4.00	4.09**
Uplift due to positive physical state	13.65	2.90	13.00	2.30	1.73
Uplift due to caring and considerate spouse	8.53	2.32	8.41	2.03	0.37
Social Support	36.27	5.46	38.14	4.08	2.76*
Family Orientation	25.96	3.45	26.32	3.07	0.74
Mental Health					
Inadequacy	17.34	4.33	16.20	4.03	1.81
Depression	10.21	3.67	12.13	4.78	2.74*
Anxiety	12.25	2.78	14.26	2.90	4.56**
Sensitivity	10.11	4.64	9.23	5.10	1.43
Anger	15.43	5.34	16.20	5.01	0.99
Tension	14.03	8.02	14.34	8.34	0.49

* $p < .05$ ** $p < .01$

seen that middle aged unemployed women experienced maximum hassles (M = 110.56), followed by older women employed in Class III category (M = 107.05). Least hassles were experienced by older women of Class II category. As seen in Figure 11.1, the younger age group of women evinced about same level of stress across all the four groups of women. Older women revealed remarkable changes in certain areas of stress with change in job level.

Thus except for Class III jobs, middle aged women reported maximum stress. It appears that role becomes most complex for women in their middle age and makes daily living highly stressful for them. It may be noted that in this study the age range of 34 to 43 years was taken as middle age. Coping with teenage children, ailing in-laws, increased responsibilities of husband and self at work place, all contributed towards making this phase of life a stressful one.

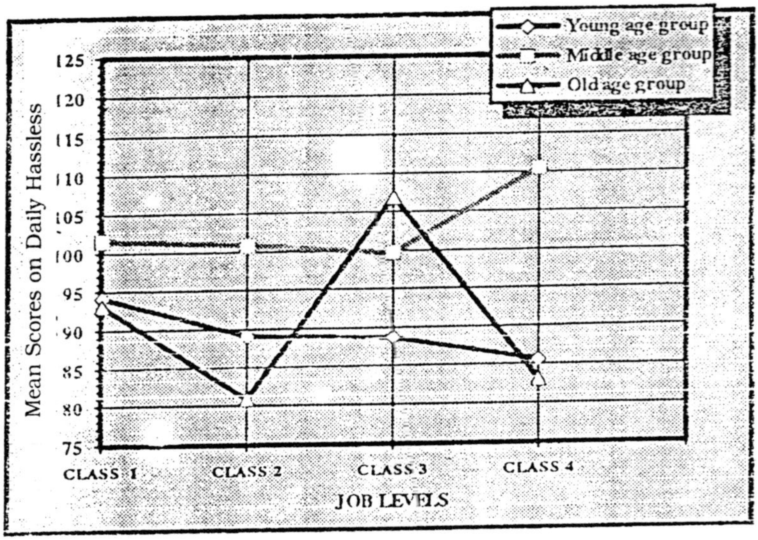

FIG. 11.1 : Interaction of age and job level for total daily hassle scores.

Relationship of Daily Hassles with other Variables

Different types of hassles were related differently with various coping strategies. Tables 11.3 and 11.4 show that to cope with the hassles due to feeling of confinement, feeling of helplessness and financial matters, the employed women did not have any preferred coping strategy and used all the strategies somewhat similarly. The unemployed group revealed no preference for any specific coping strategy for hassles due to feeling of confinement and environment related hassles.

While employed group preferred active cognitive and active behavioural strategies to cope with hassles, the unemployed group preferred religion, avoidance, tension reduction and active cognitive coping to deal with the same.

For the hassles arising out of too many expectations, interesting comparisons emerged for the two groups of women. While the employed group coped by increased self criticism, and reduced affective regulation, the unemployed group revealed a more comprehensive approach to coping as they preferred to use logical analysis, inflicting guilt on self and others, affective regulation and acceptance.

Both the groups used different strategies to cope with children-related hassles, though the employed group used more varied strategies. The two groups differed in their preference of strategies to deal with hassles owing to feelings of helplessness. Employed women preferred problem solving and acceptance and unemployed group used active avoidance and religion. Hassles due to social interaction revealed that employed women preferred religion for coping.

Social Support

Table 11.3 shows that for the employed group, social support had significant negative relationship with hassles in most of the areas. Unemployed women (Table 11.4) also yielded strong negative association between social support and daily hassles. Social support was unrelated to the worries about family members for both the groups. Social support thus, appears to have a moderating effect on the experience of hassles.

Family Orientation

Family orientation was related differently to daily hassles, for the two groups of women. As seen in Table 11.3, family orientation and daily hassles were positively related in case of employed group and negatively related in unemployed women (Table 11.4). This finding highlights the centrality of family in the lives of unemployed women.

Well Being Among Working Women

Uplift and Mental Health

The analysis revealed a significant main effect of age, $F = 3.28$, $p < .001$ as well as job level, $F = 3.60$, $p < .001$, for uplift due to effiicent management of the household. Older women experienced it most ($M = 27.23$), while in job level, unemployed women reported it most ($M = 27.81$). Responses on the Mental Health Questionnaire (MHQ) revealed that women employed in Class II jobs had best mental health, while those in Class III jobs had worst of it. Importance of the quality of job is highlighted by this finding and employment in itself does not necessarily mean greater well being.

More significant relationships between uplift and coping were seen for the employed women. For this group total uplift had significant negative relationship with introversion and inflicting guilt on self and others, i.e., emotion focussed coping. Use of avoidance as a coping strategy increased with total uplift. Use of tension reduction increased with uplift due to efficient management of household while use of religion as a coping strategy increased with uplift due to interaction. MHQ and coping strategies did not reveal any definite trend for either group of women.

Uplift, Mental Health and Social Support

Social support shared positive relationship with all the uplift factors for the unemployed women, though none of the relationships was statistically significant. For the employed group, on the other hand, some significant relationships were evident. Uplift total score, uplift due to interaction and uplift due to caring and considerate spouse, had significant positive relationship with social support. For employed women, this may point to the need for support from spouse and significant others.

TABLE 11.3 : Relationship of Factors of Daily Hassles scale with mediating variables for the Unemployed women (N = 54)

Coping Strategies	Daily hassles (Total)	Feeling of conf-inement	Too many expectat-ions	Children related	Interrup-ptions in daily life	Feeling of help lessness	Worries about family members	Environ-ment related	Financial	Social inter-actions
Logical Analysis	30	-03	37 *	36 *	10	24	36 *	-16	17	16
Tension Reduction	33 *	12	21	28	17 *	-19	20	31	09	15
Active Avoidance	28	08	09	19	36 *	34	-42 **	28	37 *	-07
Introversion	20	10	14	14	38 *	22	30	09	28	09
Religion	36 *	07	30	09	-20	39*	19	17	-19	10
Inflicting Guilt	37	12	32	11	26	18	-17	16	21	24
Self Criticism	31	14	27	38 *	-17	14	08	06	30	-43 **
Self Manipulation	18	08	21	29	19	20	12	24	18	30
Affective Regulation	24	21	35 *	19	24	28	09	20	-14	37 **
Avoidance	37 *	03	09	20	-37 *	-21	10	-17	28	20
Problem Solving	14	30	17	-24	-28	26	11	11	36 *	26
Acceptance	19	18	36 *	37 *	30	30	18	20	12	31 *
Social Support	-50 **	-44 **	-52 **	-33 *	-45 **	-30	-18	-30*	-33 *	-44 **
Family Orientation	-36 *	-17	-15	-20	42	26	30	11	15	23

Note : Decimals are omitted
** = p < 0.1
* = p < .05

TABLE 11.4 : Relationship of Factors of Daily Hassles scale with mediating variables for the employed women (N = 196)

Coping Strategies	Daily hassles (Total)	Feeling of confinement	Too many expectations	Children related	Interruptions in daily life	Feeling of help lessness	Worries about family members	Environment related	Financial	Social interactions
Logical Analysis	15	-06	-10	-16	11	-10	03	14	10	02
Tension Reduction	19 *	08	11	13	17 *	10	16	14	09	10 *
Active Avoidance	14	12	07	28 **	-05	14	08	04	14	03
Introversion	10	09	02	21 *	-02	11	03	04	09	00
Religion	14	04	01	13	17 *	07	-04	22**	15	17 *
Inflicting Guilt	12	15	14	17 *	02	15	-10	-10	07	-0
Self Criticism	21 **	13	18	19 *	18 *	12	09	12	13	14
Self Manipulation	-01	-05	-03	11	02	-09	-05	08	08	-08
Affective Regulation	22 **	14	-28 **	27 **	08	15	03	08	13	09
Avoidance	07	02	01	07	15	11	11	-00	01	·04
Problem Solving	22 **	16	15	20 *	12	17 *	13	15	15	14
Acceptance	19 *	15	19 *	13	09	21 *	02	16	08	08
Social Support	-35 **	-37 **	-38 **	-22 **	-22 **	-25 **	-10	-17	-13	-18 *
Family Orientation	-09	-06	-12	-06	-07	-06	-09	00	02	04

Note : Decimals are omitted

** = $p < 0.1$

* = $p < .05$

Both the groups of women showed a positive relationship between mental health and uplift, though it was significant only for employed women. For the Indian women embedded in the family social support appears to be a necessary ingredient for well being.

Uplift, Mental Health and Family Orientation

For the employed women, family orientation was significantly and positively related to uplift due to positive physical state but negatively related to uplift owing to caring and considerate spouse. This finding is interesting and points to the transition in the employed women's perspective. It suggests the uniqueness of husband-wife relation as an exclusive domain, separate from the rest of the family, indicative of a movement or shift towards westernized outlook.

Coping Strategies

It was found that older women used religion more than the younger women, ($M=8.78$ for younger women, $M=9.43$ for middle aged women and $M=9.96$ for older women), $F(2,238) = 4.20$, $p < .01$. It indicates that religion assumes increasingly greater value with maturity and age.

Logical analysis yielded significant main effect of job level. Thus the women of Class III jobs used it most ($M=25.56$) followed by Class II ($M=24.98$) and Class I ($M=23.50$) job women while unemployed women used it least ($M=22.94$), $F=2.41$, $p < .05$. Since coping is viewed as effort to manage specific demands, appraised as taxing by the individual, perhaps, women of Class III jobs encounter such situations at jobs where they use logical analysis significantly more for coping with the hassles.

Family Orientation

The preference for family orientation was jointly determined by age and job level. Thus middle aged women of Class I jobs were least family oriented ($M=22.80$) while younger unemployed women reported it most (M=27.77). For older women, job level did not influence family orientation. Middle aged women, employed in Class II and Class III jobs as well as unemployed women revealed similar concern for family (M=26.21, 26.29, 26.88, respectively). For younger women family orientation revealed a straight ascending pattern, as Class I women (M=24.25) reported it lesser than Class II women (M=24.58), who in turn reported it lesser than those from Class III (M=26.00), and unemployed younger women (M=27.77) reported it the most. Demands of the job, expectations and self-ideals about the husband's home and socialization at large determine the family orientation of women.

On the Job Stresses

It was found that older women experienced job difficulty most (M=6.04) while younger women experienced it least (M=5.32), F = 3.44, p <.05. This finding was by and large in the expected direction, as the supervisory support expected and given differs for different levels of jobs. In the present context job difficulty, referred to the experience of stress in the organisation because of certain job qualities, varied with age.

The joint effect of job level and age was significant for experience of inequality and constraints of change. The experience of inequality, younger and older women belonging to different age and job levels was almost similar. On the other hand, middle aged women of Class I experienced it very little, while middle aged women of Class II experienced it very much. Job nature and organisational stress related to experience of inequity were linked with chronological age. Enequity occurs where an employee feels that the compensation provided to her does not commensurate with work done. This is how perhaps appraisal acts as it changes the perception of work experience for women.

Concluding Comments

It is clear from the empirical analysis that in a predominantly patriarchal and traditional Indian society, women's employment is definitely a big event, demanding on both, the women herself and family as well as the society at large. The results revealed that women's experience of stress varied in large part with age and job status. This implies change in the quality of their roles. Social support emerged as an important variable moderating stress. The relationship between social support and daily hassles was similar for the working as well as non working women. It was found that the employed women reported more hassles, greater well being and less support while housewives reported lesser stress and well being and more support.

The role of social support in stress process has proved to be a debatable issue. Although many studies have shown that social support is a mediator of stress, others have found that it acted independently in determining the level of psychological health. It is important to note that the distinction between the main and buffering effects of social support has different implications. Disregarding the well-being aspect for a moment, unemployed women received more social support and reported lesser number of hassles. Qualitative differences in the sources of social support may have differential effect on well-being though this is yet to be ascertained by further research. Reciprocity of the support giving agent and the recipient is a key ingredient in successful supportive relationships (Caplan, 1974; Hobfoll, 1985). This has relevance to the Indian context, as it seems to reflect the transition currently taking place in the society. The traditional aspect of a woman's role is still accepted in the social network, providing support. These women, in turn, experience lesser hassles than the women who are engaged in non-traditional roles. The question is whether lesser number of stresses is due to availability of support or due to the existence of lesser sources of stress or a joint effect of both. Enhanced well-being for employed women is important, though they had reported more hassles and less support. They appear to appraise and use social support differently. While unemployed women, do not require support to combat the stress ensuing from additional roles, for the employed women resources like income, status and prestige which the employment yields appears adequate to cope with stress and to enhance well being. The relationship of social support with daily hassles in the context of women's employment is depicted in Figure 11.2. It is seen that employed women received lesser support than the unemployed women and reported more stress than their unemployed counterparts. Social support appears to moderate the stress experience for women playing traditional roles.

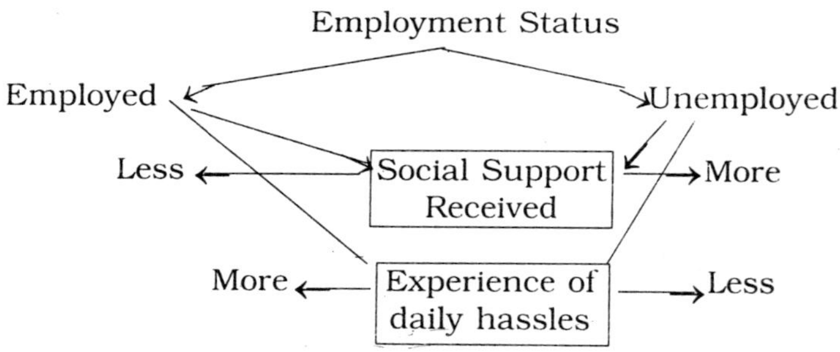

FIG. 11.2 : Relationship between employment status, social support and daily hassles.

Family orientation revealed significant negative relationship with daily hassles for the unemployed group while the employed group showed no significant relationship between the two. Unemployed women, having household activities as central to their interest benefit from stronger family orientation as, daily hassles are negatively related to it.

Both working women and housewives experience rewards and costs for their roles in their respective lives. Housewives may receive support from their spouses and others due to their role conformity, but may feel that they do not receive approval from the significant others. The employed women may feel both lack of support at home for her job and lack of support at work for her career advancement. In both cases, women who receive affirmation for whom they are and what they do, experience less psychological stress than women who did not receive such support (Aneshensel, 1986). Employment or work outside home at large seems to contribute differently to the experience of hassles for women varying in their employment status. Type of work done outside home is not so significant in structuring the experience of hassles. This finding is expected in the Indian society, where employment of women is a significant departure from their traditional role. It appears that "home as a haven" theory is not true for today's Indian woman as she is going out of house to work, facing more stresses but achieving greater well-being. Slightly greater preference of the employed women to use problem focussed strategies to cope with hassles may suggest that at least to a certain extent work related hassles are perceived as controllable. Emotional involvement, attachments and role expectations within the family may decrease the perception of control among women in dealing with family based hassles. This feeling of helplessness is somewhat compensated by an objective, outside world of work, where women may rightfully try to change the situation to their own liking.

Despite the fact that employed women receive lesser social support than their unemployed counterparts, their better well-being is fascinating. Are Indian women gradually evolving into independent, self sufficient persons, enjoying their different roles without spill over? Alternatively, is it possible that women compromise their standards of achievement in one of the roles and thereby reduce the chances of spill over? As Ramu (1989) found, when women realize that they cannot satisfactorily resolve the conflict between new economic and old domestic roles they not only compartmentalize these two roles, but also scale down their occupational aspirations in favour of maternal and conjugal obligations. Women are ready to work outside home even when they have to juggle so many roles and emotions. This readiness of the Indian women to compromise the standards of traditional roles expected of her is startling. A more extensive longitudinal design to study the consequences of work stress would be very telling. It may also be mentioned that the measure of social support used largely focussed on the support given by all the family members including the husband. It did not tap extensively the work-place support which the employed women may be receiving. It is possible that employment generates such resources for women which are so precious for them, that investments involved are relatively less than what they reap. It seems that these resources are greater than the threat, and a desirable condition of surplus resources is brought about, begetting something like 'eu-stress', a sense of control and positive association with the environment (Hobfoll, 1988). The situation emerging from the present study can be summarized as follows :

Employed Women	⇒	Problem focussed coping Less social support Low Family Orientation	⇒	Greater experience of daily Hassles
Unemployed women	⇒	Emotion focussed coping More social support High family Orientation	⇒	Lower Experience of daily Hassles

FIG. 11.3 : Linkages between employment, mediating variables and outcomes.

The results showed that unemployed women received greater social support than their employed counterparts. The traditional Indian society had divided the roles of men and women in the context of family and work. The stability of family, bringing-up children in a close knit family full of values and cultural heritage all still continue to have significance even today. Before Manu, the law giver of Indian society, women in ancient India had status equal to men. By the time women decided to come out of home, the society had evolved and maintained such fixed patterns for role enactment that it became difficult again to accommodate this work force. Change is always resisted by the tradition. Withholding support for the non-traditional roles, then should not be surprising. This is not so much with a motivation to stop women's entry into the work force, but to maintain the warm integrity of the traditional Indian home and family.

The analysis of coping strategies revealed a common pattern, across groups of women differing in age and employment status. But this needs to be qualified further, because the group of employed women had larger number of significant relationships of coping with other vairables. Earlier research had revealed that though dual-career women are hassled more frequently, they appear to be using the same set of coping strategies as housewives. It seems that for women, coping may be a process involving a combination of problem and emotion-focussed coping strategies (Alpert & Culbertson 1987).

Employment of women may be more common now but it is still competing with women's traditional roles for cultural endorsement. As stated by Callero (1994), a role may receive wide recognition and acceptance as legitimate, but at the same time may be viewed as deviant or negative.

It may be concluded that housewives' role when enacted in isolation without employment, reduced the experience of daily hassles for women. Housewives enjoyed social support for their traditional roles and expressed life satisfaction. Western literature in the area of stress has criticized the assumption of the primacy of family roles, especially that of wife and mother (Barnett & Baruch, 1985, 1987). In contrast, the overpowering existence of marriage, family and their sustainence is a normative reality in the Indian society. The traditional, socially approved role of the housewife is accepted by the Indian women and interpersonal relationship makes them satisfied. Motherhood is seen as an ultimate culmination of all of women's needs and aspriations and grants them status and fulfilment. That is not to say that housewife's role is easy or simple. On the contrary, it is highly demanding, confusing and sometimes taken for granted.

The point to consider is whether Indian women are willing to give it up for something new, or do they accept the obligations as well as gratifications after appraising the alternatives.

REFERENCES

Alpert, D., & Culbertson, A. (1987). Daily hassles and coping strategies of dual-earner and nondual-earner women. *Psychology of Women Quarterly, 11*, 359-366.

Aneshensel, C.S. (1986). Mental and employment role-strain, social support, and depression among adult women. In S.E. Hobfoll (Ed.). *Stress, Social Support and Women*. (pp. 99-114). New York : Hemisphere.

Barnett, R.C., Brennan, R.T., Raudenbush, S.W., Pleck, J.H., & Marshall, N.L. (1995). Change in job and marital experiences and change in psychological distress : A longitudinal study of dual-earner couples. *Journal of Personality and Social Psychology, 69*, 838-850.

Barnett, G.C., & Baruch, G.K. (1985). Women's involvement in multiple roles, role strain, and psychological distress. *Journal of Personality and Social Psychology, 49*, 135-145.

Barnett, R.C. & Baruch, G.K. (1987). Social roles, gender, and psychological distress. In Barnet, R.C., Biener, L., & Baruch, G.K. (Eds.). *Gender and Stress*. New York : Free Press.

Baruch, G.K. & Barnett, R. (1986). Role quality, multiple role involvement and psychological well-being in middle aged women. *Journal of Personality and Social Psychology, 51*, 578-585.

Callero, P.L. (1994). From role-playing to role-using : Understanding role as resource. *Social Psychology Quarterly, 57*, 228-243.

Caplan, G. (1974). *Support Systems and Community Mental Health*. New York : Behavioral Publications.

Chakraborty, K. (1977). Some variables in role conflict analysis : The case of middle-class working mothers. *Sociological Indica, 1*, 37-47.

Ganguly, K. (1988). *Role of perceived control in coping with stress*. Unpublished doctoral dissertation, Bhopal University, Bhopal, India.

Ghadiyally, R. (1988). *Women in Indian Society : A Reader*. New Delhi : Sage.

Hobfoll, S.E. (1988). *The Ecology of Stress*. New York : Washington, Philadelphia, London : Hemisphere, Publishing Corporation.

Hobfoll, S.E. (1985). The limitations of social support in the stress process. In I.G. & B.R. Sarason (Eds.). *Social Support : Theory, Research and Applications* (391-414). The Hague : Martinus Nijhof.

Kakar, S. (1978). *The Inner World : A Psychoanalytic Study of Childhood and Society in India*. Delhi : Oxford University Press.

Kanner, A.D., Coyne, J.C., Schaefer G., & Lazarus, R.S., (1981). Comparisons of two models of stress measurement : Daily hassles and uplifts versus major life events. *Journal of Behavioral Medicine, 4*, 1-39.

Kumar, U. (1986). Indian Women and Work : A paradigm for research. *Psychological Studies. 31* 147-160.

Lazarus, R.S., & Cohen, J.B. (1977). Environmental stress. In I. Altman & J.F. Wohlwill (Eds.), *Human Behavior and the Environment : Current Theory and research.* New York : Plenum.

Lazarus, S., & Scotch, N.A. (1970). *Social Stress.* Chicago : Aldine.

Long, J. & Porter, K.L. (1984). Multiple roles of midlife women : A case for new directions, in theory research and policy. In G. Baruch & J. Brooks-unn (Eds.) *Between Youth and Old Age : Women in the Middle Years* (pp. 109-160). New York : Plenum.

Mehta, R. (1975), *Divorced Hindu Women.* Delhi : Vikas.

Nandy, A., & Kakar, S. (1980). Culture and personality. In Udai Pareek (Ed.). *A Survey of Research in Psychology. 1971-76,* Part I. Bombay : Popular Parkashan.

Pushpa Sundar, (1981) Characteristics of female employment : Implications of research and policy. *Economic and Political Weekly. 16,* 863-71.

Ramu, G.M., (1989). *Women. Work and Marriage in Urban India : A Study of Dual and Single Earner Couples.* New Delhi : Sage.

Singh, S. (1990). *Organizational Stress and Executive Behaviour.* New Delhi : Shri Ram Centre for Industrial Relations and Human Resources.

Thakar, G. (1994). *Rewards and Costs of Employment : Case of Working Women.* Unpublished doctoral dissertation, Bhopal University, Bhopal.

Thakar G., & Misra, G. (1995). Correlates of daily hassles among dual career women. *Journal of the Indian Academy of Applied Psychology, 21,* 93-101.

Thakar G., & Misra, G. (1988). *Role of age and type of family in coping with daily hassles among employed women.* Unpublished manuscript, Bhopal University, Bhopal, India.

Vandewater, E.A., Ostrove, J.M., & Stewart, A.J. (1997). Predicting women's well-being in midlife : The importance of personality development and social role involvements. *Journal of Personality and Social Psychology. 72,* 1147-1160.

12

Environmental Stress and Human Behaviour

DINESH NAGAR

The current upsurge of interest in the study of man-environment relationship has assumed a critical dimension in technocratic industrial societies. During the last two decades or so the delicate ecological balance existing on 'spaceship earth' is disturbed largely because of the emission of noxious gas in the atmosphere, acid rain, acidification of ground, traffic noise, and congestion. The adverse effects of these ecological irritants have heightened the awareness of community-environment crisis and have perplexed the scientists, administrators, policy-makers, and social workers to think and take necessary steps towards resolving the problem of ecological imbalance. Although, rapid industrialization which is one of the prime source of man-environment disharmony has assured a number of economic benefits, the danger prevails (see Marsella, 1998 for a review of issues). Even the preliminary safeguards to ensure safety and health of the community are lacking in many of the dangerous chemical plants. Our past experience conforms the fact that zero-order risk free chemical and nuclear industries are inconceivable and sufficient evidence exists that not only the people of the third world countries were victimized by the industrial accidents but also countless marine and human casualities were reported in the most advanced countries of the world like USSR, USA and Germany in the 80s. The suddenness and intensity by which the global eco-cetestrophe adversely affects the big strata of the community is immediately noticed not only because of its incalculable human and material cost but also due to greater publicity. However, people fail to notice or are unaware of the dangerous psychological effects of silent ecological stressors which impinge on them in their day-to-day lives. The objective of this paper is to highlight the potential impact of some of the physical environmental stressors which pose potential threats to cognitive, emotional, and behavioural functioning of humans.

In recent years the area of psychological stress has made significant advance in understanding the relationship between physical environmental stresses and well-being. It deals with the impact of a wide range of mostly negative outcomes that otherwise seem to defy adequate explanation. With the beginning of influential work of Selye (1956) and Lazarus (1966), followed by a series of well-designed experimental studies of Glass and Singer (1972) on unabated noise, the environmental stress concept has led to ample amount of research on the properties of environment and its relationship with human behaviour and health.

One of the prominent concerns of environmental psychology for the last two decades has been the understanding of underlying psychological processes through which physical environment and behaviour are linked. Sufficient evidence exists regarding the facilitative/inhibitory environmental conditions that are capable of enhancing/blocking the optimal human functioning. Furthermore, various psychological factors like perceived control, stress tolerance, coping resources, and personality dispositions may moderate the adverse impact of environmental stressors on human social behaviour, health and well-being (See Baum & Paulus, 1987; Evans & Cohen, 1987; Paulus & Nagar, 1989 for review).

In the present context the term physical environment refers to the structure, the lay-out and the interior of the building as well as ambient conditions like temperature, crowding, and noise. The usage of the term ambient stressor is similar to that of Campbell (1983). He argues that it is heuristically useful to view global, acute phenomena that are negatively valued, non-urgent, physically perceptible and intractable conditions of the physical environment as ambient stressors.

The conventional definitions of stress vary depending on their emphasis on either situational factors interfering with the desired goal or emphasizing the response to stressors. Both these approaches to understanding environmental stressors suffer from several methodological weaknesses (Evans & Cohen, 1987; Lazarus & Cohen, 1977). In recent past process oriented models of stress (Lazarus & Folkman, 1984;) have emerged which take into account the psychological reality of the stress process more adequately. Such an approach views stress as a dynamic transaction between the person and his environment mediated by several variables like cognitive appraisal and coping. According to Lazarus and Folkman (1984) the mediating constructs (e.g. appraisal, coping) must be studied as processes occurring over time that continuously alter or change the relationship between environmental stressors and stress related outcomes. The process oriented models tend to examine how the individual appraises the misfit between environemntal attributes and human needs. The severity of the stress and its long-term consequences for the individual are affected by many factors like characteristics of the stressful situation, importance of the misfit to the individual, perceived awareness of the misfit, and the coping strategies available to the individual for establishing congruence between individual's need and environmental demands (Baum, A., Singer & Baum, C., 1982). Before discussing the sources of environmental stressors it is pertinent to examine the contemporary perspectives and psychological mediation of environmental stressors.

Physiological Perspectives

The first systematic treatment of stress phenomenon was developed by Selye (1956, 1976). The General Adaptation Syndrome (GAS) on which his physiological model is based includes three stages: alarm, resistance and exhaustion.

His model focuses on bodily defense against physical challenge to maintain a state of homeostasis.

Selye (1956) in his model, had made no attempt to distinguish between responses to physiological and psychological stressors and has not analyzed the mechanisms that trigger the GAS. In contrast, Mason (1968) has emphasized on the relationship between psychological response and emotional arousal as a specific stress response. He has also suggested that psychological threats are necessary for adrenal stimulation in the stress responses. Even relatively minor changes in the environment are sufficient in activating the hypothalamus for adrenal secretion. Frankenhaeuser and Johanson (1986) have discussed extensively the role of adrenal system explaining the causes of psychological arousal; effort and distress in work environment under the condition of stimulus underload as well as stimulus overload. Finally, evidence exists regarding the coping processes which may influence the psychological responses to stress.

Psychological Perspectives

The importance of psychological variables both as mediators of physical stressors (Glass & Singer, 1972) and as independent stressors (Paulus, & Nagar, 1989) has been increasingly emphasized by the researchers. Responses to stressors are evaluated by the degree to which they are perceived as potentially harmful or threatening. The primary appraisal of each stressor will depend upon a number of personal and situational factors, including attitude towards the stressor, evaluation of its costs and rewards, knowledge about its consequences, past experience about the aversive properties of the stressor, the duration of the stressor and the degree of controllability. If the individual appraises the stressful situation as upsetting, threatening or harmful, the secondary appraisals are made. During these processes people turn their attention to different modes of coping with the threat which may be either manipulative or accommodative.

Psychological Mediation of Environmental Stressors

Not everyone react similarly to the physical sources of stress. In fact people vary greatly in their reactions to environmental stressors like crowding and noise. The critical question thus, has been: what are the psychological mediators that intercede between objective measures of density and the subjective or behavioural responses? While most environmental psychologists accept the mediational processes of appraisal, there is very little research examining the mediating variables in the context of density and crowding which may help explaining and predicting psychological well-being, and related outcomes.

In crowding-literature the most investigated construct mediating between environmental stressors and outcome measures has been perceived loss of control. The Glass and Singer (1972) study on noise illustrates the fact that unpredictable stressors produce more negative effects on human functioning. The provision of control over environmental stressors has been found to significantly reduce their aversive impact (Cohen, 1980; Glass & Singer, 1972). Thus, empirical linkages between crowding and perceived control have been established. It has been shown that perceived or actual control over high density can alleviate some adverse effects of crowded conditions (Sherrod & Cohen, 1979). In a similar vein a series of studies conducted by Saegert and her colleagues (Langer & Saegert, 1977; Saegert, Mackintosh, & West, 1975) reveal that individuals who were forewarned about impeding crowding conditions in retail stores reported less crowding related stress and displayed significantly higher level of performance than those who were not forewarned.

Evidence suggests that different cultural groups develop different psychological or socio-cultural mechanisms to minimize the adverse effect of physical stresses like temperature and dense environments (Altman & Chemers, 1983; Schmidt, 1983). Pandey (1990) has explored the reciprocal linkages between the people, culture and the physical environment. Homes constructed by peole living in different parts of the world vary significantly not only in terms of layout, design and material used but also in terms of cultural considerations. For instance, to minimize the adverse effects of excessive heat and oppressive cold people in Middle east construct homes with high ceilings and ventilation while Eskimo igloos conserve heat to protect themselves from high intensity wind and freezing cold. In rural India young family members display a general tendency to sleep outside in the open field partly to provide other senior members their desired level of privacy. Empirical evidence is available that individuals from scarce resource environments show a tendency of heightened competition tolerance (Jain, 1987). In addition, the high level of crowding experienced in the home environment may enhance the threshold of crowding tolerance (Nagar, Pandey & Paulus, 1988). Similarly, the role of cultural coping mechanisms in response to crowding and diversity has been noted by many scholars (Altman & Chemers, 1983; Pandey, 1990; Rapoport, 1980).

Various features of residential design are capable of facilitating or inhibiting social contact (Osmond, 1957). Some architectural designs are crime prone and create a feeling of anonymity in the high-rise residential environments. An important task for environmental psychologist is to examine how the physical setting contributes to mediating the adverse effects of environmental stressors.

Types of Environmental Stressors

On the basis of eight major dimensions i.e. perceptual salience, predictability, controllability, positive or negative value, sudden or gradual onset, importance, type of adjustment required and duration of exposure, three major types of environmental stressors may be identified: (a) Cataclysmic phenomena, (b) daily hassles, and (c) ambient stressors (Campbell, 1983; Evans & Cohen, 1987; Lazarus & Cohen, 1977).

Cataclysmic Stressors

It refers to sudden catastrophes, unique and powerful single events that demand major adaptive responses and affect large number of people. These events include natural disasters, technological disasters, sudden emission of poisonous gas in the atmosphere and so forth. The eco-catastrophe resulted from the leakage of toxic MIC gas at Bhopal is one example of cataclysmic environmental event. The occurrence of this environmental tragedy was sudden, powerful, uncontrollable and disastrous affecting the collective psyche of the entire Bhopal community in central India. In this disaster more than 3000 people died and over 2,00,000 others were injured in which thousands of the gas exposed victims are still suffering from serious mental, psychosomatic and physical disorders (Weir, 1987; Hazarika, 1987; Everest, 1986). The Bhopal gas tragedy cannot be dismissed as an isolated incident, specially after the nuclear accident at Chernobyl in Russia and the gas tragedy at Shri Ram Chemical Industry in Delhi. The psychological after effects of cataclysmic events are examined both in the east as well as in the west (Baum, Fleming & Davidson, 1983; Misra, 1988). For instance, a longitudinal study conducted by Misra (1988) attempts to look for the pattern, of psycho-social development of MIC exposed children. The results of this study clearly reveal that the MIC exposed group children displayed significantly lower level of performance on cognitive and motor tasks as compared to their non exposed counterparts. In addition, the exposed group reported greater incidence of psychiatric symptoms like temper tantrums, stubbornness, poor development of speech, and enuresis than control group.

Daily Hassels and Ambient Stressors

Daily hassels range from the ordinary distrubances in the family and conflicts regarding work, to various aspects of the physical environment (Caspi, Bolger, & Eckenrode, 1987; Evans & Cohen, 1987). Daily hassles are characterized by more or less circumscribed events which are stable, non-urgent and appear for a short duration and may cause negative mood state, reduce well-being and health problems. For the most part, daily hassles are routine conditions and require only minor adaptive responses (Lazarus & Cohen, 1977). However, evidence exists that adaptive responses to daily hassles are not always minor in nature (DeLongis, 1982). In contrast, the term ambient stressor refers to chronic, and global conditions of the physical environment which are relatively more continuous and vary in intensity such as air pollution, traffic noise, congestion and residential crowding. The term 'ambient' connotes the background conditions. Ambient physical conditions generate psychological discomfort only when they block the attainment of salient goals. In these conditions ambient stressors come into forefront of consciousness at cognitive, emotional and psychological levels. Another property of these stressors is that they are low on perceptual salience and their motivational salience is variable (Baum, Singer & Baum, 1982; Evans, Jacobs & Frager, 1982). On the other hand, daily hassles have greater perceptual salience and variable motivational salience. Until recently most of the studies on crowding have been conducted in Euro-American countries which are relatively non-crowded. Thus, to provide better generalization the present overview on crowding will attempt to integrate the results of the key studies conducted both in crowded countries like India with those studies done in relatively less crowded Euro-American countries.

The term crowding has been defined in a variety of ways. One common distinction is made between density as an objective physical condition of spatial construction and crowding as a subjective experience when density forces goal blockage, interference, and mental and psychological discomfort (Stokols, 1972). Other studies employ measures of internal and external density. In the primary residential environment the internal density is measured by utilizing the person/room index, number of residents in the home and so forth. In contrast, external density in the secondary environment is measured by census data, number of apartments per unit/per acre (Gove, Hughes & Galle, 1979). Conditions of high density can come about in three distinct ways-increasing the number of inhabitants but keeping the amount of space while keeping the number of inhabitants constant (spatial density) and reducing the interpersonal distance (social distance) between individuals. Each of the three dimensions of density has shown to have an unique, independent, and diverse effect on the inhabitants (Baum & Paulus, 1987).

Studies on Animals

Initial attempts with most dramatic findings on crowding have come from animal studies. The Calhoun's (1962) studies with rodents revealed stress related negative effects of crowding. In one study the rats were left free to breed profusely in an enclosed colony and sufficient food was made available to them. The results reveal that normal maternal behaviour deteriorated and the higher infant mortality led to complete extinction of the colony. Similar evidence of crowding induced pathological maladies has been reported by other scholars working on animal population (Christian, Flyger & Davis, 1960; Myers, Hale, Mykytowycz, & Hughes, 1971). The results are very consistent and seem to provide a basis for theorization at human level. However, many scholars have questioned the generalizability of animal results for human population (Freedman, 1979).

Correlational Studies on Human Population

Much of the early research done in the urban settings tried to related crowding strain experienced by urban residents to various indices of pathology (e.g. mortality, juvenile deliquency, admission to mental hospital, crime rate). The evidence, however for a density-pathology relationship is mixed. Strong supportive evidence for density-related health problems was reported in Germany

(Manton & Myers, 1977), Netherlands (Levy & Herzog, 1974), United States (Galle, Gove, & McPherson, 1972), Honolulu (Schmitt, 1966), and India (Pandey, 1978; Pandey & Nagar, 1987, 1988; Jain, 1987). In contrast, several studies suggest a weak relationship between urban density and negative effect (Winsborough, 1965) or even no effect (Cholden & Roneck, 1975; Mitchell, 1971).

Inconsistency in the results regarding the direction and magnitude of density-pathology relationship may primarily be because of the problems in infering causal relationship and lack of adequate control over the confounding variables. In addition, the obvious possibility that individuals who gravitate towards congested and crowded areas are prone to anti-social tendencies, as well as mental and physical problems can not be ruled out. Furthermore, the various density measures employed may not accurately reflect the perceived crowding. Familiarity with the neighbourhood and residents, architectural design of external and internal space and tolerance level are likely to influence the perceived crowding experience (Paulus & Nagar, 1987; Paulus, 1988).

Experimental Studies

Another phase of crowding research involved laboratory studies. Typically, a variety of effects of short-term crowding were observed on various measures of task performance, emotional state, and social inclination. Most sessions last for less than an hour, and the subjects are asked to perform on various cognitive tasks in diverse density conditions. Such studies provide a fairly consistent picture regarding debilitated performance on cognitively complex tasks in highly dense laboratory conditions both in the Euro-American context as well as in India (Jain, 1987; Nagar & Pandey, 1987; Paulus *et al.*, 1976), though, some studies have reported inconsistent results (Freedman, Klevansky, & Ehrlich, 1971). It appears that a number of factors like degree of perceived control, use of multiple tasks, and nature of the task used seem to determine whether or not crowding effects are found (Paulus &

Matthews, 1980). A recent study by Nagar *et al.* (1988) seems to provide evidence regarding the influence of previous residential crowding experience on sensitivity to laboratory crowding. Their results indicate that respondents with a background of high level of crowding in the residential environment showed relatively greater crowding tolerance by performing significantly better on cognitively complex tasks as compared to their low experience of crowding counterparts. It appears that laboratory crowding does not hamper the performance on simple cognitive tasks (Evans, 1979; Nagar *et al.*, 1988; Paulus *et al.*, 1976).

Brief encounters with high density condition not only engenders the negative emotional state in the respondents (Evans, 1979; Jain, 1987; Nagar *et al.*, 1988) but can also affect the physiological responses such as skin conductance (Aiello, Epstein & Karlin, 1975), palmer sweeting (Saegert, 1978), blood pressure and heart rate (Evans, 1979). In conclusion, the results reported from the controlled laboratory studies demonstrate adverse effects of density on cognitive task performance, emotional state, and physiological responses.

Field Studies

Field studies of crowding have been conducted in a wide variety of settings ranging from family dwellings, college dorms, to prisons, and naval ships. Crowding in these and other residential settings is essentially a group phenomenon. The problems created in this environment are primarily due to difficulties in coordinating the activities and disruption of interpersonal communication with others. The negative effects of density are observed only if the individual perceives the space in the residential environment as insufficient (Stokols, 1972).

In a typical residential environment people are generally forced to share the limited space with other residents. The impact of these environments on individuals are pervasive, prolonged, and inescapable. In the Indian context comprehensive assessment of the psychological consequences of crowding was studied by Jain (1978).

He found definite relationship between culturally relevant concept of competition tolerance and adaptation to high density living conditions. In a subsequent study Jain (1983) reported relationship between various objective density measures with subjective experiences of crowding and resultant adverse affective consequences. These results were supported in other studies (Kamal & Jain, 1984; Jain & Misra, 1990; Tripathi, 1996). Anand (1983) has reported negative effect of high density on the quality of life, perceived control, health and personal space. S.K. Tripathi (1986) has reported a field survey of Varanasi in north India. He noted that the experience of crowding was greater under high density conditions and its magnitude was greatest among older people. However, younger males felt greater stress than their female counterparts from high density area. High density yielded greater negative behavioural effects, poor adjustment and neuroticism. The work of Ruback and Pandey (1991) on Indian villagers suggests that the spatial density does not have independent effects on physcial health, mental health or interpersonal relations. However, they noted that individual's perception of control which is an indicator of social density was found to be significantly related to various health related measures. Prakash and Tripathi (1996) have noted that physical as well as psychological environment in villages has changed drastically in the last few decades. The pattern of production, consumption and disposal of goods and services in villages is resulting in rapidly deteriorating environment.

The diverse effects of residential crowding come from the Chicago study conducted by Gove, Hughes and Galle (1979). They utilized both the objective and psychological indicators of crowding to examine their relationship with a host of pathological measures. The results of this study indicate that crowding experience acts as a mediator between density and pathology. This study has utilized the measures of perceived crowding based on loss of control and privacy, it is surprising that only a few studies have tried to examine directly the nature of this experience (Baron & Rodin, 1978; Gove *et al.*, 1979; Montana &

Adamopoulos, 1984; Saegert, 1978; Jain, 1987, 1997). However, these scholars, have examined only limited dimensions of crowding experience. The Nagar and Paulus (1989) study has incorporated most of the dimensions of residential crowding experience. Factor analysis suggested evidence of four distinct components: spaciousness, positive or supportive interactions, negative or disruptive interactions, and uncontrollable disturbance. Interestingly, these four components of perceived crowding were unique in predicting various outcome measures like psychological well-being, psychosomatic symptoms, emotional state, and home and neighborhood evaluations. For instance, the uncontrollable disturbance was the most potent predictor of reported symptoms, with negative relationship adding further to the predictive power. Space satisfaction and negative relations in home both predicted psychological well-being and emotional state. In the context of social interaction-demand model, the disruptive interactions may most closely represent the interference component.

There are individual and cultural differences in sensitivity to crowding. Individuals who differ in status within the household, such as children, may be more prone to the ill effects of residential crowding partly because they have less control over environment relative to the senior members of the house (Baldassare, 1979; Epstein, 1981). In a crowded country like India the inhabitants of high density living environment develop high competition tolerance which, in turn, mitigates some of the ill effects of density (Jain, 1978). Similarly, evidence of cross-situational effect of crowding was demonstrated in a study conducted in India by Nagar *et al.* (1988). The study of Evans, Palsane, Lepore and Martin (1989) showed that high density living conditions weakens the social support bonds which results in adverese effects on psychological health. This study suggests that social support acts as an endogenous variable in the stress - health relationship.

Research on Residential Design

Dormitory design and social behaviour

In typical college dorms a large number of residents are

accommodated around undifferentiated, shared spaces where the level of social density is high. Baum and his associates (Baum & Valins, 1977; 1979), have examined the effects of dormitory crowding on social behaviour of inhabitants. In one of their studies, students living in suite style dorms with double loaded long corridor dorms were compared with their counterparts living in short corridor dorms. Irrespective of the variation along architectural dimensions, all residents availed equivalent square footage of space. Results indicated that residents of long corridor dorms felt more helpless and acted more competitively than did residents living in accommodations of a different architectural arrangement. Thus long corridor residents were more likely to encounter unwanted social interaction than were short corridor or suite residents. It appears that when the jurisdiction over space was clear, residents would actively regulate their social interaction consistent with their need.

At Rutgers University Karlin, Epstein, and Aiello (1978) investigated the effects of tripled students living in double loaded corridor dormitory rooms originally intended for two person occupancy with double students living in similar dorm type. This study indicated that not only did tripled students escaped to alternative locations but they also reflected more disappointment and stress than doubled students. In addition, significant drop in the grade point averages was found for both tripled men and women relative to their counterparts living in double seated rooms. However, evidence exists that the adverse effects of living in crowded dorms seems to go away in subsequent years, when the room density was reduced (Karlin, Rosen & Epstein, 1979). It seems that the introduction of additional people into spatially restricted settings may strain an individual's ability to adapt and adversely influence group development and satisfaction. Evidence suggests that when three students are housed to a room designed for double occupancy, stress and social disruption occurs (Aiello, Epstein, & Karlin, 1975; Baum & Vallins, 1977). Tripling in double occupancy dormitory rooms lessens resident's sense of control and is aversive, but this effect is mediated by the interpersonal relationship that develops among the residents. The problem of dormitory crowding is intensified when one resident felt that he or she was 'left out' by the other two room mates. The Karlin *et al.* study (1979) suggests that females and not men showed a tendency of coalitions and left their dorms by the end of the semester.

The field studies conducted in the crowded dormitory environment provide a generally consistent picture that density in a real world setting can have diverse ill effects. Similar results are obtained with Navy personnel on ships as well as in prison environment (Dean, Pugh & Gunderson, 1978; Paulus, 1988). These reults can be best explained in the light of perceived control and interpersonal orientation of residents.

Built Environment and Social Behaviour

Despite our lack of awareness the design of the built environment may cause stress. The architectural design of the built environment is operationalized here as a socio-physical structure where physical elements interact with salient behavioural processes and block important individual goals and needs of its users. By constructing different types of architectural design we have created a third environment that intervenes between natural and psychological realms. The buildings and spaces of architectural environment may facilitate or hinder social behaviour of their users thereby making some responses more likely than others. The influence of the built environment has been examined in many ways. Some scholars have studied the role of architectural design on social behaviour. For instance, the state of St. Louis in order to elaborate the quality of life of slum inhabitants constructed a high rise public housing project. This project which was hailed in 1950s as a prototypic architectural design, was destroyed for the faulty design which made it a dangerous place to live. The design of Pruitt-complex facilitated anomie, alienation and was prone to crime (Jeffery, 1971). Yankey (1972) observed that the architectural features of this housing complex provided a very poor fit between the needs of the residents and the arrangement of residential space. The interior architecture failed to support social expectations of its inhabitants which resulted in 'atomization' of social network and dissatisfaction among the users. There is evidence of negative outcomes resulting from an interaction between design dysfunction and blockage of important goals both in prisons (Paulus, 1987) and college dormitories (Baum & Valins, 1977).

With regard to residential environment both physical and functional proximity among residents influence the probability of friendship formation and cohesive group development (Festinger, Schachter, & Back, 1950). In addition, the sociopetal arrangement of the housing units, common access to facilities, and common stairways are some potent factors that are likely to enhance social contact among residents. The number and quality of one's friendship in the residential environment are good predictors of overall life satisfaction because other people may provide useful ways of coping in times of stress and may be a source of comfort (Unger & Wandersman, 1985). A recent study conducted on U.S. Army families by Paulus, Nagar and Camacho (1991) has reported the strong effects of psychological factors like degree of housing choice, comparison of present housing with past housing and expectation of impending improvement in housing on overall housing satisfaction.

Apart from physical and functional proximity among residents defensible space modifications may reduce crime rates in high rise buildings and residential compounds. Crime is a symptom of stress caused by inappropriate and faulty design of residential environment which destroys social network among inhabitants (Newman, 1972). Defensible space in residential areas may be created through environmental engineering. To this end the following considerations are important: (1) The design of the residential units must be created in ways that provide residents natural surveillance. Inmates and users can overlook common areas of the residential units without opening their main door and hence are aware of the intruders. (2) Symbolic markers also provide residents a sense of property ownership. (3) Improving the quality of high rise may enhance the feeling of pride in residents. (4) The cul-de-sac type of physical arrangment of units, common access to facilities like mail boxes, and use of common lounges, may increase the opportunity of social contact among residents in the course of time. Hallways broken by doors that clusters a number of apartments together may facilitate the appropriate use of space and enhance the chances of group cohesion (Osmond, 1957).

Concluding Observations

Both noise and crowding have effects on human health and well-being that can be characterized as stress-effect. The importance of psychological factors and their potential to predict various outcomes are examined in the context of various theoretical models like behavioural constraint, overload, social interaction and ecological (Baum & Paulus, 1987; Paulus & Nagar, 1989, for reviews). Within the field of environmental psychology the area of crowding stress represents the most extensive theoretical and empirical enterprise. It has implications for a wide range of environmental issues like architectural designing of offices and factories as well as high rise residential complexes. The field of crowding has facilitated and generated relevant research in the area of personal space, territoriality and community development (Paulus & Nagar, 1988; Unger & Wandersmann, 1985).

Ecological degradation is assuming alarming proportions and there is increasing threat to the well-being of human and animal life on the planet earth. The situation in developing countries like India has become critical due to increase in consumerism, limited resources and unmindful urbanization and industrialization. The human intervention has interfered with the quality of air, water and food products. Psychological studies are limited. Only concerted efforts by multidisciplinary teams of researchers can address these issues. So far psychologists have been concerned with very limited aspects of stress.

Despite advancement both theoretical and practical several gaps exist in the area of environmental stress in particular. A better conceptual understanding of the relationship between stress and cognition is needed. Our understanding of the effects of multiple stressors on health, cognition and well-being is very limited. The issue of additive and multiplicative effects of stresses is unresolved.

In addition, insufficient evidence based on inferences exist regarding how an individual develops tolerance to handle the adverse effect of ambient stressors and how costly is the adaptation or what are the limits of tolerance. More research is needed in this direction so as to develop a better perspective on stress and its ill effects.

Another gap in this area is lack of appropriate indices of stress. With the exception of a few crowding studies (Evans, 1978), there has been essentially no work on verbal and non-verbal indices of stress during exposure to environmental stressors. Research on adaptive processes and environmental stressors has focused primarily on habituation, performance after effects, and indices of health status. However, there had been very little research on how coping with one stressor affects our ability to deal with another source of environmental demand.

With regard to crowding and noise it is also pertinent to explore the environmental parameters and situational factors/contexts that are more likely to produce negative effects. We do know that ambient stressors are capable of producing ill effects. We also know that some degree of stimulation is essential to concentrate properly on various mental tasks and physical work. However, in order to enhance our knowledge it is essential to know at what level of noise and crowding the individual can perform optimally.

There is also a growing concern among psychologists that their research is not taken seriously by the policy makers. A framework presented by Ruback and Innes (1988) suggests two dimensions along which the relevance and irrelevance of psychological research can be considered: (a) the number of policy variables investigated, and (b) the extent to which the dependent measures are useful to the practitioners or policy-makers. In order to make the psychological research practically relevant the need is to select those dependent measures that have higher utility and are measured not at the individual level but at the system level. In addition, selection of the policy variables must be clearly operationalized so as to facilitate the decision about what should be changed. The need is to communicate the implications of research findings to policy makers as clearly and directly as possible. Thus, environmental research should be conducted in natural environment taking both policy variables, that can be changed and dependent variables that are of high practical utility. Pursuing the research of this order will not only enhance the visibility of the discipline of psychology but will create global awareness among the masses about the environmental issues affecting the harmonious relationship between man and his physical environment.

REFERENCES

Aiello, J., Epstein, Y., & Karlin, R. (1975). Effects of crowding on electrodermal activity. *Sociological Symposium, 14*, 42-57.

Altman, I., & Chemers, M. (1983). *Culture and Environment*. New York: Cambridge University Press.

Anand, M. (1983). *Indwelling and outdwelling experience of crowding and social, cognitive and affective responses*. Unpulbished master's dissertation. Allahabad University.

Baladassare, M. (1979). *Residential Crowding in Urban America*. Berkeley: University of California Press.

Baron, R.M., & Rodin, J. (1978). Personal control as a mediator of crowding. In A. Baum, J. Singer, & S. Valins (Eds.) *Advances in Environmental Psychology* (Vol. 1, pp. 145-190). Hillsdale, NJ: Erlbaum.

Baum, A., Fleming, R., & Davidson, L. (1983). Natural disaster and technological catastrophe. *Environment and Behavior, 15*, 333-354.

Baum, A., & Paulus, P. (1987). Crowding. In D. Stokols & I. Altman (Eds.), *Handbook of Environmental Psychology* (pp. 533-570). New York: Wiley.

Baum, A., Singer, J.E., & Baum, C. (1982). Stress and the

environment. In G.W. Evans (Ed.). *Environmental Stress* (pp. 15-44). New York: Cambridge University Press.

Baum. A., & Valins. S. (1979). Architectural mediation of residential density and control: Crowding and the regulation of social contact. In L. Berkowitz (Ed.). *Advances in Experimental Social Psychology* (Vol. 12). New York: Academic.

Baum. A., and Valins. S. (1977). *Architectural and Social Behavior: Psychological Studies of Social Density*. Hillsdale. N.J.: Erlbaum.

Calhoun. J.B. (1962). Population density and social pathology. *Scientific American*, *206*, 139-148.

Campbell, J. (1983). Ambient stressors. *Environment and Behavior, 15*, 355-380.

Caspi. A., Bolger. N., & Eckenrode. J. (1987). Linking person and context in the daily stress process. *Journal of Personality and Social Psychology*, *52*, 184-195.

Cholden. H., & Roneck. D. (1975). *Density and pathology: The issue expanded*. Paper presented at the meeting of the population Association of America. Seattle, WA.

Christian. J., Flyger. V., & Davis. D. (1960). Factors in the mass mortality of a herd of silka deer cervus nippen. *Chespapeake Science*, *1*, 19-95.

Cohen. S.A. (1980). After effects of stress on human performance and social behaviour: A review of research and theory. *Psychological Bulletin*, *88*. 82-102.

Dean. L., Pugh. W., & Gunderson. E. (1975). Spatial and perceptual components of crowding: Effects on health and satisfaction. *Environment and Behavior*. *7*. 255-226.

DeLongis. A., Coyne. J., Dakof. G., Folkman. S., & Lazarus. R.S. (1982). Relationships of daily hassels. uplifts. and major life events to health status. *Health Psychology*. *1*, 119-136.

Epstein. Y. (1981). Crowding stress and human behavior. *Journal of Social Issues*. *37*. 126-143.

Evans. G. (1978). Crowding and the development process. In: A. Baum & Y. Epstein (Eds.). *Human Response to Crowding*. Hillsdale. N.J.: Erlbaum.

Evans. G.W. (1979). Behavioral and physiological consequences of crowding in humans. *Journal of Applied Social Psychology*, *9*. 27-46.

Evans. G.. Palsane. M.N.. Lepore. S.J.. & Martin. J. (1989). Residential density and psychological health: The meditating effects of social support. *Journal of Personality and Social Psychology*. *57*. 994-999.

Evans, G., Jacobs, S.V., & Frager, N. (1982). Behavioral responses to air pollution. In A. Baum & J. Singer (Eds.) *Advances in Environmental Psychology* (Vol. 4) pp. 237-270. Hillsdale, NJ: Erlbaum.

Evans, G., & Cohen, S. (1987). Environmental stress. In D. Stokols & I. Altman (Eds.), *Handbook of Environmental Psychology* (pp. 371-610). New York: Wiley.

Everest, L. (1986). *Behind the Poison Cloud.* Hyderabad, Banner Press.

Festinger, L., Schachter, S., & Back, K. (1950). *Social Pressures in Informal Groups.* New York: Harper and Row.

Frankenhaeuser, M., & Johanson, G. (1986). Stress at work: Psychological and psychosocial aspects. *International Review of Applied Psychology, 35*, 287-299.

Freedman, J.L. (1979). Reconciling apparent differences between the responses of humans and other animal to crowding. *Psychological Review, 86*. 80-85.

Freedman, J., Klevansky, S., & Ehrlich, P. (1971). The effect of crowding on human task performance. *Journal of Applied Social Psychology, 1*, 7-26.

Galle, O., Gove, W., & McPherson, J.M. (1972). Population density and pathology: What are the relations for man? *Science*, 23-30.

Glass, D.C., & Singer, J.E. (1972). *Urban Stress: Experiments on Noise and Social Stressors.* New York: Academic.

Gove, W., Hughes, M., & Galle, O. (1979). Overcrowding in the home: An empirical investigation of its possible pathological consequences. *American Sociological Review, 44*, 59-80.

Hazarika, S. (1987). *Bhopal: The Lessons of a Tragedy.* New Delhi: Penguin Books.

Jain, U. (1978). Competition tolerance in high-low density urban-rural areas. *Journal of Social Psychology, 105*, 297-298.

Jain, U. (1987). *The Psychological Consequences of Crowding.* New Delhi: Sage Publications.

Jain, U. (Ed.) (1997). *Perspectives on Environment and Behaviour.* New Delhi : Har Anand.

Jain, U., & Misra, G. (1990). Experience and consequences of crowding. In: G. Misra (ed.) *Applied Social Psychology in India.* (pp. 265-278). New Delhi: Sage Publication.

Jain, U. (1983). Effect of population density on human social behaviour and coping in dense environment. New Delhi: Indian Council of Soical Science Research.

Jeffery, C.R. (1971). *Crime Prevention Through Environmental Design.* Beverly Hills: Sage Publications.

Karlin, R., Epstein, Y., & Aiello, J. (1978). Strategies for the investigation of crowding. In A. Esser & B. Greenbie (Eds.), *Design for Community and Privacy*. New York: Plenum.

Karlin, R., Rosen, L., & Epstein, Y. (1979). Three into two doesn't go: A follow up on the effects of overcrowded dormitory rooms. *Personality and Social Psychology Bulletin, 5,* 391-395.

Langer, E.U., & Saegert, S. (1977). Crowding and cognitive control. *Journal of Personality and Social Psychology, 35,* 175-182.

Lazarus, R.S. (1966). *Psychological Stress and the Coping Process.* New York: McGraw-Hill.

Lazarus, R.S., & Cohen, J. (1977). Environmental stress. In: J. Wohlwill & I. Altman (Eds.), *Human Behavior and Environment.* (pp. 9L-127), New York: Plenum.

Lazarus, R.S. & Folkman, S. (1984). *Stress, Appraisal, and Coping.* New York: Springer.

Levy, L., & Herzog, A. (1974). Effects of population density and crowding on health and social adaptation in the Netherlands. *Journal of Health and Social Behavior, 15,* 228-240.

Mason, J.W. (1968). A historical review of the stress field. *Journal of Human Stress, 1,* 6-12.

Manton, K.G., & Myers, G. (1977). The structure of urban mortality: A methodological study of Hanover, Germany (pt. 2). *International Journal of Epidemiology, 6,* 213-223.

Marsella, A.J. (1998). Urbanization, mental health and social deviancey : A review of issues and research, *American Psychologist, 53,* 624-634.

Misra, G. (1988). *Psycho-social competence in children in MIC exposed areas of Bhopal.* Paper presented at the Workshop on developmental norms of children, National Institute of Public Cooperation and Child Development, New Delhi.

Mitchell, R. (1971). Some social implications of high density housing. *American Sociological Review, 36,* 18-29.

Montana, D., & Adamopoulos, J. (1984). The perception of crowding in interpersonal situations: Affective and behavioral responses. *Environment and Behavior, 16,* 643-666.

Myers, K., Hale, C.S., Mykytowycz, R., & Hughes, R. (1971). Density, space, sociality and health. In A.H. Esser (Ed.) *Behavior and Environment.* New York: Plenum.

Nagar, D. (1990). Review of Psychological Consequences of Crowding. *Vikalpa, 13,* 77-80.

Nagar, D., Pandey, J., & Paulus, P.B. (1988). The effects of residential crowding on reactivity to laboratory crowding and noise. *Journal of Applied Social Psychology, 18.* 1423-1442.

Nagar, D., & Pandey, J. (1987). Affect and performance on cognitive tasks as a function of density and noise. *Journal of Applied Social Psychology, 17,* 147-157.

Nagar, D., & Paulus, P. (1989). *Residential crowding experience scale: Assessment and validation.* Unpublished manuscript. The University of texas at Arlington.

Newman, O. (1972). *Defensible Space.* New York: Macmillan.

Osmond, H. (1957). Function as a basis of psychiatric ward design. *Mental Hospitals, 83,* 235-245.

Pandey, J. (1978). Effects of crowding on human social behaviour. *Journal of Social and Economic Studies, 6,* 85-95.

Pandey, J. (1990). The environment, culture, and behavior. In: R. Brislin (Ed.), *Applied Cross Cultural Psychology,* Sage.

Pandey, J., and Nagar, D. (1987). Experiences of indwelling and outdwelling crowding and social psychological consequences. *Social Science International, 3,* 1-9.

Pandey, J., and Nagar, D. (1988). Residential crowding in India: Its social psychological consequences. Paper presented at *The 24th International Congress of Psychology,* Sydney.

Paulus, P. (1988). *Prison Crowding: A Psychological Perspective.* New York: Springer-Verlag.

Paulus, P., Annis, A., Seta, J., Schkade, J., & Matthews, R. (1976). Crowding does effects task performance. *Journal of Personality and Social Psychology, 34,* 248-253.

Paulus, P., & Matthews, R. (1980). Crowding, attribution, and task performance. *Basic and Applied Social Psychology, 1,* 3-14.

Paulus, P., & Nagar, D. (1987). Environmental influences on social interaction and group development. In C. Hendrick (Ed.) *Group Process and Intergroup Relations. Review of Personality and Social Psychology* (Vol. 14, pp. 68-90). Beverly Hills, CA: Sage.

Paulus, P., & Nagar, D. (1989). Environmental influences in groups. In: P.B. Paulus (Ed.) *Psychology of Group Influences.* Hillsdale, NH: Lawrence Erlbaum Associates.

Paulus, P., Nagar, D., & Camacho, L. (1991). Environmental and psychological factors in reactions to apartments and mobile homes. *Journal of Environmental Psychology, 11,* 143-161.

Prakash, A. & Tripathi, M. (1976). Environmental change and its psychological impact : A case study of a village. *Trends in Social Science Research, 3,* 35-45.

Preet Kamal, & Jain, U. (1984). *Effects of Populaton density on mental health*. Paper presented at the Indian Psychiatric Conference, Udaipur, Rajasthan.

Rapoport, A. (1980). Preference, habitat selection and urban housing. *Journal of Social Issues, 36*, 118-134.

Ruback. B., & Innes, C. (1988). The relevance and irrelevance of psychological research: The example of prison crowding. *American Psychologist, 43*, 683-693.

Ruback, R.b. & Pandey, J. (1991). Crowding, perceived control, and relative power: An analysis of households in India. *Journal of Personality and Social Psychology, 21*, 345-374.

Saegert, S. (1978). High density environments: Their personal and social consequences. In: A. Baum and Y.M. Epstein (Eds.), *Human Response to Crowding*. Hillsdale, N.J.: Erlbaum.

Saegert, S.C., Mackintosh, E., & West, S. (1975). Two studies of crowding in urban public spaces. *Environment and Behavior, 7*, 159-184.

Schmitt, R.C. (1966). Density, health and social disorganization. *American Institute of Planners Journal, 32*, 38-40.

Schmidt, D.E. (1983). Personal control and crowding stress: A test of similarity in two cultures. *Journal of Cross-Cultural Psychology, 14*, 221-239.

Schmidt, D.E., & Keating, J.P. (1979). Human crowding and person control: An integration of the research. *Psychological Bulletin, 86*, 680-700.

Selye, H. (1956). *The Stress of Life*. New York: McGraw-Hill.

Selye, H. (1976). *Stress in Health and Disease*. Woburn, Mass: Butterworth.

Sherrod, D.R., & Cohen, S. (1979). Density, personal control, and design. In A. Baum and J.R. Aiello (eds.) *Residential Crowding and Design*. New York: Plenum.

Stokols, D. (1972). On the distinction between density and crowding: Some implications for future research. *Pscyhological Review, 79*, 275-277.

Sundstrom, E. (1986). *Work places: The psychology of the physical environment in offices and factories*. Cambridge, Cambridge University Press.

Tripathi, H.G.R. (1996). Effect of quality of surrounding on crowding stress. *Journal of Personality and Clinical Studies, 12*, 49-54.

Tripathi, S.K. (1986). *Effects of Crowding on Human Behaviour*. Unpublished doctoral dissertation, Kashi Vidyapeeth, Varanasi.

Unger, D., & Wandersman, A. (1985). The importance of neighbors: The social, cognitive and affective components of neighboring. *American Journal of Community Psychology, 13*, 139-169.

Weir, D. (1987). *The Bhopal Syndrome*. San Francisco. Sierra Club Books.

Winsborough, H. (1965). The social consequences of high population density. *Law and Contemporary Problems, 30*, 120-126.

Yancey, W.C. (1972). Architecture, interaction and social control: The case of a large scale housing project. In J.G. Wohlwill and D.H. Carson (Eds.). *Environment and the Social Sciences: Perspectives and Applications* (pp. 126-153), Washington, D.C.: American Psychological Association.

13

Stress and Mental Health in Childhood and Adolescence

MALAVIKA KAPUR

Research into stress and life events has received some attention in India, in the adult population. Saxena and Mohan (1982) have highlighted the need for larger sample size, events list suitable for Indian population, control sample, community survey especially with reference to clinical population, use of interview methods, reliability studies and inclusion of new concepts. Sharma (1988) in a review of the work in the area, reported definite advancement in research with reference to adult population. Apart from describing the methodological issues common to Western and Indian settings, he has highlighted the need to study implications of poverty, transitional nature of the society, the person-environment fit, and the role of other mediating factors. However, research in child and adolescent population is conspicuously absent, with very little published literature (Malhotra, Kaur & Nehra, 1992; Rangaswamy & Kamakshi, 1983). However, some research where stress has been incidentally studied can be found.

It is a timely endeavour to conceptualise stress research with reference to child and adolescent population with special focus on methodological issues in the Indian context, (See Kapoor, 1995, 1997 for details). A perusal of western research reveals that theoretical models and empirical research do not always have a 'good fit'. The present chapter attempts to highlight, some salient western theoretical perspectives, methodological issues, and implications of available research data in the area of child and adolescent mental health in India.

Theoretical Perspectives

To understand the child's overwhelming response to stress, several theoretical constructs have been put forth in the western context. These are described by Anthony (1988) as follows:

(i) A model of self-induced pathology according to which some individuals are prone to a helpless or hopeless response as a part of giving up or given up pattern of behaviour, in response to environmental pathogens or constitutional vulnerabilities (Schmale, 1972).

(ii) A model according to which the individual differences in vulnerability to stress-induced conditions are seen as related to expectations of the individuals and can be controlled from external or internal sources (Rotter, 1966). The internal locus of control has been equated with competency, coping ability and relative invulnerability to stress (Campbell, Converse & Rodgers, 1976).

(iii) A model based on laboratory research on physiological and psychological responses to stress, according to which there are individual differences in vulnerability, manifested in response styles of suppressing or being hyperalert to stressful stimuli. It has been reported that suppression or possibly an unconscious mechanism of denial may lead to better recovery (Cohen & Lazarus, 1973). Extreme degree of denial, however, may lead to risk taking and reckless behaviour. This was described by Sandman (1972) as narrowing of perception as if blinkers were worn by those individuals.

(iv) A comprehensive model, specially applicable to children is the one, according to which presence of social support, such as family and social networks determines the response to stress (Caplan, 1976). Hence interpersonal context along with individual differences should be taken into account.

(v) A model which focuses on the developmental context which includes the time dimension, and explores the effects of stress being cumulative over time or providing an "inoculation" effect.

(vi) A model which focuses on coping styles enabling the child to work through stress. Janis (1958) has highlighted work of "worrying" as realistic working through of stressful events and Lindemann (1944) described work of 'grieving' leading to successful negotiation of bereavement.

Post traumatic stress disorder (PTSD) is an exclusive syndrome related to stress, as manifested in dreams, art work reflecting the stress and reliving the events reflecting stressful events man-made or otherwise. Reactions of children to higher degree of stress are varied, and range from mild and transient to acute psychopathology, at the core of which is overwhelming anxiety. As the child grows older, the clusters grow larger and more complex (Anthony, 1988).

The first three models have limited application, and all the models described only segmentally explain stress and response to stress especially in children and adolescents. There is a need for an integrated approach to view stress from holistic and longitudinal perspectives.

Emerging Trends in the Developed Nations

There are three broad approaches to the study of relationship of stressful life events and psychiatric illness.

(a) Chronic adversity;
(b) circumscribed stressful events; and
(c) the contention that stressors are additive in their effects especially in children.

Studies in the earlier two decades focused more on children who were exposed to markedly adverse circumstances of family life and deprived psychosocial conditions which led to the concept of *child-at-risk* (Anthony & Koupernik, 1974; Madge, 1982). More recently, research has been carried out on the effects of recent life events on psychiatric disorders (Goodyer, Kolvin and Gatezanis, 1985, 1986). Recent life events scales, based on adult versions have been used, with nonpsychotic disorders such as conduct, emotion (mild and severe) and somatic groups. When compared to the controls, the psychiatric groups had significantly excessive events with negative impact. They suggested that the nature of events may affect different disorders in a varied fashion. They also studied the nature of timing of onset of illness and stressors, and suggested that multiple events had closer temporal link with onset than single events, ranging from 4 to 16 weeks for multiple events. The Goodyer studies used Paykels' criteria of *independence* of the event from the psychiatric problems and *objective* negative *impact*, and concluded that stressful events increased the risk for psychiatric disorders. They exert long-term, short-term and rapid effects to some extent, dependent on the number of events, and that there was additivity in some cases, of principally increasing the likelihood of a short-term effect. Goodyer *et al.* (1965) have also highlighted the advantage of obtaining personal appraisal of stressors from the children.

It is thus, necessary to examine whether life events have different aetiological relationship in childhood disorders in comparison to adult disorders. McFarlane's (1988) prospective study of primary school children following a natural disaster of devastating bushfires in Australia, sheds some light on the nature of this relationship. It suggested that role of stressful life events in emotional and behavioural problems may neither be mechanically additive nor an all-or-none effect. The findings suggested that the children whose parents were psychologically distressed were more likely to be adversely affected by the disaster, than as a direct impact of the disaster. Thus, rather than the nature of the disaster, the implications of it on the child's immediate family were of concern. The conventional life events scales fail to take into account of these complex interactions of the stressful events, the children and their families.

Garmezy and Rutter (1983), Compas (1987) and other investigators have suggested crucial links between experiencing distressing events and adjustment. Rossman (1992) studied the perception of stressful events and what they did to feel better, in a sample of six to twelve year olds. The coping strategies were of seeking social support of caregivers and peers, distraction, avoidance, calming oneself, and expression of anger and distress. Age and gender differences were found in coping responses.

Self appraisal of stressful events in fifteen year olds was studied by McGee and Stanton (1992) provides insight into the sources of distress in adolescents. Four types of stressful life circumstances were elicited, i.e., problems of self-image and independence, academic and physical competence, moving of residence and school. Girls reported higher levels of distress. Distress was associated with poor family and social support, maternal depression and parental separation. Poor social competence and high distress were independent and additive predictors of mental health disorders. To quote Robbie Rossman's (1992) succinct statement, that the impact of most of the studies is reduced in several ways : *conceptually* — by not taking into account of the potential primacy of emotional regulation piece of coping task for children; *methodologically*, by the absence of instruments to assess general coping strategies; *developmentally*, by the lack of serious attempts to view coping within one age group as possible progression of previously developed schemes; and *strategically* by not examining the coping — adjustment link, at different levels of stress.

Rutter (1983) has emphasized that in considering stressful stimuli, individual differences are crucial. The elements involved in these individual differences include personal characteristics, vulnerability and protective factors, the individuals' cognitive appraisal of the event and his process of coping with it. Vulnerability factors may increase the stress, whether they are acute in nature or occur against a background of chronic psychosocial adversity. Thus, a fit or mismatch between the temperament and adversity is an important dimension of stress research.

Indian Studies in Community and Clinic Setting

Community Settings

Kapur (1990) in a study of 150 normal rural and semi-urban pre-school children elicited certain emotions and responses to situations in the child's daily life. Rural children felt sad when no food was given, while their semi-urban counterparts felt sad when they were beaten up, scolded or their demands were not met. Majority of them responded by crying or keeping quiet. The children feared animals, insects, strangers and punishment by parents. Rural children responded by avoiding the situations and coming home while semi-urban children became quiet or cried. Anger was provoked when they were beaten or were denied something. The rural children responded by being quiet, whereas semi-urban boys hit back; girls in general became quiet or threw temper tantrums. This study made use of mostly mothers' observation of the children. According to the mothers, expression of happiness shown was by jumping, smiling, kissing and hugging in these pre-schoolers. The parents belonged to low social economic strata, with stable rural families. The children were screened for malnutrition. In this predominantly rural community, these stable though poor families protected their children from adult pre-occupation with stressors. This study highlighted the need to observe nature of emotional responsiveness to the various situations, in the very young children and how the information can be elicited from the mothers.

In an epidemiological study of 1,535 school going, five to eight year olds from middle class urban background, Shenoy (1992) studied a sample of 164 disturbed children and 171 normal children, and reported chronic stressors in the disturbed group. These stressors consisted of alcoholism in the fathers, and neuroticism in the mothers. The fathers were often indifferent while the mothers were hostile rejecting or overprotective or overambitious. In addition, the siblings were hostile and the disturbed children had difficulties with the peers. The study suggested that chronic stressors at home and with peers had significant association with psychiatric problems.

From an epidemiological survey of 408 urban middle class 8 to 11 year old school children, the effects of recent life events were studied on 18 psychiatrically disturbed and matched sample of 18 normal children (Sarkar, 1990). She reported the number of stressful events in the past one year being significantly larger in the disturbed children. There were significant correlations between stressful life events, behaviour problems and adjustment. Academic problems were present in 60 per cent, of poor acceptance by the peers in 50 per cent, illness or operation in 40 per cent, and change of residence was reported with equal frequency in both the groups.

In an epidemiological study of 663 adolescent girls, Dalal (1989) in a group of 79 disturbed girls found the number of stressful events to be significantly higher when compared to a control group of 78 non-disturbed girls. The checklist of 20 developmental and 20 non-developmental stressors were equally high in the disturbed groups. This group of adolescent girls from middle class background showed little preoccupation with heterosexual matters or sexual pre-occupations.

Arulmani (1989) in a study of 15 disturbed and 15 competent adolescent boys from extremely impoverished background, found both the groups to have equal number of stressors in most of the areas. However, the disturbed adolescents had higher stressors in interpersonal relationships and pertaining to self. Coping behaviour patterns of the competent adolescents had high flexibility and they had larger reportoires of coping responses. Their coping styles included seeking social support, self control, accepting responsibility, planned problem solving and positive self appraisal. The disturbed adolescents used escape avoidance as the main coping response. The study appeared to suggest that a healthy family matrix was essential for effective coping even under extreme adverse circumstances.

Studies in Clinic Settings

Sonpar (1982) studied 40 non-psychotic psychiatrically disturbed and 40 normal controls, divided equally, into early and late adolescent groups, from urban middle class, on the Vincent and Rosenstock modification of Coddington Scales. She found that the greater number of stressful events in the disturbed adolescents was more of daily hassles than major events. Early adolescent boys had significantly higher number of stressful events than girls, while girls had significant history of anxious personality. Thus, the interplay of temperament and stressful life events proved to be an important ingredient of psychopathology in adolescence.

Malhotra, Kaur and Nehra (1992) in a study of 80 psychiatrically disturbed and 100 normal children in the age range of 4-14 years, using Monagham modification of Coddington Scale found the psychiatrically disturbed had significantly higher stress scores though the number of recent life events was somewhat similar in both groups. However, the younger children showed higher association between number of life events and disturbance. In addition, normal children showed significant increase in the number of life events and stress scores with increasing age. The study suggested closer association between psychiatric illness and recent life events in the younger age than in older age groups.

A study by Rangaswamy and Kamakshi (1983) of 30 adolescent hysterics in the age range of 13 to 17 years, using Coddington Scale, reported that 88 per cent of the hysterics had significant life stress before the onset. The onset was preceded by unpleasant personal experiences, impersonal life events and school problems. In these 30 adolescents, in 13 per cent there was death of parents, and in the other 13 per cent hospitalization while breaking up of friendship was present, not being allowed to participate in extracurricular activities by the parents in 23 per cent, and increased arguments between the parents in 10 per cent. Kaur (1987) found similar trend in somatoform disorders. Uma (1988) in a clinical group of 70 hysteric children in the age range of 8 to 12 years, reported that stressors had a significant role to play in precipitating hysterical symptoms. The precipitating home events were parental quarrells, and punishment or scolding by the relatives. It was observed that though the events were not severe by themselves, but they were experienced for the first time by the children. Precipitating events at school were change of school, punishment by the teachers, fights with peers and stress of academic work. The third group of stressors consisted of fearful experiences when the child was alone, such as 'seeing ghosts', skeletons, dead bodies and feeling of being pushed — when no one was around (these, interestingly, are culturally acceptable precipitants for such responses). In addition, fearful experience with strangers or mentally ill person and sexual assault or conflicts also have been encountered especially in adolescents (Ninan & Kapur, 1989). Chronic stressors have been reported to be significantly high in school, and in the family context being disciplinary-styles, discordant relationships, overinvolvement, anomalous family situations and mental disturbance in the family. Thus, in the Indian clinical settings, there is a strong association between stressful recent life events and onset of hysterical and somatoform symptoms.

Daniel (1989) studied the psychosocial stressors in 33 conduct disordered, 33 with mixed disorders of conduct and emotion, and 33 emotion disordered 8 to 12 year old children, and compared them to those of normal controls. There was significant marital disharmony in the parents of the three clinic groups. Parents of the conduct disordered were hostile and rejecting, while the parents of the emotion disordered, and those with mixed disorder of emotion and conduct, were overprotective. High sibling rivalry was present in all the three groups, more so in the conduct disordered group. Peer interaction was especially in the emotion disordered but not in the other three groups. These findings are similar to those found in the western literature.

The above studies highlight the need to explore the nature of association between chronic stressors, recent life events and specific syndromes. This may lead to better understanding of role of stress in each of these disorders. These need to be carried out in groups belonging to urban or rural population, with varied socio-economic backgrounds, caste and religion. The dimension of resilience and competencies in children especially with disadvantageous backgrounds is necessary. Obviously, the research should span across ages, gender, and ideally be longitudinal in nature.

Methodological Implications

Tools of Assessment

Some stressors may be common across cultures and may be age, gender and ethnospecific. Conventional tools of assessment such as Coddington Scale and the modified versions developed in the west, and are specially downward extension of tools in use with adults, are of limited value. Ideally, ethnographic methods should form the basis of construction of the tools. Listing of items and judging their severity by the experts is an acceptable technique of tool construction. Yet in the study of stress, subjective appraisal of stress has greater significance than opinion of the experts.

Developmental Context

The stages of physical, cognitive, language, emotional, social, moral and sexual development, determine what the stressors are and whether these are perceived by the child or the adolescent as stressors.

(a) Stress in infancy and preschool years: From the time of conception an infant is subjected to experiences which may be considered as stressful, especially the developmental milestones and tasks. Yet, these are critical to negotiating the necessary developmental stages. Starvation or chronic illness may result in significant developmental lag. Events potentially stressful such as having peers or school entry may help in the well-being and development. For example, defensive responses such as crying, social withdrawal characterized by listlessness, and poor interaction with caretakers can occur in response to extreme forms of child abuse. Whether these behaviour repertoires persist at later stages needs to be studied. Kagan (1983) asserted that stress must be viewed as interaction between "want and response", and cannot be studied in isolation. At present there is substantial literature to show that enduring difficulties do exert unwanted effects on infants (Rutter, 1983). The children whose mothers could not nurture their children as they had psychiatric or personality disorders, could not provide an environment for normal development (Ghodsian *et al.*, 1984; Richman, 1977; Pound *et al.*, 1985). Resilience in the young infants is shown by the evidence that the stressors have to be chronic and long lasting, and also that children respond with rapid recovery when adverse conditions are replaced with congenial ones.

(b) Stress in middle childhood: In the middle childhood the family continues to protect children from stress or being cause of stress. The developmental tasks of these age groups are different from those of early childhood. Goodyer (1988) describes them under the three categories i.e., peer relations, cognitive development and behavioural response to stress. Increasing number of peer relations provides the child with more life events within school along with social and play activities. These could be self esteem-enhancing or stressful. Cognitive development enhances the exploration of the world, which may lead to mastery or personal failure. Unlike the young children who evoke care-eliciting responses, middle childhood children show affective responses such as sadness, misery and anger, or

behavioural responses such as disruptiveness or school refusal, in response to stress.

(c) Stress in adolescence: Increasing social development leads to widening social network and decreases the time spent at home. Responses to stressful events may be likely to be more personal, and may be perceived more differently than of the parents. Recent research appears to suggest that adolescents may more reliably report stressors than their mothers (Moncke & Dobbs, 1985). Sexual events often may be reported by only the adolescents and not by the others. Protective nurturing may be essential to an infant, but may be totally undesirabe for an adolescent. Confiding relationship of the young child with the mother yields to confiding relationship with a friend in an adolescent.

Some of the areas studied extensively in the field of stress in the West are divorce, birth of sibling and bereavement. In India, these priorities are yet to clearly emerge.

Stress and Coping

Dimensions of coping behaviour too need to be studied from a developmental perspective, as described in the previous section. The coping could be at an emotional or cognitive or at a social support-seeking level. Emotional responsiveness grows out of simple reflexes to simple association and to the emergence of planful emotional responsive behaviour, by the age of two or three years. Kopp (1989) described five types of behaviour i.e., visual or physical avoidance, distraction, self-soothing, problem-oriented behaviour and care-eliciting behaviour. Campas *et al.* (1988) described emotion focused and problem focused behaviours and found them to be variable. Problem solving may increase with age and strategies to control distress may increase in importance and number during school age.

A coping style which may be effective at one age may be totally unsuitable at another age. A particular style of coping may be totally appropriate in one situation while being wholly inappropriate in another. Flexibility and situation appropriateness of effective coping need to be explored. This may be determined, to a large part by the cultural expectations. On the other hand, individual vulnerabilities set limits to one's coping, effective or otherwise.

Robbie Rossman (1992) highlights the need to have non domain-specific, empirically derived self report inventory to study the coping behaviour. The coping behaviour may be determined by temperamental predisposition, past experiences and specific circumstances.

Stress and Temperament

Study of competency and resiliency rests not only on the coping styles but the basic temperamental characteristics from which they emerge. Temperament and child rearing practices in the infancy continually influence each other.

McCall synthesized the approaches to the concept of temperament as follows :

> "Temperament consists of relatively consistent, basic dispositions inherent in the person, that underlie and modulate the expression of activity, reactivity, emotionality and sociability. Major elements of temperament are present in early life, and those elements are likely to be strongly influenced by biological factors. As development proceeds, the expression of temperament increasingly becomes more influenced by experience and context" (cf. Goldsmith *et al.*, 1987).

The studies of temperament in the Indian setting so far have made use of the framework suggested by Thomas and Chess. Malhotra *et al.* (1986) in their study of 100 normal and 100 psychiatrically disturbed children found that the model was equally applicable with minor modifications and arrived at 5 factors. Daniel (1989) and Shenoy (1992) used the same model to relate temperament to externalizing and internalizing disorders and found significant association between the disorders and certain temperamental traits. However, there are studies which report significant cross-cultural differences in temperament.

Several of the ancient Indian texts classify the adult personality traits, based on "trigunas" i.e., Satvik, Rajasik and Tamasik temperaments. These are considered to be innate predispositions which are traced not only to infancy, but beyond it, to previous birth. It is possible to interpolate and view the temperamental traits as being present at birth, without invoking the concept of "karma" attributed to previous births.

It is interesting to look at these traits against the backdrop of western research on temperament. The three dimensions are described as being different, in sleeping and eating proclivities with Tamasiks characterized by excessive indulgence, Rajasiks by discriminatory or fussy eating; while the Satviks by moderation and with control of sleeping and eating functions. Tamasiks are described as low in activity, low in sociability, with lack of concern for others and with cruel disposition, with need for immediate gratification, and have persistent negative moods of fear and depression; they lack the ability to discriminate between good and bad and right and wrong. The Rajasiks are characterized by high activity, persistence, and are too sensitive and volatile in their emotionality; they have an overriding need to socialize because of their need for recognition of their achievements, material or otherwise; they also indulge in fantasy.

While the Tamasik and Rajasik temperamental styles are similar to the dimensions described by the Western researchers, the Satvik dimension stands out alone. Satvik temperament is characterized by activity, emotionality, sociability, is moderated by cognitive and emotional control, and can be an 'ideal' temperament. Rajasik temperament can be considered to be ideally suited for materialistic cultures. The Satvik temperament represents a hardworking, altruistic person with efficient control of cognition and emotionality, and is considered as an ideal model in the Hindu ethos. In the context of current emphasis on the study of positive mental health, 'invulnerable', 'competent' or 'hardy' children, the Satvik framework is an eminently suitable model. It shows that temperamental dimensions could be extended to include such positive dimensions. This Indian model consists of 8 psychosocial and 9 biosocial dimensions. The biosocial dimensions were very similar with the western temperamental dimensions (Kapur, 1995).

Stress and Social Support

The effects of stress may be attenuated by family and social supports. The evidence that young children respond to stress with distress, leading to emotional or behavioural problems, makes it crucial to study the nature of social support, particularly in the family contexts and with the peer group. Aspects of traditional child rearing practices which offer social support need to be conserved. The western concept of social support appears to be unidirectional in practice even with children and adolescents and thus is simplistic for example, the social support in the peer group. The support giver and the recipient often change their roles depending on the situation. A competent, a resilient child or adolescent is characterized by their give-and-take relationship. Thus, being 'dependent' is culturally acceptable, and it is equally important in the Indian ethos to be "interdependent" and "dependable". Thus, social support is "situation specific", mutual and not unidirectional. It is not a "contract" of the kind practiced in the western cultures. It has strong affinity with altruistic mode of life. Thus, a child who seeks help, can also help a friend and take care of his parents when they are in need of it, cannot being considered a "parental" child, (a term with pathological connotation). This aspect of social support in consonance with Satvik temperament, and is the very essence of mental health or well being or competency.

Policy Perspectives

(i) Stress is a part of human existence and hence cannot be predicted or totally eliminated. Thus focus should be on research into area where it is possible to alleviate distress.

(ii) In the community, the focus should be on obtaining normative culture-specific data of the families of the very young, and the coping styles of the older children and adolescents. But eventually the material gathered can be used for public education.

(iii) In the clinical settings the research should lead to planning of effective intervention strategies in different clinical groups.

(iv) In the community, with at-risk populations, such as slum or street children, institutionalised or working children, the research should be interventive. It is unethical to sensitize such a vulnerable population to its miseries and not do anything to alleviate distress. Research for the sake of research should be discouraged. Interventive research is a must for the developing countires.

To sum up, stress research in childhood and adolescence needs to be viewed from a developmental context, is interactional in nature, is to be studied across ages, gender and ethnic groups, preferably from a longitudinal perspective with effective use of ethnographic methods. Unfortunately, the research in India has been cross-sectional, static and based on western tools of assessment of the adult mould, wherin aspects of individual vulnerability, social support, styles of coping are sadly neglected. Interventive research is needed, especially in the developing countries.

REFERENCES

Anthony, J.E. (1988). The response to overwhelming stress in children : Some introductory comments. In J.E. Anthony, & C. Chiland, (Eds.) The child in his family. *Perilous Development: Child Raising and Identity Formation Under Stress.* (Vol. 8) 3-16. New York: Wiley.

Anthony, E.J., & Koupernick, C. (1974). (Eds.) *The Child and His Family: Children at Psychiatric Risk.* New York: Wiley.

Arulmani, G. (1989). *Patterns of Coping with Psychosocial*

stressors Among Indian Adolescents. Unpublished M.Phil thesis. Bangalore University. Bangalore. India.

Campbell. A.. Converse. P.E.. & Rodgers. W.L.. (1976). *The Quality of American Life.* New York: Russel Sage Foundation.

Caplan. G. (1976). The family as a support system. In G. Caplan. & M. Kallilea. (Eds.). *Support Systems and Mutual Help : Multidisciplinary Explorations* (pp. 19-36). New York: Grune & Stratton.

Cohen. F.. & Lazarus. R.S. (1973). Active coping processes. coping dispositions and recovery from surgery. *Psychosomatic Medicine. 35.* 375-389.

Compas. B.E. (1987). Coping with stress during childhood and adolescence. *Psychological Bulletin. 101.* 393-403.

Compas. B.E.. Malcarne. V.L.. & Fondacaro. K.M. (1988). Coping with stressful events in older children and young adolescents. *Journal of Consulting and Clinical Psychology. 56.* 405-411.

Dalal. M. (1989). *Prevalence and pattern of psychological disturbance in school going early adolescent girls.* Unpublished M.Phil. Bangalore University. Bangalore India.

Daniel. E. (1989). *Study of disorders of emotion and conduct.* Unpublished doctoral dissertation. Bangalore University. Bangalore. India.

Gargmezy. N.. & Rutter M. (1983). *Stess. Coping and Development in Children.* New York: McGraw-Hill.

Gohdsian. M.. Zajicek. E.. & Wolkind. S. (1984). A longitudinal study of maternal depression and childhood behavior problems. *Journal of Child Psychology and Psychiatry. 25.* 97-109.

Goldsmith. H.H.. Buss. A.H.. Plomin. R.. Rothbart. M.K.. Thomas. A.. Chess. S.. Hinde. R.A.. & McCall. R.B. (1987). Round table: What is temperament: Four approaches. *Child Development. 58.* 505-529.

Goodyer. I.. Kolvin. I.. & Gatzanis. S. (1985). Recent undesirable life events and psychiatric disorder in childhood and adolescence. *British Journal of Psychiatry. 147.* 517-523.

Goodyer. I.. Kolvin. I.. & Gatzanis. S. (1986). Do age and sex influence the association between recent life events and psychiatric disorders in children and adolescents? A controlled enquiry. *Journal of Child Psychology and Psychiatry. 27.* 681-697.

Goodyer. I.M. (1988). Stress in childhood and adolescence. In F. Fisher. & J. Reason. (Eds.). *Handbook of Life Stress. Cognition and Health.* New York: Wiley.

Janis. I. (1958). *Psychological stress.* New York: Wiley.

Kagan. J. (1983). Stress and coping in early development. In N. Garmezy & M. Rutter (Eds). *Stress. Coping and Development in Children.* New York: McGraw-Hill.

Kapur. M. (1990). *Early childhood stimulation and optimum mental development.* Unpublished data. WHO- NIMHANS Project.

Kapur. M. (1995). *Mental Health of Indian Children.* New Delhi: Sage.

Kapoor. M. (1997). *Mental Health in Indian Schools.*New Delhi Sage.

Kaur. S. (1987). *A clinical study of somatoform disorders in children.* Unpublished M.D. thesis. Postgraduate Indstitute of Medical Education and Research. Chandigarh.

Kopp. C.B. (1989). Regulation of distress and negative emotions: A developmental view. *Developmental Psychology. 25.* 343-354.

Lindemann. E. (1944). Symptomatology and management of acute grief. *American Journal of Psychiatry. 101.* 141-148.

Madge. N. (1982) (Ed.). *Families at Risk.* London: Heinemann Medical Books.

Malhotra S.. Varma. V.K.. & Verma. S.K. (1986). Temperament as determinant of phenomenology of childhood psychiatric disorders. *Indian Journal of Psychiatry. 28.* 263-276.

Malhotra. S.. Kaur. R.. & Nehra. R. (1992). Life events in psychiatrically sick children. *Indian Journal of Psychiatry. 34.* 222-230.

McFarlane. A.C. (1987). Life events and psychiatric disorder: The role of a natural disaster. *British Journal of Psychiatry. 151.* 362-367.

McFarlane. A.C. (1988). Recent life events and psychiatric disorder in children: The interaction with preceding extreme adversity. *Journal of Child Psychology and Psychiatry. 29.* 677-690.

McGee. R.. & Stanton. W.R. (1992). Sources of distress among New Zealander adolescents. *Journal of Child Psychology and Psychiatry. 33.* 999-1010.

Moncke. E.. & Dobbs. R. (1985). Measuring life events in an adolescent population : Methodological issues and related findings. *Psychological Medicine. 15.* 841-850.

Ninan. T.. & Kapur. M. (1981). A study of hysteria in early adolescence. *NIMHANS Journal. 7.* 43-48.

Pound. A.. Cox. A.D.. Puckering. C.. & Mills. M. (1985). The impact of maternal depression on young children. In J.E. Stevenson (Ed.). *Recent Research in developmental psychopathology*. Oxford: Pergamon.

Rangaswami, K., & Kamakshi, G. (1983). Life events in hysterical adolescents. *Child Psychiatry Quarterly, 15*, 26-33.

Richman, N. (1977). Behavior problems in preschool children: Family and social factors. *British Journal of Psychiatry, 131*, 523-527.

Robbie Rossman, B.B. (1992). School-age children's perceptions of coping with distress: Strategies for emotion regulation and the moderation of adjustment. *Journal of Child Psychology and Psychiatry, 33*, 1373-1397.

Rotter, J.B. (1966). Generalized expectancies for internal versus external control of reinforcement. *Psychological Monographs, 80*, 609.

Rutter, M. (1983). Stress, coping and development : Some issues and some questions. In N. Garmezy & M. Rutter (Eds.). *Stress, Coping and Development in Children*. New York: McGraw-Hill.

Sarkar, A. (1990). *Prevalence and pattern of psychological disturbances in 8-11 year old school going children*. Unpublished M.Phil. dissertation, Bangalore University, Bangalore, India.

Sandman, C.C. (1972). Psychophysiological parameters of emotional expression. *Dissertation Abstracts International, 33*, 2356-2357.

Saxena, S., & Mohan, D. (1982). Life event research : A review of methodology (with special reference to India). *Indian Journal of Psychiatry, 24*, 322-328.

Schmale, A.H. (1972). Giving up as a final common pathway to changes in health. *Advances in Psychosomatic Medicine, 8*, 20-40.

Sharma, S. (1988). Stress and anxiety. In J. Pandey (Ed.). *Psychology in India. The State-of-the-Art*. Vol. 1 (pp. 191-248). New Delhi: Sage Publications.

Shenoy, J. (1992). *Psychological disturbances in 5-8 year old school going children*. Unpublished doctoral dissertation, Bangalore University, Bangalore, India.

Sonpar, S. (1982). *Psychopathology of adolescence*. Unpublished doctoral dissertation, Bangalore University, Bangalore, India.

Uma, H. (1988). *Study of childhood hysteria*. Unpublished doctoral dissertation, Bangalore University, Bangalore, India.

14

Problem Behaviour in Primary School Children

NEELAM SOOD and GIRISHWAR MISRA

Problem behaviour is commonly seen in children. Studies and surveys of children's and parents' perceptions of problem behaviours show that a large number of children who are generally considered normal often evince disturbed behaviours, such as tantrums, destructiveness, fearfulness, and hyperactivity to some degree at times during their growing years. Such behaviours may evoke varied reactions in adults, ranging from confusion, worry, embarrassment, fear or even repulsion. In a given socio-cultural setting, adults may find these behaviours as not normal, atypical, strange or more often than not as annoying because they carry with themselves their own set of norms or standards with which they evaluate the appropriateness of child behaviour. How are these norms formed against which we render judgemental decisions about normality or abnormality and how realistic are these judgements? How do children develop such behaviour patterns and what are the underlying processes that maintain them? How and when the behaviour of children is conceptualised as problem behaviour? These are important issues that emerge in understanding problem behaviour among children. This chapter discusses some of these issues. Further, it seeks to understand the contextual variables that contribute in predicting the incidence of problem behaviour and reports the psycho-social correlates of problem behaviour based on an empirical analysis.

Identifying and defining disordered behaviour is a complex matter that depends on many factors. Since normal and abnormal behaviours are considered to be on a continuum, any child may be more or less problematic only with regard to particular characteristics. It is a matter of degree. Further, because the criteria for defining disordered behaviour are mainly social, these are always relative, and are also likely to change over a period of time. These may vary according to the particular society/culture, family, setting, age and sex of the child in question, or the evaluating agent etc.

Adults' judgements about child behaviour problems can differ markedly as a function of their cultural context. This is illustrated in a study that compared adults in the United States and Thailand, two countries where social values and perspectives on childhood differ markedly (Weisz *et al.*, 1988). Thais, compared with Americans rated both over-and under controlled problem patterns as less serious, less worrisome to a parent and/teacher, more likely to improve with time and less unusual. These findings appear to be consistent with the core teachings of Thai Buddhism which proposes that everyone experiences unhappiness, every condition changes and that an individual's behaviour does not reflect enduring personality. Thais may have therefore rated seriousness and worrisomeness relatively low in part because they were more confident than were Americans that the problems would improve over time.

The families also set different behavioural standards. In an interesting study, two groups of New York City families: well educated, middle class and working class Puerto Rican families were compared (Korn & Gannon, 1983). For their five year old sons the middle class families reported two and a half times as many problems as the Puerto Rican families. The kind of problems reported differed in the two groups of families. They seemed related to sub-cultural values and child management practices. Many more middle class than Puerto Rican families set a standard bedtime and did not allow their children to take a bottle to bed with them. They also reported more sleep problems. In contrast, Puerto Rican families placed high value on 'good' behaviour, disciplined their children more severely, and reported more discipline problems.

Socio-cultural norms depend on other contextual variables. One of these is the social setting. Energetic running may be acceptable in the playground but would create havoc in the classroom. Children are expected to act in certain ways in certain situations, to meet the situational norms. Norms are also specified according to the sex and the age of the children. In most societies males are expected to be relatively more aggressive, dominant, active and adventurous; females to be more passive, dependent, quiet and sensitive. These gender stereotypes strongly guide judgements about normality. Developmental norms are also important. For instance, temper tantrums in a three-year-old are less likely to be labeled a problem than in a seven-year-old. Several other factors may be considered in evaluating children's behaviours. Behaviours that meet age norms may still be judged as disturbed if they occur too frequently or are too intense or insufficiently intense or endure over too long or too short a period of time. It is not unusual for a child to display fear, but fearfulness may be a problem if it occurs in an excessive number of situations, is extremely intense and does not weaken over time.

The socio-cultural norms do change over time due to broad social changes in ideas about mental health, e.g. nail biting once seen as a sign of degeneration, is now considered quite harmless. Finally, the subjective feelings of others play a role in identifying problem behaviours. Since childhood disorders are often identified by adults, adult attitudes, sensitivity, tolerance and ability to cope are bound to influence how children are perceived.

Research on Problem Behaviour: An Overview

Research output in this area has been derived mainly from the analysis of clinical data. There is a dearth of studies on problem behaviour as seen in general population. Child psychiatry has remained largely a neglected field in psychiatric research. Prabhu (1980) in his review highlighted the need for meaningful, relevant and theory-based research and for longitudinal studies. Sitholey (1992), observed that though the facilities for child mental health care have gradually expanded during the last few decades, the hopes raised by the ICMR task force recommendations (1980) were yet to be fulfilled.

Some of the salient trends that can be discerned from the review of available research on problem behaviour in children are summarized here.

Most of the studies report a high prevalence rate of behaviour disorders. These ranged between 6 to 10 per cent (Achenback & Edelbrock, 1981; Grahm, 1979; Rutter, Tizard, Yule, Grahm & Whitmore, 1976). Bower (1981) estimated that about 10 per cent of school age children are emotionally handicapped. The extensive Isle of Wight study indicated that 6.8 per cent of 10-11 years old were reported as needing clinical services (Rutter, 1989). From a review of studies Cotler (1986) estimated that in middle childhood about 7 per cent of all children exhibit severe to moderate disorders and about 15 per cent show mild problems. Another review reported 14 to 20 per cent as an estimate of moderate to severe disorders in children and adolescents (Bradenburg, Friendman & Silver, 1990).

Clinic-based studies report a broader range in prevalence estimates of behaviour disorders in children. These have been reported to be ranging between 1.99 per cent (Malhotra & Chadha, 1987), 3.3 per cent (Malhotra & Chaturvedi, 1984), 4.6 per cent (Singh & Gupta, 1970), 9 per cent (ICMR, 1983), 16.9 per cent (Dagar & Singh, 1981) to as high as 33 per cent (Murthy *et al.*, 1974). An earlier study had reported the same to be as high as 36 per cent (Bassa, 1962).

Almost all studies report a higher prevalence rate of problem behaviour in boys (Rubin & Balow, 1978; Werry & Quay, 1977). Incidence of conduct disorders like aggression, dislike for school, attention demanding behaviour and restlessness have been reported to be higher among boys (Banik, 1972). Incidence of such problems such as overactivity, attention demanding behaviour, temper tantrums and lying has been reported to be significantly higher among boys while problems such as excessive modesty, shyness and fears were found to be more common among girls.

Definite trends are not discernible with regard to association between age and incidence of problem behaviour among children. Many studies have reported declining trends in problem behaviour with increase in chronological age (Dagar & Singh, 1981; Werry & Quay, 1977). Muralidharan (1973) reported that problems such as sleeping and eating difficulties, habit disorders, aggression and delinquent behaviour decrease with age.

Interesting findings that deal with differences related to sibling order have been reported in some studies. For example, in an investigation, withdrawal and internalization patterns of adjustment were more common among first-born boys in contrast to more aggressive and competitive patterns of adjustment among non-first-born boys. Among the four sibling groups studied, the first-born girls manifested more problems and evinced the most conflicting modes of adjustment. Dagar and Singh (1981) reported that first-born and last-born children in the family were more prone to develop behaviour problems as compared to children at mid-ordinal positions. Very little difference in the incidence of behaviour deviations has been reported between only children and children with siblings.

Some studies also report incidence of other problems in the children who manifest disordered behaviour (e.g. difficulty in visuo-motor coordination, visuo-motor perception in hyperactive children) indicating the possibility that behaviour disorders occur in combination with other problems or many problems can occur together (Chawla, Sahasi, Sunderam & Mehta, 1981).

It has been noted that the results of the clinic-based studies vary a great deal with regard to the type of problem behaviour reported. Evidently, this depends upon the setting in which the particular clinic is functioning. In any case, the findings from clinic-based studies can not be generalized for the general population. Paucity of the studies done in the general population also becomes quite evident while scanning the available research evidence.

Another important observation on the studies conducted so far is with regard to age-range of the children studied. Age differences are either not studied (Banik, 1972) or children of various ages are combined under a very broad group as 0-12 years (Verghese *et al.*, 1973). Use of broad age group is likely to camouflage age trends in the problem behaviour under study. The studies where age differences have been taken into account, dealt with only one or two problems like enuresis or hyperactivity etc. As children grow and move through various stages over the years, changes that occur in them are phenomenal. Physically, intellectually, socially and emotionally, the variations are legion. Behaviour disorders of chidren therefore, must be viewed in relation to their ages and developmental stages. In his recent review of child psychiatric research in India, Sitholey (1992) has pointed out that "the entire group of children has been considered as a whole" (p. 49). As such, it is necessary to study various groups of children such as pre-schoolers, primary school children and adolescents etc. separately. Further, age differences must be studied by comparing children in a single year age group for each problem under study, separately.

It is believed that the early years of school attendance, ages 6 to 10 years are the most common period of onset reported for all childhood behaviour problems. Also, as we know, many behaviour problems can occur together in children, the research studies must be so planned that there is a built-in scope for tapping various types of problems. For this purpose, use of comprehensive measures is essential.

Incidence of Behaviour Problems and Its Correlates: An Empirical Analysis

The present study was formulated to assess the incidence of problem behaviour in the middle childhood i.e. the age group of 6-11 years. It was planned to examine the variation in problem behaviour as related to age and sex of the children. In addition the study also attempted to assess the home environment of the children and the disciplinary methods used by their parents. The social competence and intelligence of children were also measured. Association between problem behaviours and selected background variables describing parent and family characteristics (e.g., education and occupation of the parents, family income, size of the family, mother's employment, long absence of the father) was also examined. The manner in which the background and contextual variables contribute in predicting problem behaviour and social competence of the children was also investigated.

A sample of 375 children aged 6-11 years (*mean=8.40, SD=1.47*) was drawn from three public schools (co-educational) located in south Delhi. There were seventy five children in each of the five age groups included in the study i.e. 6-7, 7-8, 8-9, 9-10 and 10-11 years. The sample comprised 201 boys and 174 girls. The parents of these children also participated in the study.

The parents' age ranged between 21-52 years. The modal ages of fathers and mothers were 40 and 32 years, respectively. Fathers (99.2%) had education at graduation level or above. In case of mothers 48 per cent had education upto matriculation level. Rest of them were educated above graduate level. Most of the fathers were professionals employed in private sector (63.6%) or Government sector (12.5%). About 20 per cent were entrepreneurs and the rest were non-professionals engaged in various fields such as farming, politics and social work etc. About 50 per cent of the mothers were employed. They generally spent about 8 hours out of home. A large number of families were nuclear (57.6%), the rest were either joint or extended (42.4%). Mean size of family was 5.4, but modal size was 4. Most of the families had a per person income as Rs. 2500 and above (55.2%), while 44.8 per cent had a monthly per person income below Rs. 2500.

Fathers of 44 children were absent for long from their

families, mainly due to their job demands (35) or other reasons such as death (7) or divorce (1) or mental illness (1). In 80 families, parental discord was reported, with parents having fights almost everyday (25), or once a week or so (55). In 28 families, it was reported, that there was no open disagreement ever between the parents.

Five measures were used to collect pertinent data about the parents, home environment, disciplinary methods used by the parents, problem behaviours, social competence and intelligence of the children.

Home Environment Scale. To assess the home environment of children a schedule based on home Observation of the Measurement of the Environment (HOME) (Caldwell's 1968) was used. The items were modified to suit the requirements of the study. The retest reliability was estimated at .82. Information was collected on 20 items pertaining to physical environment, intellective climate and affective climate of the home.

A schedule was designed to elicit informtion regarding the disciplinary methods used by the parent. The retest reliability was estimated at .81. The measure consisted of a set of 10 situations of the typ that are likely to occur in homes. The parent was asked to imagine himself/herself and the child in those situations and indiate the three most likely response that these situations would evoke.

Child Behaviour Checklist (CBCL), devised by Achenbach at the Deparment of Psychiatry, University of Vermont, U.S.A. was employed to study problem behaviour in children. This checklist has been successfully used in many studies (Achenbach, Verhulst, Baron & Althaus, 1987; Malhotra, 1984). Slight modifications were made in the measure to make it culturally relevant. the checklist used for the study consisted of 110 behaviour problem items. The items on CBCL were subsumed under the following ten sub scales: Schizoid or Anxious; Depressed; Uncommunicative; Obsessive-Compulsive; Somatic Complaints; Social Withdrawal; Hyperactive; Aggressive; Delinquent; and Other Problems.

Social competence was assessed on three sub-scales. These were activites scale, social scale and school scale.

Draw-A-Man Test was used to assess intelligence of children through their drawings adapted from Goodenough's technique by Phatak (1966). The scale has been revised (Phatak, 1984) and now provides separate norms for boys and girls of 2.5 to 16.5 years of age. It has 25 scoring points for major body parts and their proportions. Each child was given a sheet of paper and asked to make a full drawing of a man as best as he/she could, in the space provided. The drawings were then scored by assigning weightage as per the manual.

Incidence of Behaviour Problems

Total scores on Child Behaviour Checklist (CBCL), the measure of problem behaviour obtained for 110 items separately for boys and girls by each age-group are presented in Figure 14.1.

The incidence of problem behaviour was higher in the first two age groups, decreased in the middle age group and then increased again in subsequent age groups. This shows that the children in the age group of 8-9 years manifested least number of problems. Two peak points are seen at the age group 7-8 years and 10-11 years, with the former age group reporting the highest incidence. The overall trend in the incidence of problem behaviour in boys and girls is also somewhat similar i.e. there is first an increase in the incidence in the second age group i.e. 7-8 years, then decrease in the next one or two age groups and then an increase again in the last age group. The major difference however, between boys and girls is in the age groups where the problem behaviour was least. While the dip in the curve is seen at the middle age group i.e. 8-9 years in case of girls, the same is found to be in the next age group i.e. 9-10 years in case of boys (Fig.14.1).

The mean comparisons revealed that age differences were not significant. Sex differences were very clear. Girls reported lower incidence of problem behaviour than boys in all the age groups consistently. The analysis of total CBCL scores revealed significant main effect of sex ($F(1,365) = 7.35$, $p < .01$). Boys shared significantly greater

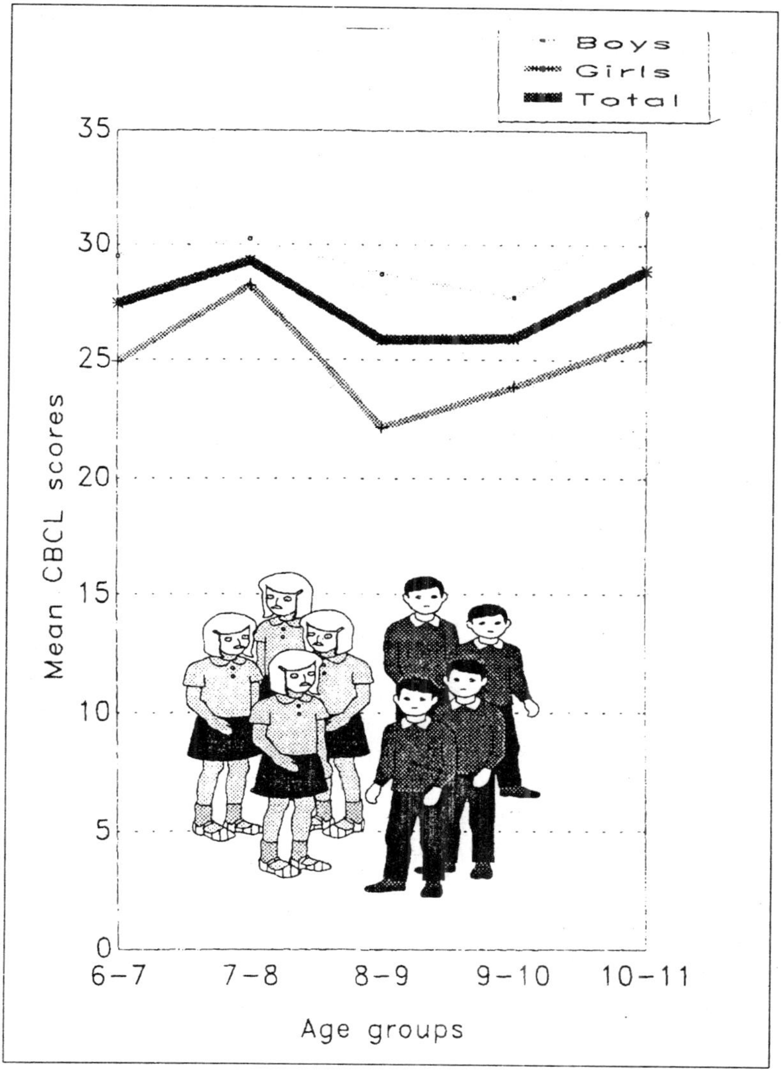

FIG. 14.1 : Total Problem Behaviour Scores
(By Age and Sex)

number of problems (*M=29.52, SD=16.61*) than girls (*M=25.02, SD=14.58*). The main effect of age as well as the interaction of age x sex did not reach significance level.

The frequency distributions of CBCL scores for both boys and girls were skewed towards the lower end as seen in Figures 14.2 and 14.3. Both boys and girls (almost 70%) had scores between 5 and 35. However, the major difference between boys and girls were with regard to the distribution of their scores on the extremes. There were fewer boys who obtained a score of less than 5 on CBCL (8%) as compared to girls (14%). The reverse was true with regard to the other end of the distribution. Twenty four per cent boys received a score higher than 35, while the corresponding percentage for girls was sixteen.

Age and Sex Differences

In all, there were twenty-three problems, where the difference between boys and girls was found to be significant. Out of these, boys had higher scores on twenty problems which were asthma, bragging, lack of concentration, hyperactivity, cruelty to animals, daydreaming, destroying own things, destroying others' things, accident-proneness, hanging around children who get in trouble, being impulsive, physical attack on people, poor school work, being clumsy, compulsions, strange behaviour, sleep walking/talking, excessive talk, teasing a lot, and being unusually loud.

The girls had higher scores on three problems which included need to be perfect, aches/pains without medical reasons and being too concerned with neatness.

As regards age differences, there were only thirteen problems where the difference was significant.

Six problems where an increase was noted with age were asthma, lack of concentration, nervousness, aches/ pains without medical reasons, screaming a lot, and speech problems.

Decline with age was noted in seven problems. These were bragging, crying a lot, accident proneness, feeling

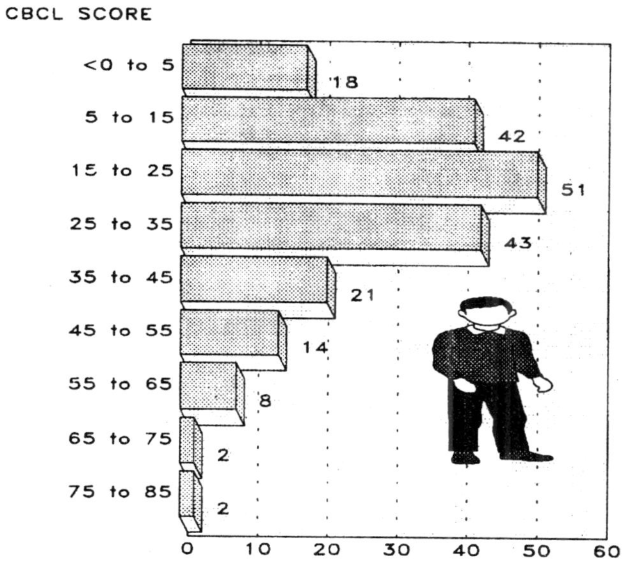

FIG. 14.2 : Frequency Distribution of CBCL Scores (Boys)

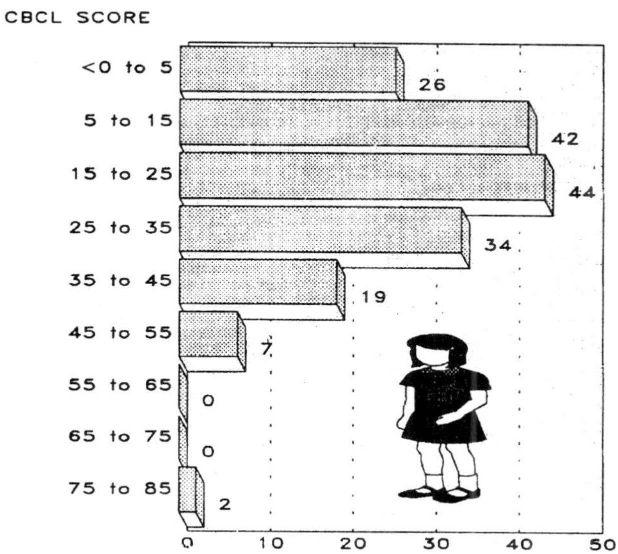

FIG. 14.3 : Frequency Distribution of CBCL Scores (Girls)

too guilty, overeating, being overweight and poor school work.

Out of 110 problems under study, 39 endorsed by parents in case of 125 or more children i.e. at least one-third or more of the sample (Table 14.1).

TABLE 14.1 : Problems Shown by One-third or More Children for Each Age Group and Sex

CBCL ITEMS	Age Groups (in years) 6-7		7-8		8-9		9-10		10-11	
	Boys N=41	Girls N=34	Boys N=39	Girls N=36	Boys N=40	Girls N=35	Boys N=40	Girls N=35	Boys N=41	Girls N=34
Acts too young				+						
Argues a lot	+	+	+	+	+	+	+	+	+	+
Bragging	+		+		+		+		+	
Can't concentrate	+	+	+	+	+	+	+	+	+	+
Obsession	+	+	+	+	+	+	+	+	+	
Hyperactive	+	+	+	+	+	+	+	+	+	+
Too dependent	+	+	+	+	+		+	+		
Lonely			+	+						
Cries a lot			+	+						
Demands attention	+	+	+	+	+	+	+	+	+	+
Destroys own things	+								+	
Disobedient	+		+	+	+	+	+	+	+	+
Doesn't eat well	+	+	+	+	+	+	+	+	+	+
Poor peer relations		+	+							
Lacks guilt	+		+			+				
Easily jealous	+		+	+			+			
Fears	+	+	+	+		+		+		+
Needs to be perfect	+	+	+	+	+		+	+	+	+
Feels unloved						+	+			
Feels persecuted		+								
Accident prone	+		+		+			+		
Hangs around with children who get in trouble					+					
Impulsive	+		+		+			+		
Likes to be alone	+	+								
Physical problems		+		+						
Prefers older children	+	+	+	+	+	+	+	+	+	+
Prefers younger children	+	+	+	+	+	+	+	+	+	+
Self-conscious	+	+	+	+	+			+	+	+
Shy or timid	+	+	+				+			
Sleeps little			+							

(*Contd.*)

TABLE 14.1 (*Contd.*)

Stores up unneeded things	+		+			+				+
Stubborn, sullen,or irritable	+	+	+	+	+	+	+	+	+	+
Moody	+	+	+	+	+	+	+	+	+	+
Sulks a lot	+		+				+			
Talks a lot	+	+	+	+	+	+	+	+	+	+
Teases a lot	+				+		+		+	
Temper tantrums			+	+			+		+	+
Too concerned with neatness or cleanliness	+	+	+	+	+	+	+	+	+	+
Unusually loud			+						+	

Looking at Table 14.1, one finds that there were certain problems which were endorsed by parents for both boys and girls for all age-groups. These included:

- To argue a lot
- Lack of concentration
- Hyperactivity
- Demanding a lot of attention
- Not eating well
- Need to be perfect
- To prefer playing with older children
- To prefer playing with younger children
- Being stubborn, sullen or irritable
- Sudden changes of moods or feelings
- Talking too much
- Too concerned with neatness or cleanliness

Three problems reported exclusively by parents of boys for more than one-third of the sample were bragging/ boasting (all ages), getting hurt a lot/accident-proneness (all ages except 9 years) and being impulsive or to act without thinking (except 9 years).

It was noted that mean scores of boys were higher on all the sub scales except for somatic complaints where girls reported marginally higher incidence than boys. Significant main effect of sex, however was obtained only on four sub scales, as revealed from ANOVA results. These sub scales were Obsessive-Compulsiveness. Hyperactivity, Aggression and Delinquency. Hyperactivity and delinquency were reported to be much higher in boys than girls. Incidence of aggression and obsessive-compulsive behaviour was also significantly higher in boys as compared to that of girls.

The age effects indicated that there was a somewhat increasing trend in the incidence with regard to problems subsumed under sub scales like depression, obsessive-compulsive behaviour, somatic complaints, hyperactivity, aggression and delinquency. The incidence was seen as the maximum in the age group 10-11 years, for all these problems except for depression which was highest in the age group 7-8 years. The other sub scales, where a somewhat declining trend was noted included anxiety, uncommunicative behaviour, social withdrawal and 'other problems'. These problems were reported as maximum in the age group 6-7 years. The only exception to this was the category 'other problems' which peaked in the age group 7-8 years.

It was found that the main effect of age was significant only for two sub scales, i.e. social withdrawal and hyperactivity. The earlier observation of least incidence was confirmed with regard to six sub scales. In other words, the incidence of problem behaviour was least in 8-9 years old children for problems categorized under six sub scales i.e. schizoid or anxious; uncommunicative; somatic complaints; social withdrawal; hyperactivity; and 'other problems'.

Contextual Variables and Problem Behaviour

In order to examine the relationships between background variables such as education and occupation of parents; length of time the mother was away from home; any long absence of father due to his job or other reasons etc., correlations of these variables were computed with the total problem behaviour scores of children as well as scores on ten sub scales of CBCL. Table 14.2 shows the correlation values.

TABLE 14.2 : Correlations between Problem Behaviour Scores and Background and Other Variables (N=375)

Background Variables	Total CBCL Score	CBCL Subscales I	II	III	IV	V	VI	VII	VIII	IX	X
Father's Education	-02	-20**	-02	-11	-08	03	01	-02	07	-01	-01
Mother's Education	05	-02	05	-04	06	-01	01	02	08	-00	02
Father's Occupation	07	00	03	08	10	03	09	07	04	01	05
Mother's Employment	-05	-16*	-06	-08	-01	-12	-9	-05	00	-03	-06
Hours spent out by mother	-08	-18**	-09	-10	-02	-15*	-13	-04	-02	-03	-06
Type of Family	09	09	06	13	08	-03	07	06	03	06	14*
Size of Family	08	14	14*	08	09	00	08	05	02	02	06
Per capita income	15*	-27**	-26**	-25**	-16*	-08	-06	-08	-03	-04	-07
Child's Birth-order	-08	-02	-08	-06	-07	-01	-03	-04	-10	-03	-05
Absence of Father	13	03	05	05	16	07	01	05	16*	06	13
Parental Discord	19**	10	11	21	16	09	11	13	13*	07	19**
Home Environment Score (HES)	-18**	-10	-10	-17*	-12	-17*	-19**	-25**	-08	-15*	-12
Parent's Reasoning in Discipline	-17*	00	-03	-04	-12	-04	-09	-14*	23**	-12	-11
Social Competence	-28**	-16*	-17*	-22*	-12	-19**	-30**	-32**	-22**	-26**	-15*
Draw-A-Man Test Score	-09	-05	-05	-11	-04	-01	-12	-07	-07	-03	-12
Home Environment											
Physical	-18**	-20**	-18**	-18**	-18**	-20**	-19**	-07	-07	-08	
Intellective	-14*	-01	-02	-12	-04	-13*	-17**	-25**	-08	-17*	-08
Affective	-15*	-09	-07	-14*	-11	-13	-13*	-19**	-06	-12	-13*
Social Competence											
Activity	-14*	-14*	-12	-18**	-06	-11	-25**	-22**	-06	-17**	-00
Social	-25**	-12	-15*	-18**	-11	-19**	-23**	-23**	-22**	-19**	-17*
School	-19**	-6	-05	-08	-07	-05	-15*	-29**	-16*	-23**	-15*

Note: Decimals are omitted. * p <.01 ** p <.001

Key for Subscales: I- Schizoid or Anxious, II - Depressed, III - Uncommunicative, IV - Obsessive-compulsive, V- Somatic Complaints, VI - Social Withdrawal, VII - Hyperactive, VIII-Agressive, IX - Delinquent, X-Other Problems.

It emerged that the level of father's education; mother's occupation and the number of hours spent by her on work out of home everyday; income and size of the family; long absence of the father; and parental discord were significantly correlated with the incidence of problem behaviour in children. Level of father's education was negatively correlated with sub scale I of CBCL i.e. "Schizoid or Anxious". This sub scale included problem behaviours like fear of school, nightmares, being anxious, clinging to adults etc. This shows that the children of educated parents had less anxiety or the children whose fathers' level of education was low, experienced greater anxiety. There was also a significant inverse relationship between mother's employment as well as the daily hours spent out on her job and anxiety in children indicating thereby that incidence of problem behaviour was lower in those children whose mothers were employed and spent time out of home everyday. Interestingly, somatic complaints in children also correlated significantly with the daily hours spent by mother on her job out of home i.e. children had fewer somatic complaints where mothers spent longer hours out of home. Income of the family also seemed to affect the total problem behaviours for children as well as for behaviours on the sub scales such as : Schizoid or Anxious; Depressed; Uncommunicative; and Obsessive - Compulsive. The lower was the income of the family, higher was the likelihood of behaviour problems such as : feeling lonely, crying a lot, feeling worthless/ unloved, nervous, anxious, sad, confused, secretive, obsessed, overtired, compulsive behaviour etc. or *vice-versa.*

Long absence of father was also positively associated with aggression in children. It may be recalled here, that father were mainly absent or away from the families due to their job demands and absence was taken as long when it was three months or so at a stretch. The families where fathers were away for longer duration, children evinced behaviours such as being stubborn, being loud, bragging, arguing, demanding attention, fighting, disobeying, poor peer relations, cruelty to animals, excessive talking, teasing, short temper and being moody etc. A significant positive relationship was also observed between parental discord and aggression in children. In the sample studied, parental discord was reported in 25 per cent families. Of these, 31 per cent reported to have fights almost everyday and 69 per cent reported the frequency to be once a week or so. The other behaviour problems evinced by children, when frequency of parental discord was higher, were: poor eating/over eating, lack of guilt, bedwetting, whining, accident proneness, or physical problems like eyes/skin rash etc. without medical reasons. These problems were also correlated with the type of family indicating the higher incidence in children from joint/extended families as compared to those from nuclear families.

Some Other Correlates of Problem Behaviour

Correlations were also computed between CBCL scores with each of the four mediating variables to understand the relationships. An inverse relationship was found between frequency of problem behaviour and home environment, clearly indicating that the quality of home environment is associated with problem behaviour in children (Sood & Misra 1995). The more stimulating the home environment is, lesser is the occurrence of behaviour problems in children. As seen in Table 14.2, the correlations of home environment were significant with behaviour problems such as being uncommunicative, somatic complaints, social withdrawal, hyperactivity, and delinquency.

There was a negative relationship between 'reasoning' used by parents in disciplining their children and problem behaviour in children particularly hyperactivity and aggression. In other words, greater use of reasoning in parental disciplining methods was related with occurrence of lower levels of hyperactivity and aggression in children (Sood, 1998).

Social competence was inversely and significantly correlated with total CBCL scores of children i.e. the lower was the occurrence of behaviour problems in children the higher was the social competence or vice versa. Specifically, the children who evinced high levels of anxiety, depression, uncommunicativeness, somatic complaints, hyperactivity, aggression and delinquency, were seen to be less competent socially.

Intelligence was also negatively correlated with problem behaviour in children, though it was not significant.

Correlation values obtained between the three components of home environment and social competence scales have been indicated in Table 14.2. The physical component of home environment was significantly related to most of the problem behaviours studied. This component of the Home Environment Scale, it may be recalled, comprised adequacy of living and play space for children, safety and cleanliness of the home environment and availability of play materials etc. This means that the children who are living in less desirable physical conditions of the home are more likely to develop anxiety, depression, uncommunicative and obsessive-compulsive behaviour pattern, somatic complaints, social withdrawal and hyperactivity.

Intellective component of the home environment (quality of home environment in terms of stimulation available for the mind) was also inversely and significantly related with somatic complaints, social withdrawal, hyperactivity and delinquency in children. Emotional components of the home environment also inversely correlated with problem behaviour in children. It implies that the higher is the level of love and warmth in the home environment, lesser is the likelihood for the child to uncommunicative, hyperactive, socially withdrawn and evince other problems relating to eating, whining, acting like opposite sex, cruelty to animals etc.

Multiple Regression Analyses

In order to understand the contribution of different variables to the occurrence of problem behaviour, stepwise multiple regression analyses were done separately for the ten sub scales of the CBCL. The predictors included education and occupation of parents, length of time spent out of home by mother, type, size and income of the family, child's birth-order, long absence of father, parental discord, home environment, parental reasoning in discipline, social competence and intelligence. Analyses were done for boys and girls separetly. The results are presented in Tables 14.3 and 14.4.

In case of problem behaviour in boys, four variables which accounted for 14 per cent of variance in the total problem behaviour score included social component of the competence scale, parental reasoning, physical environment of the home and absence of the father from home for a long period (Table 14.3). Anxiety was related to family income and social competence which together

TABLE 14.3 : Results of Step-wise Multiple Regression Analysis for Prediction of CBCL Scores among Boys (N=201)

Criterion Variables	Predictors	Multiple R	R^2	Adjusted R^2	F
Total CBCL Score	Social scale	.283	.080	.075	17.36***
	Parental reasoning	.324	.105	.096	11.65***
	Physical environment	.351	.123	.109	9.23***
	Father's absence	.377	.142	.125	8.14***
Schizoid or Anxious	Per capita income	.308	.094	.090	20.87***
	Social scale	.376	.141	.132	16.32***
Depressed	Per capita income	.235	.055	.050	11.64**
	Social scale	.307	094	.085	10.33**
	Social scale	.283	.080	.075	17.43***
Uncommu-nictive	Per capita income	.365	.133	.125	15.30***
	Parental discord	.403	.162	.149	12.74***
	Physical environment	.203	.041	.036	8.56*
Obsessive-compulsive	Father's absence	.272	.074	.064	7.91**
	Parental reasoning	.315	.099	.085	7.25**
	Mother's education	.342	.117	.099	6.50**
Somatic complaints	Physical environment	.293	.085	.081	18.69***
	Social scale	.335	.112	.103	12.54***
Social withdrawal	Physical environment	.278	.077	.072	16.69**
	Social scale	.327	.107	.098	11.86***
	Per capita income	.353	.125	.111	9.39***
	Social scale	.277	.077	.072	16.64**
	School scale	.354	.125	.116	14.20***
Hyperactive	Intellective environment	.383	.147	.134	11.31***
	Mother's education	.409	.167	.150	9.85***
	Parental reasoning	.432	.186	.165	8.95***
	Parental reasoning	.222	.049	.044	10.37*
Aggressive	Social scale	.285	.081	.072	8.81**
	Father's absence	.326	.106	.093	7.83**
Delinquent	School scale	.253	.064	.059	13.71**
	Social scale	.316	.099	.090	10.98***
Other problems	Social scale	.204	.041	.037	8.71*
	School scale	.273	.074	.065	7.98**
	Parental discord	.329	.108	.094	7.97***

* p < .01 ** p <.001 *** p <.0001

accounted for 14 per cent of variance. The same two variables were also important determinants of depresion and uncommunicative behavioural tendencies in boys. Parental discord added to these two variables in explaining uncommunicative behaviour pattern of boys. Physical environmental father's absence, parental reasoning and education of the mother were significant determinants of obsessive-compulsive behaviour in boys. Physical environment, and social competence of boys were

TABLE 14.4 : Results of Step-wise Multiple Regression Analysis for the Prediction of CBCL Score among Girls (N=174)

Criterion Variables	Predictors	Multiple R	R^2	Adjusted R^2	F
Total CBCL score	Physical environment	.279	.078	.072	14.59**
	Per capita income	.332	.104	.094	9.99**
	Physical environment	.280	.078	.073	14.69**
Schizoid or Anxious	Family size	.369	.136	.126	13.52***
	Mother absence hours	.422	.178	.163	12.27***
	Father education	.459	.211	.192	11.31***
	Mother's education	.485	.235	.212	10.34***
	Per capita income	.296	.087	.082	16.59**
Depressed	Activity scale	.358	.128	.118	12.64***
	Family size	.395	.156	.141	10.51***
	Physical environment	.420	.176	.157	9.07***
	Per capita income	.269	.078	.067	13.49**
Uncomm-unicative	Activity scale	.333	.110	.100	10.66***
	Parental discord	.368	.136	.120	8.91***
Obsessive-compulsive	Physical environment	.275	.075	.070	14.10**
	Family size	.344	.118	.108	11.51***
	Per capita income	.376	.141	.126	9.33***
Somatic complaints	Physical environment	.168	.028	.022	4.99*
Social withdrawal	Physical environment	.264	.070	.064	12.97**
	Activity scale	.340	.115	.105	11.18***
Hyperactive	School scale	.294	.086	.081	16.36**
	Physical environment	.340	.115	.105	11.18***
Aggressive	Parental reasoning	.206	.042	.037	7.67*
	Social scale	.267	.071	.060	6.58*
Delinquent	Activity scale	.173	.030	.024	5.34
Other problems	Physical environment	.198	.039	.033	7.04*

* $p < .01$ ** $p < .001$ *** $p < .0001$

significantly related to somatic complaints and social withdrawal in children, accounting for almost 11 per cent of variance. Family income added an increment to variance in social withdrawal in boys. Social and school components of competence scale, intellective component of the home environment, education of the mother, and use of reasoing by parents in disciplining their children were important variables for hyperactivity in boys. Aggression in boys was related to parental reasoning, social competence and absence of the father from the home for long.

Physical environment and family income were the most significant predictors for problem behaviour in girls. As can be seen in Table 14.4, physical environment is the variable that accounts for variance in almost all the problems. In addition to physical environment, size of family, mother's absence hours and education of parents were significant predictors of anxiety in girls, accounting for 23.5 per cent of variance. Depression in girls was related to family income, activity component of the competence scale, family size and physical environment of the home. Income, activity component and parental discord accounted for 13.6 per cent variance in uncommunicative behaviour pattern in girls. Obsessive-compulsive behaviour in girls was predicted by physical environment of the home, family size and income of the family. Physical environment was the only predictor for somatic complaints in girls. Apart from physical environment, activity component predicted hyperactivity in girls. Parental reasoning and social scale contributed significantly to aggression in girls.

Concluding Comments

It is clear from the results of the present study that problem behaviours are commonly seen in children. Out of 110 problems, 39 were endorsed by 1/3rd or more parents. This means that 125 or more children in the study sample had evinced problems. Recent studies from various countries confirm that such behavioural problems are commonly reported (Campbell, 1983; Cotler, 1986).

The important issue, however, is to understand that some of the problems seen in children during early years may simply be part of growing up crisis and are likely to get resolved with time. These are transient problems and thus may not require professional help. The problems that deserve serious attention are the ones that persist and predict later disturbance. For example, children who show hyperactivity are reported to display academic and social deficits during adolescence and many display some continuation of maladaptive behaviours into adulthood (Weiss & Hechtman, 1986). Childhood aggression and antisocial behaviour are relatively stable over time into adulthood (McMahon & Forehand, 1988).

The results of this study showed that boys had significantly higher incidence of problems such as bragging, hyperactivity, cruelty to animals, accident-proneness, impulsivity, physical attacks on people, teasing a lot, being unusually loud etc. (Sood, 1997). The sub scales of CBCL where higher incidence in boys was reported included obsessive-compulsive behaviour, hyperactivity, aggression and delinquency. Sixty per cent or more boys in the sample were hyperactive at every age group. Empirically derived syndromes involving this kind of problems such as aggression, oppositional, destructive, and antisocial behaviour have been identified in a wide variety of studies (Achenbach & Edelbrock, 1989; Quay, 1986).

Boys are known to be more vulnerable to the ill-effects of environment. There could be biological or social influence including family influences on child's behaviour itself that influence his interactions with others. At present, there is no conclusive evidence of a genetic component. However, it may be reasonable to hypothesize an increased genetic component in anti-social behaviour that persists from childhood into adult life (Rutter *et al.*, 1990). This hypothesis need to be addressed by future research.

Though it is often assumed that parental behaviour causes childhood conduct disorders, it may actually be that the reverse is true or the relationship may be at least reciprocal. Anderson, Lytton, and Romney (1986) found that mothers of conduct-problem boys and mothers of normal boys both interacted more negatively with conduct-problem boys. They suggested that the child's behaviour is the influence in these interactions, not the mother's.

Age differences have been found to be significant for 13 items of CBCL. The problems that increased with age included — asthma, lack of concentration, nervousness, aches/pains without medical reasons, screaming a lot; and speech problems. The problems that decreased with age were: bragging, crying a lot, accident-proneness, feeling too guilty, overeating/being overweight and poor school work. The study also indicated certain age trends in problem behaviour. As detailed out earlier the incidence of certain problems was least in the age group of 8-9 years. These included-cruelty to others, disobedience, unable to concentrate, poor peer relations, trouble sleeping, being unhappy and withdrawn etc. The reverse trend i.e. the peak in the problem behviour around the middle age group was also observed with regard to problems such as stubborn behaviour, lack of guilt, showing off, threatening people, screaming etc. Certain problems like restlessness, obsessions, etc. did not change much with age. By and large problems subsumed under sub-scales of depression, obsessive-compulsive behaviour, somatic complaints, hyperactivity, aggression and delinquency increased with age while, anxiety, uncommunicative behaviour, social withdrawal etc. declined with increase in age.

It is possible that the age at which disorders are first noticed is not actually the age when disorders had arisen. For example, certain problems like attention-deficit etc. are generally noticed around the time children start their schooling.

However, there is a need for longitudinal research in this area that may produce conclusive evidence of age-effects on behavioural problems in children.

Social Context and Problem Behaviour

The study has shown a negative, significant relationship between family income and incidence of problem behaviour in children, meaning that problem behaviour is more freqently seen in families of lower income level. The specific behaviour problems that were seen to be negatively related with family income were — anxiety, depression, being uncommunicative and obsessive-compulsive behaviour. This is in agreement with findings from other research studies, as available evidence indicates that children from lower SES have increased vulnerability to behaviour disorders (Mehta, 1969). Caste and SES have also been shown to be associated with problem behaviour in children (Kalra, 1975).

It may be argued that the association between income of the family and problem behaviour is due. not to any causal link between the two, but rather due to some other variable that is the result of poverty. Income of the family may be the net result of a cluster of variables such as parent's education, occupation, type and size of the family. Further, family income is an important determinant of the kind of the housing, food, clothes, general well-being, stimulation in the home environment, supervision of the child, and time spent by parents with the child. It could be due to any of the factors or due to interaction among some of these. It could be due to the consequences of poor level of income of the family such as poor living conditions and intra familial discord etc. Thus income of the family per se may not be the real factor that causes problem behaviour in children. It seems that the real issue is about the relevant mechanisms that operate in the families with the lower income and the interactions among these that produce problem behaviour in children.

At one time, much emphasis was placed on broken homes as a cause of delinquency. The fact of family break up was considered to be damaging as broken homes were indeed statistically associated with delinquency. A possible explanation is the presence of family discord and quarreling (Rutter, 1971, 1982). Is it the break up of home per se or the family discord? Studies have shown that divorce/separation is strongly associated with delinquency whereas parental death is only very weakly so, showing thereby that it is the family discord that is more important than break up per se.

Further, family discord in unbroken homes was also seen to be causing delinquency. Temporary separation also predisposes to conduct disorderes if it arises due to discord. Empirical findings are also available to indicate that reduction in discord is followed by diminution in the risk of conduct disturbance. Thus it can be concluded that discordant relationship is the underlying relevant mechanism that is important in the emergence of delinquency rather than family break up per se.

Results of the study show that the incidence of problem behaviour is likely to be higher in families where the parents have a discordant relationship. Aggression in children was also higher in such families. Problems such as poor eating/over-eating, lack of guilt, bed-wetting, whining, accident-proneness etc. were also higher in families where there was parental discord. It is believed that children learn what they live. Children's observations of parental interactions influence their behaviour. Warm, loving, accepting, cooperative attitude of the parents towards each other as well as towards the child is likely to foster positive feelings in the child and may contribute a great deal towards his healthy, wholesome development. Less conflict and greater cooperation are associated with fewer problems in children (Hetherington, Stanley-Hagan, & Anderson, 1989). On the other hand, parents who engage in a great deal of marital conflict or aggression may serve as models for their children. It may also be possible that such parents direct higher than usual rates of conflictual and aggressive behaviour at others as well, including the child. Since the child is unable to understand the reason for such aggression etc. he or she may develop fear or may be nervous or confused. These feelings may surface as one or the other problem in his behaviour.

The results also showed an association between father

absence and aggression in children. Other studies also show relationship between divorce and father-absence with conduct disorders particularly in boys (Guidubaldi & Perry, 1985; Hetherington, Cox & Cox, 1985). Fathers serve as role models for boys. In the absence of the father, the boy may try to model his father's behaviour and thus act assertive or aggressive.

Associations between various facets of the home environment and behaviour problems in children have been noted in this study. A negative relation was seen between overall home environment and total behaviour problem scores of the children implying that the higher the quality of home environment, lower is the likelihood of behaviour problem in children and vice versa. Specifically, children from poor quality home environments are likely to manifest problems such as uncommunicative behaviour, somatic complaints, social withdrawal, hyperactivity and delinquency.

Poor physical conditions in the home were associated with problems such as anxiety, depression, obsessive-compulsive behaviour, somatic complaints, social withdrawal and hyperactivity in girls and obsessive-compulsive behaviour and somatic complaints in boys. Most of these problems are associated with broad brand internalizing syndrome (Achenbach & Edelbrock, 1978). These reactions may be due to feelings of inadequacies, or responses to some perceived threats or some unconscious conflict or impulses in children. Intellective climate of the home was related to hyperactivity in boys.

While these associations enhance our understanding about behavioural pathology, these certainly can not be understood as direct influences on behaviour. Influence of the environment is exerted via the child's perceptions and interpretations of the environment. None of the above variables such as family income, employment of mother, size of the family, absence of father etc. may be sufficient in itself to produce behaviour in children. These could cause the behavioural problem in children only in complex interaction with each other and with other factors such as parental discord, age, sex and temperamental characteristics of the child etc.

REFERENCES

Achenbach, T.M., & Edelbrock, C.S (1978). The classification of child psychopathology: A review and analysis of empirical efforts. *Psychological Bulletin, 85*, 1275-1301.

Achenbach, T.M., & Edelbrock, C.S. (1981). Behavioral problems and competencies reported by parents of normal and disturbed children aged four through sixteen. *Monographs of the Society for Research in Child Development, 46*. (Whole No. 188).

Achenbach, T.M., Verhulst, F.C., Baron, G.D., & Althaus, M. (1987). A comparison of syndromes derived from the child behaviour checklist for American and Dutch boys aged 6-11 and 12-16. *Journal of Child Psychology and Psychiatry, 28*, 437-453.

Achenbach, T.M., & Edelbrock, S.C. (1989). Diagnostic, taxonomic, and assessment issues. In T.H. Ollendick & M. Hersen (Eds.). *Handbook of Child Psychopathology*. (2nd ed.). New York: Plenum.

Anderson, K.E., Lytton, H., & Romney, D.M. (1986). Mother's interactions with normal and conduct-disordered boys: Who affects whom? *Developmental Psychology, 22*, 604-609.

Banik, N.D.B., Sushila, N., Krishna, A., & Raj, L. (1972). Behaviour problems of primary school children. *Indian Paediatrics, 9*, 757-761.

Bassa, D.M. (1962). An analysis of cases attending child guidance psychotherapy centres. *Indian Jounal of Psychiatry, 4*, 139.

Bower, E.M. (1981). *Early Identification of Emotionally Handicapped Children in Schoo*. (3rd ed.) Springfield, Ill: Charles C. Thomas.

Brandenburg, N.A., Friedman, R.M., & Silver, S.E. (1990). The epidemiology of childhood psychiatric disorders: Prevalence findings from recent studies. *Journal of the American Academy of Child and Adolescen Psychiatry, 29*, 76-83.

Campbell, S.B. (1982). Developmental perspectives in child psychopathology. In T.H. Ollendick, & M. Hersen (Eds.). *Handbook of Child Psychopathology* (pp. 13-40). New York: Plenum.

Chawla, P., Sahasi, G., Sundaram, K.R., & Mehta, M. (1981). A study of prevalence and pattern of hyperactive syndrome in primary school children. *Indian Journal of Psychiatry,*

23, 313-323.

Cotler, S. (1986). Epidemilogy and outcome. In J.M. Reisman (Ed.), *Behavior Disorders in Infants, Children and Adolescents.* New York: Random House.

Dagar, B., & Singh, M.V. (1981). Behaviour disorders in a community child guidance centre. *Archives of Child Health, 23*, 140-145.

Grahm, P.J. (1979). Epidemiological studies. In H.C. Quay. & J.S. Werry (Eds.). *Psychopathological Disorders of Childhood* (2nd ed.). New York: Wiley.

Guidabaldi, J., & Perry, J.D. (1985). Divorce and mental health sequelae for children: A two-year follow up of a nationwide sample. *Journal of American Academy of Child Psychiatry, 24*, 531-537.

Hetherington, E.M., & Cox, M., & Cox, R. (1985). Long-term effects of divorce and remarriage on the adjustment of children. *Journal of the American Academy of Child Psychiatry, 24*, 518-530.

Indian Council of Medical Research. (1983). *Multicentre study of the patterns of child and adolescent disorders:* Unpublished final report of the task force project. New Delhi ; Author.

Korn, S.J., & Gannon, S. (1983). Temperament, cultural variation, and behavior disorder in preschool children. *Child Psychiatry and Human Development, 13*, 203-212.

Malhotra, S., & Chaturvedi, S.K. (1984). Patterns of childhood psychiatric disorders in India. *Indian Journal of Paediatrics, 51*, 235.

Malhotra, S., & Chadda, R. (1987). Specific development disorders in children attending child guidance clinic. *Indian Journal of Psychiatry, 29*, 343.

McMahon, R.J., & Forehand, R. (1988). Conduct disorders. In E.J. Mash & L.G. Terdal (Eds.), *Behavioral Assessment of Childhood Disorders*, (2nd ed.). New York: Guilford.

Mehta, K. (1969). *Psychological study of the problem child:* Unpublished doctoral dissertation, University of Jodhpur, Jodhpur, India

Muralidharan, R. (1973). Age trends in behaviour problems of children. In T.E. Shanumgam (Ed.). *Research in Personality and Social Problems.* (pp. 107-128). Madras : Madras University.

Murthy, R.S., Ghosh, A., & Verma, V.K. (1974). Behaviour disorders of childhood and adolescence. *Indian Journal of Psychiatry, 16*, 229.

Phatak, P. (1966). *Draw-A-Man test for Indian Children.* Poona:

Anand Agencies.

Phatak, P. (1984). A revision and extension of Phatak Draw-a-Man scale for Indian children of age group 2 ½ to 16 ½ years. *Psychological Studies, 29*, 34-46.

Prabhu, G.G. (1980). Deviance and pathology. In U. Pareek (Ed.). *A Survey of Research in Psychology 1971-1976 Part I.* (pp. 260-303). Bombay: Popular Prakashan.

Quay, H.C. (1986). Conduct disorders. In H.C. Quay & J.S. Werry (Eds.), *Psychopathological Disorders of Childhood,* (3rd ed.). New York: Wiley.

Rubin, R.A., & Balow, B. (1978). Prevalence of teacher identified behavior problems: A longitudinal study. *Exceptional Children, 45.* 102-111.

Rutter, M. (1971). Parent-child separation: Psychological effects on the children. *Journal of Child Psychology and Psychiatry, 12,* 233-260.

Rutter, M. (1982). Epidemiological-longitudinal approaches to the study of development. In W.A. Collins (Ed.), *The concept of development. Minnesota Symposium on Child Psychology,* Vol. 15, (pp. 105-144). Hillsdale, NJ: Erlbaum.

Rutter, M., Bolton, P., Harrington, R., Le Couteur, A., Macdonald, & Simoff, E. (1990). Genetic factors in child psychiatric disorders-I. A review of research strategies. *Journal of Child Psychology and Psychiatry, 31*, 3-37.

Rutter, M. (1989). Isle of Wight revisited: Twenty-five years of child psychiatric epidemiology. *Journal of the American Academy of Child and Adolescent Psychiatry, 28,* 633-653,

Rutter, M., Tizard, J., Yule, W., Graham, P., & Whitmore, K. (1976). Research report: Isle of Wight studies, 1964-74. *Psychological Medicine, 6,* 313-332.

Singh, M.V., & Gupta, S. (1970). Behaviour problems as seen in a child guidance clinic. *Paediatric Clinics of India, 5,* 145-148.

Sitholey, P., & Chakrabarti, S. (1992). Child psychiatric research in India: Epidemiology, assessment and treatment. In S. Malhotra; A. Malhotra, & V.K. Verma (Eds.), *Child Mental Health in India,* (pp. 42-65). Delhi: MacMillan.

Sood, N., & Misra, G. (1995). Home environment and problem behaviours in children. *Journal of Personality and Clinical Studies, 11*, 23-32.

Sood, N. (1997). *Behaviour Problems in Children.* New Delhi : Geetangali.

Sood, N., (1998). Pattern of family interaction and problem behaviour in children. *Journal of Research and Applications in Clinical Psychology. 1*, 19-35.

Verghese, A., Beig, A., Senseman, S.A., Rao, S.S., & Benjamin, V.A. (1973). Social and psychiatric study of representative group of families in Vellore town. *Indian Journal of Medical Research, 61*, 608.0

Weisz, J.R., Suwanlet, S., Chaiyasit, W., Weiss, B., Walter, B.R., & Anderson, W.W. (1988). Thai and American perspectives on over-and undercontrolled and child behaviour problems: Exploring the threshold model among parents, teachers, and psychologists. *Journal of Consulting and Clinical Psychology, 56*, 601-609.

Werry, J., & Quay, H. (1977). The prevalence of behavior symptoms in younger elementary school children. *American Journal of Orthopsychiatry, 41*, 136-143.

15

Self-Instructional Training and Mental Health in Children

SUDHAKAR RATH

Self-Instructional treatment has proved to be one of the most promising cognitive-behavioural treatment approaches in the area of child mental health. The research on verbal control of behaviour suggests a developmental progression by which the child's inner private speech comes to assume a functional role in changing non-verbal behaviour. This approach stems from the theoretical rationale of verbally-mediated self-control advocated by Soviet psychologists namely Luria (1961) and Vygotsky (1962). They proposed a stage theory of development in which a child's overt and covert self-verbalisations ("Second Signal System") gradually gain control over non-verbal behaviour. For Luria (1961), self control is a matter of the internalisation of speech. During the developmental course of speech, the content of self verbalisation is transformed from self-stimulatory language with no task solving or planning function to self guiding language with problem-solving or goal-oriented functions (Hughes, 1988; Kazdin, 1982; Kendall & Siqueland, 1989).

The growing internalisation of speech can alter perception, can facilitate or allow more intelligent interaction with the world, and can initiate and inhibit action. Although the age related developmental stages laid down by Luria had been challenged by many Western psychologists (Meichenbaum, 1980), the underlying theory and developmental model provided a practical and very useful sequence for conceptualising and designing many cognitive self-guidance treatment programmes. Meichenbaum and Goodman (1969, 1971), Kendall and Finch (1979), and Kendall and Braswell (1984) were the pioneers who developed verbal self-instructional treatment paradigm to train impulsive children to talk to themselves as a means of developing self-control.

The VSI Paradigm

The Verbal self-instructional (VSI) training regimen involved a step-by-step sequence which includes : (a) the therapist models the task performance and talks out loud while the child observes (cognitive modelling), (b) the child performs the task, instructing himself aloud under the guidance and direction of the therapist (overt guidance), (c) the therapist models task performance while whispering the self-instruction, followed by (d) the child performs the tasks, whispering to himself (faded self-guidance), (e) the therapist performs task using covert self-instructions with pauses and behavioural signs of thinking (e.g., stroking chin or raising eyes towards the ceiling) and (f) the child performs the task using covert self-instructions.

The contents of verbalisation modeled by the therapist and rehearsed by the child include several performance relevant skills : (a) problem definition (What is it I have to do?"); (b) problem approach ("I have to look at all the possibilities"); (c) focusing attention ("I have to concentrate and mind only what I am supposed to do"); (d) coping statements ("If I make a mistake I can continue more slowly") and (e) self-reinforcement ("Great, I did it, that was good").

Promises of VSI Training

A consistent theme appears from the literature that VSI treatment procedures appear to hold considerable promise for generalised changes since they are directly related to the issue of cognitive strategies. VSI training is a form of self-control that children learn through verbal mediation and this can be implemented to interrupt or inhibit a sequence of behaviour, thoughts, or actions (Kazdin, 1982; Manning, 1990). By mastering self control over thought patterns and behaviour children can develop independence and become less dependent upon the source of outside environmental control. Since, the locus of control is implanted within the child, it is expected that the treatment effects should be maintained and generalised to other problem situations, even when external supports are withdrawn (Dush, Hirt & Schroeder, 1989; Eifert, 1984).

Since the rationale of the VSI is based on a natural developmental phenomenon with sequence of gaining verbal mediational control over cognition and behaviour, it should provide a source of natural nurturance to the naturally occurring sequence of self-control skills (Cole & Kazdin, 1980). It also provides a remedial procedure for children who are delayed in verbal self-control (Kendall, 1985) and can lead to the development of automatic covert verbal self-control. Self-instructional training also has the potency to enhance general coping skills in a wider variety of contexts than the situation specific responses provided by operant procedures (Rath, 1992). This method can be tailored to different training tasks and to different verbal styles as per individual child's need, because content and sequence of the training procedure are independent of the tasks used in the treatments (Kendall, 1981). The child can be an active collaborator in generalising and implementing the treatment package.

RESEARCH EVALUATION

Impulsivity

Meichenbaum and Goodman (1969, 1971) were the pioneers who developed and empirically demonstrated the merit of self-instructional treatment paradigm in primary grade impulsive children. The training package induced improvements in various problem-solving measures (e.g.,

MFFT task, Porteus Maze and performance on WISC) both in post test and a one month follow-up. The major problem of the study was that the statistical power was very low and no attempt was made to indicate on which measures there were significant results versus only trends. Also, no effects were obtained on class room measures as rated by the teachers. In a second study S-I training plus cognitive modelling was compared with cognitive-modelling and attention control strategy. Data revealed that both the modelling and modelling plus self-instruction produced changes in MFFT latencies but S-I was essential to decrease in errors in MFFT problem-solving. These studies for the first time demonstrated that S-I training is meaningful not only as a means to change behaviour through verbal mediation but as a means to develop problem-solving skills which facilitate a change in overt behaviour.

Kendall and Finch (1978) evaluated the efficacy of the S-I treatment programme by randomly assigning impulsive subjects either to treatment or control group. The subjects in the treatment group received six 20 minutes sessions of training in VSI and a response-cost contingency with psycho-educational materials. Results indicated that treatment groups significantly performed better on the MFFT and showed improvement in classroom behaviour compared to the control group. However, the improvement on these measures was unfortunately confounded with pretest differences. Arnold and Forhand (1978) studied separate and combined effects of self-instruction and response-cost to train impulsive pre-schoolers. All treatment groups improved on pre-school version of the MFFT. Only groups receiving S-I training showed generalisation to similar tasks in classroom assessment.

Rath (1992) and Rath and Routray (1991) examined the relative efficacy of VSI training and motivational manipulations of response-cost and reward when offered separately and in combination in the remediation of an impulsive cognitive style in Scheduled Tribe and Scheduled Caste children. Results revealed that VSI treatment was found to be superior in facilitating generalisation of treatment effects across different tasks (i.e., reading comprehension) and different settings (i.e., self-control behaviour in classroom situation). The S-I training combined with response cost operant procedures produced most effective results in terms of treatment efficacy, generalisation and maintenance in case of impulsivity.

Hyperactivity and Aggressive Behaviour

In a most comprehensive and extensive self-instructional training programme consisting of 24 sessions with hyperactive children over a 3 month period, plus atleast 6 sessions with each child's teacher and 12 sessions with the child's parents, Douglas *et al.*, (1976) provided strong supportive evidence for the effectiveness of self-instructional procedures with hyperactive children. Cognitive modelling, self-verbalisation, and self-reinforcement were used on a wide range of cognitive tasks, academic problems and social situations. Results revealed significant and desired changes in post-test as well as in 3 month follow-up in cognitive problem-solving measures, measures of frustration, intolerance and reading. But treatment effects did not generalise to school behaviour rated by teachers. It was difficult to assess which were the active components in that programme since only a single no-treatment control group was employed. Again, whether the lack of generalisation was due to the insensitivity of the behaviour checklist used by teachers or insufficient attention to classroom behaviour in training remain for further work.

Bugenthal, Whalen and Henker (1977) and Bugenthal *et al.*, (1978) evaluated two behaviour change procedures on hyperactive boys aged 7 to 12 in relation to the attributional style of the children. They were provided with instructions in self-controlling speech or social reinforcement contingency. Half of the subjects in each group were given Retalin and the other half were unmedicated. Findings revealed that the children's attributional style (luck vs effort) was a major determinant of treatment effectiveness. The self-instructional programme was effective and better maintained for the effort or internal attributing children and the non-medicated children. However, there was no significant change in the classroom behaviour suggesting a lack of transfer effect of the treatment. In addition to providing supporting evidence for the value of self-instructional training, these results suggested a relevant subject variable (i.e., attributional style) which might be used to make individual intervention more efficient and effective. Barkley, Copeland, and Sivage (1980) demonstrated that a self-control treatment involving self-instruction, self-monitoring and self-reinforcement was effective in improving hyperactive children's misbehaviour and attention to tasks but failed to improve children's classroom achievement scores. Watson and Hall (1977) combined self-instruction training with the "think aloud" programme in the treatment of hyperactives and reported improvements on teacher ratings of behaviour as well as classroom reading tasks. Hinshaw, Henker, and Whalen (1984b) reported that self-instructional training enhanced self regulation in an anger inducing situation.

Working on a sample of aggressive boys Camp, Blom, Herbert and Van Doornínck (1977) developed a self-instructional programme called "think aloud" to improve the solution of intellectual and social problems. The treatment group showed significant improvement on a variety of measures but the positive results were qualified by an important observation that the trained children also gave more aggressive solutions. Thus, the training did not apparently increase constructive solutions to the hypothetical social problems. Moreover, the trained and untrained aggressive children showed no significant difference in their disruptive classroom behaviour. Robin, Schneider and Dolnick (1976) reported significant reduction in the rate of teacher rated aggressive behaviour due to self-instructional treatment programme introduced into two special classes. However, decreasing trend observed in the extended baseline indicated the possibility of confounding effects with time factor. Born-Stein and

Quevillion (1976) examined the utility of VSI training with pre-school boys whose classroom behaviour was disruptive, aggressive, undersirable and overactive. Training programme included self-instruction, modelling, and reinforcement. Results revealed that decrease in disruptive behaviour and increase on task behaviour from 11 per cent before treatment to 78 per cent after training. Five month follow-up training showed that on the task, classroom behaviour was maintained at 71 per cent level. Although the effectiveness of self-instructional training has been demonstrated for specific behavioural domains, in circumscribed contexts, for relatively short period of time and with non-clinical samples of children, the promises have been found to be weak in strength, some what inconsistent, difficult to replicate and neither as predictable nor as widespread as one would expect (Whalen, Henker & Hinshaw, 1985). To date, no convincing evidence is available attesting to the facilitation of long-term maintenance. Only few studies have assessed durability of changes over period exceeding 3 months and these studies reveal only limited maintenance. Medication plus self-instruction training again has not been shown to be superior to medication in hyperactive children although a few hopeful isolated studies reported that self-instruction plus methlyphenidatte yields better results (Hinshaw, Henker & Whalen, 1984a), Horn, Chatoor and Conners (1983) compared medication to a combination of self-instruction and self-monitoring in classroom and found superior results in case of self-instruction and self-monitoring. In summary, the literature on self-instructional training on hyperactivity and aggressive behaviour reveal that there are isolated findings suggesting the potential effectiveness of this approach, yet there is no conclusive evidence that VSI is superior to other intervention techniques whether the yardstick consists of units of durability, generalisation or refractory behaviour domains (Whelen *et al.*, 1985).

Learning and Reading Disabilities

Ryan, Short and Weed (1986) reviewed research on the

relevance of cognitive-behaviour modification for remediation of reading difficulties and pointed out that major causes of such problems are lack of metalinguistic awareness and cognitive motivational problems. The VSI training programme can be of immense help in improving the performance of reading disabled children. Graham and MacArthur (1988) investigated the impact of VSI programme in improving the performance of reading disabled children on essay writing using a multiple baseline single subjects design. Data showed that VSI has not only effective in maintaining the treatment effects but also generalised to a wide range of cognitive and behavioural measures. Miller, Giovenco and Rentire (1987) examined the benefits of SI on the comprehension monitoring programme of disabled and good readers. The findings suggested that poor and disabled readers performed at a level comparable with their higher ability peers. Blandford and Lloyd (1987) examined the effect of VSI on learning disabled children in their hand-writing performance including, letter formation, letter proximity to the line, letter height and word spacing. Subjects' hand-writing improved markedly after training and the improvement persisted over time. Manning (1990) demonstrated that the VSI has been very useful training package to enhance several academic tasks of low-achievers which provides the skill to cognitively plan, organise and monitor strategies in problem-solving situations. Bivens and Berk (1988) observed that the reading disabled children lack a battery of verbal self-regulatory skills where VSI can help. Leon and Pepe (1983) observed that VSI is superior to any of the traditional methods in improving student's performance.

Other Behaviour Problems in Children

Self-instructional training programme has also shown considerable promise in remediation of a variety of childhood psychological and behavioural problems. Manning (1990) investigated the impact of cognitive self-instruction programme upon a fourth grade student exhibiting poor self-management skills (i.e., inability to focus attention, follow through and finish academic assignments). It included the components of modelling, practicing, cueing applied for 4 months. Results indicated that significant improvements were made in the deficient behaviours. Gottman, Gonso and Schulder (1976) included self-instructional training with social skills and listening skill training in order to modify social interactional patterns of socially withdrawn children and obtained encouraging results. Vahn (1988) used cognitive behavioural training paradigm to develop social skills, cognitive restructuring, coping skills and anxiety management. Agran, Fodor, and Moore (1986) investigated the effects of VSI package on the job task sequencing. Findings indicated that training increased job task sequencing. Target behaviours were maintained upto 3 months and supported the use of self-instruction in vocational training. Cohen and Schleser (1984) studied the developmental status of the child and its importance in self-instructional training. The developmentally sophisticated concrete operational children who received self-instructional training showed greater generalisation of problem-solving abilities to new tasks. Self-instructional training procedures have also been found to be useful in improving targeted classroom behaviour (Corno, 1987), enhancing arithmetic skill (Leon & Pepe, 1983), promoting a child's tolerance for resisting temptation (Mahoney & Nezworski, 1985) and decreasing disruptive and non-productive classroom behaviours (Dulcan, 1980).

Some Unresolved Issues

In general, although it is increasingly clear from theoretical perspective and empirical research that self-instructional procedure is an effective method in modifying varieties of cognitive and behaviour problems in children, several unresolved issues have been raised. Attempts have been made to review and evaluate the efficacy of self-instructional method. Conclusions have ranged from generally favourable (e.g., Kendall, 1985; Mahoney & Kazdin, 1979; Meichenbaum & Burland, 1979), to skeptical (e.g., Ledwidge, 1978), to findings of serious methodological and conceptual problems (i.e., Dulcan, 1986; Gresham, 1985; Mahoney & Nezworski, 1985; Whalen, Henker & Hinshaw, 1985). What is the objective method of evaluating the exact mediational role of self-verbalisations? How can one assess the amount of self-instruction used during the covert stage of training? Is it at all necessary and practical to use overt self-instruction for some classes of responses, especially in a classroom situation?

In addition to the above questions, several other important issues have been raised. The self-instructional treatment consists of multifaceted intervention techniques including modelling, overt and covert verbalisation and rehearsal, prompts, feedback, reinforcement or response cost in addition to training in the specific task strategies. Many potentially unspecified dimensions of VSI can be expected to influence the treatment outcome. Examples include (a) mix of cognitive, affective, motivational and behavioural elements, (b) relative focus on skill acquisition versus performance, (c) degree of involvement of parents, teachers and peers, (d) frequency, duration and sequencing of treatment sessions and (e) quality of purposeful programming for maintenance and for generalisation. The wide variations in these dimensions and other factors may be responsible for the inconsistent and even contradictory results that appear in the literature (Whalen *et al.* 1985). Not much empirical research has been done to determine the relative contribution of the above components. For example, self-reinforcement and coping strategies have been found to be successful in modifying problem behaviours (Cole & Kazdin, 1980; Kendall *et al.* 1981) Modelling alone is a powerful modification agent and so also response-cost procedures. Efforts may be made to determine the relative efficacy of different components included in the VSI programme. Again the role of self-talk remains a critical area in need of further investigation.

The other disturbing aspect of VSI programme is that there is no unequivocal evidence that effects of VSI training have produced generalised cognitive improvements. If there is any lasting change in cognition and behaviour it should manifest over a variety of problem situations, across settings and wide range of measures. When investigators have tried to measure the impact of training using a wide range of measures performance improvements have been limited to few psychometric and perceptual motor tasks. Generalisation to academic performance or achievement is rare and generalisation from cognitive task performance to social-adaptive behaviour tends not to be found (Whalen *et al.* 1985). However, against this scenario of hopelessness, there are few hopeful studies on the empirical horizon. Kendall and Braswell (1982) reported generalisation from training session to teacher rated classroom behaviours but not to parent-rated home behaviours. Rath (1992) reported generalisation effects across different tasks (i.e., reading, achievement and cognitive problem-solving domains) as well as across different settings (i.e., teacher ratings of classroom behaviour). However, Barkley *et al.* (1980) failed to find transfer from experimental to regular classroom situation. Although VSI training approach holds promise for generalised change both in cognitive and behavioural domains such promise still remains largely unfulfilled. However, recently generalisation strategies have been programmed into the treatment through multiple training sessions, training situations, trainers and settings. Teachers, parents and peers have been trained and encouraged to continue the treatment in natural, home and playground situations but without any significant success (Wholen *et al.* 1985).

A surprising aspect of self-instructional treatment literature is that there has been very little concern among researchers to realise the importance of developmental factors and "subject variables" as active moderators of treatment efficacies. Achenbach (1982) has been among the most vocal advocates of a developmental orientation to child psychopathology. Research findings have been accumulating in the recent literature that the effectiveness of the self-instructinal training may very well depend on such factors as the developmental level or status of the child (such as age, cognitive stage, complexity of the tasks used), type of child being trained, attributional style of the child, personality, cognitive style and cultural, sub-cultural affiliation of the child. (Copeland, 1982; Dush, Hirt & Schroeder, 1989; Kazdin, 1982). For example, the effectiveness of VSI may be determined by the cognitive stage, such as pre-operational vs operational stage of the child. Pre-operational children benefit most from the self-instruction where as concrete-operational children spontaneously employ different strategies to meet task demands (Schleser, Meyers, & Cohen, 1981). Bugenthal, Whalen and Henker (1977) found that children possessing internal locus of control benefitted more from the VSI training than children possessing external locus of control. Barkley *et al.* (1980) found that children with higher IQ or mental ages better respond to the VSI training than cognitively less mature children. Younger children profit more from the VSI training when the content and sequence of training are explicit and more structured whereas older children less structured VSI training paradigm is more effective. The above findings highlight the fact that the personality characteristics, attributional style, cognitive maturity and developmental status of the children should be considered and examined before tailoring and administering self-instructional regimen (Craighead, Meyers & Craighead, 1983; Rath, 1992). Another disturbing aspect of self-instructional training package is that much of the research has been carried out with the normal populations or with children who have problems that fall within a sub-clinical range of severity as reported by teachers, parents or psychologists. Although this research is important, its generalisability to actual clinical applications of treatment as a psychotherapeutic technique is less convincing rather uncertain. After two decades of research in this area, it is necessary to firmly establish its utility in actual clinical populations (Dush *et al.* 1989).

In summary, although the potential merits of self-instructional approach holds a greater promise for remediation of varieties of child-clinical problems, unfortunately there remains a wide gap between theoretical expectation and practical achievement in terms of actual research and treatment. Self-instructional training reveals failure to replicate, a limited number of examples of the maintenance of treatment effects and an inconsistency in the evidence for treatment generalisation. Further research should be conducted in the above mentioned directions to make self-instructional treatment programme an effective therapeutic procedure in child clinical psychology.

REFERENCES

Achenbach, T.M. (1982). *Developmental Psychopathology*. New York: Wiley.

Agran, M., Fodor, D.J., & Moore, S. (1986). The effects of self-instructional training on job task sequencing: Suggesting a problem-solving strategy. *Education and Training of the Mentally Retarded, 21*, 273-281.

Arnold, S.C., & Forehand, R. (1978). A comparison of cognitive training and response cost procedure in modifying cognitive styles of impulsive children. *Cognitive Therapy and Research. 2*, 183-187.

Barkley, R., Copeland, A., & Sivage, C. (1980). A self-control class room for hyperactive children. *Journal of Autism and Developmental Disorders, 10*, 75-89.

Bivens, J.A., & Berk, L.E. (1988). *A Longitudinal Study of the Development of Children's private speech.* Paper presented at the annual meeting of the American Educational Research Assoication, New Orleans.

Blandford, B.J., & Lloyd, J.W. (1987). Effects of a self-instructional procedure on handwriting. *Journal of Learning Disabilities, 20*, 342-346.

Bornstein, P., & Quevillon, R. (1976). The effects of a self-instructional package on over-active pre-school boys. *Journal of Applied Behaviour Analysis, 9*, 179-188.

Bugenthal, D.B., Whalen, C.K., & Henker, B. (1977). Causal attributions of hyperactive children and motivational assumptions of two behavior change approaches: Evidence for an interactionist position. *Child Development, 48*, 874-884.

Bugenthal, D.B., Colins, S., Collines, L., & Chaney, L.E. (1978). Attributional and behavioral changes following two behavior management interventions with hyperactive boys : A follow-up study. *Child Development, 49*, 247-250.

Camp, B.W., Blom, G.E., Hebert, F., & Van Doorninck, W.J. (1977). "Think Aloud": A programme for developing self-control in young aggressive boys. *Journal of Educational Psychology, 69,* 129-135.

Cohen, R., & Schleser, R. (1984). Cognitive development and clinical interventions. In A.W. Meyers & W.E. Craighead (Eds). *Cognitive Behavior Therapy with Children,* (pp. 45-68). New York: Plenum Press.

Cole, P.M., & Kazdin, A.E. (1980). Critical issues in self-instructional training with children. *Child Behavior Therapy, 2,* 1-23.

Copeland, A.P. (1982). Individual difference factors in children's self-management: Towards individualised treatments. *Self-Management and Behavior Change from Theory to Practice,* New York : Pergamon Press.

Craighead, W.E., Meyers, A.W., & Craighead, L. (1985). A conceptual model for cognitive behavior therapy with children. *Journal of Abnormal Child Psychology, 13,* 331-342.

Douglas, V.I., Parry, P., Marton, P.R., & Garson, C. (1976). Assessment of a cognitive training programme for hyperactive children. *Journal of Abnormal Child Psychology, 4,* 389-410.

Dulacan, M.K. (1986). Comprehensive treatment of children and adolescents with attention deficit disorders : The state of the art. *Clinical Psychology Review, 6,* 539-569.

Dush, D.M., Hirt, Mol., & Schroeder, H. (1989). Self-statement modification in the treatment of child behavior disorders : A meta analysis. *Psychological Bulletin, 106,* 197-106.

Eifert, G.H. (1984). Cognitive behavior therapy : A critical appraisal of its theoretical empirical bases and therapeutic efficacy. *Australian Psychlogist, 19,* 179-191.

Gottmen, J., Gonso, J., & Schulder, P. (1976). Teaching social skills to isolated children. *Journal of Abnormal Child Psychology, 4,* 179-197.

Grahm, S., & Mac Arthur C., (1988). Improving learning disabled students skills at revising essay produced on word processor: Self-instructional strategy training. *Journal of Special Education, 22,* 133-152.

Gresham, F.M. (1985). Utility of cognitive-behavioral procedures for social skills training with children : A critical review. *Journal of Abnormal Child Psychology, 13,* 411-423.

Hinshaw, S.P., Henker, B., & Whalen, C.K. (1984a). Cognitive-behavioral and pharmacologic interventions for hyperactive boys: Comparative and combined effects. *Journal of*

Consulting and Clinical Psychology, 51, 739-749.

Hinshaw, S.P., Henker, B., & Whalen, C.K. (1984b). Self-control in hyperactive boys in anger inducing situations : Effects of cognitive behavioral training and methylphenidate. *Journal of Abnormal Child Psychology, 12*, 55-77.

Horn, W.F., Chatoor, I., & Conners, C.K. (1983). Addictive effects of dexedrine and self-control training. A multiple assessment. *Behavior Modification, 7*, 383-402.

Hughes, J.N. (1988). *Cognitive-Behavior Therapy with Children in Schools*. New York : Pergamon.

Kazdin, A.E. (1982). Current developments and research issues in cognitive - behavioral interventions. *Social Psychology Review, 11*, 75-82.

Kendall, P.C., & Finch, A.J.Jr. (1978). A cognitive behavioral treatment for impulsivity. *Journal of Consulting and Clinical Psychology, 46*, 110-118.

Kendall, P.C., & Finch, A.J. Jr. (1979). Analysis of changes in verbal behavior following a cognitive - behavioral treatment for impulsivity. *Journal of Abnormal Child Psychology, 7*, 455-463.

Kendall, P.C. (1981). Cognitive behavioral interventions with children. In B.B. Lahey & A.E. Kazdin (Eds). *Advances in Clinical Child Psychology*, Vol. 4, New York : Plenum Press.

Kendall, P.C. (1985). Toward a cognitive - behavioral models of child psychopathology and a critique of related interventions. *Journal of Abnormal Child Psychology, 13*, 357-372.

Kendall, P.C. & Zupan, B.A. (1981). Individual versus group application of cognitive-behavioral self-control procedures with children. *Behavior Therapy, 12*, 344-359.

Kendall, P.C, & Braswell, L. (1982). Cognitive behavioral self-control therapy for children: A components analysis. *Journal of Consulting and Clinical Psychology, 50*, 672-689.

Kendall, P.C. & Braswell, L. (1984). *Cognitive-behavioral Therapy for Impulsive Children*. New York : Guilford Press.

Kendall, P.C., & Siqueland, L. (1989). Clinical decision making in child/adolescent therapy. In A.M. Nezu & C.M. Nezu (Eds.) *Clinical decision-making and judgement in the Practice of Behavior Therapy : A Problem-solving Perspective*. Champagne, IL : Research Press.

Ledwidge, B. (1978). Cognitive behavior modification : A step in the wrong direction? *Psychological Bulletin, 85*, 353-375.

Leon, J.A. & Pepe, H.J. (1983). Self-instruction training for remediation of arithmetic deficits. *Exceptional Children, 50*, 54-60.

Luria, A.R. (1961). *The Role of Speech in the Regulation of at Normal and Abnormal Behaviour.*

Mahoney, M.J., & Kazdin, A.E. (1979). Cognitive-behavior modification : Misconceptions and premature evaluation. *Psychological Bulletin, 86,* 1044-1049.

Mahoney, M.J., & Nezworski, M.T. (1985). Cognitive-behavioral approaches to children's problems. *Journal of Abnomral Child Psychology, 13,* 467-476.

Manning, B.H. (1990). Cognitive self-instruction for an off task fourth grader during indiependent academic tasks : A case study. *Contemporary Educational Psychology, 15,* 36-46.

Meichenbaum, D.H., & Godman, J. (1969). Reflection Impulsivity and verbal control of motor behavior. *Child Development, 40,* 485-497.

Meichenbaum, D.H., & Goodman, J. (1971). Training impulsive children in talk to themselves. *Journal of Abnormal Psychology, 77,* 115-126.

Meichenbaum, D., & Burland, S. (1979). Cognitive behavior modification with children. *School Psychology Digest, 8,* 426-433.

Miller, G.E., Giovenco, A., & Rentires, K.A. (1987). Fostering comprehension monitoring in below average readers through SIT. *Journal of Reading Behavior, 19*(4), 379-394.

Rath, S. (1992). Cognitive-Behavior intervention with disadvantaged tribal school children : An empirical study *Indian Journal of Clinical Psychology, 19,* 4-9.

Rath, S., & Routray, P.K. (1991). *Self-instructional Training on Scheduled Caste children : A Component Analysis.* Unpublished paper, Utkal University.

Robin, A. Schneider, M., & Dolnick, M. (1976). The Turtle technique : An extended case-study on self-control in the class-room. *Psychology in the School, 13,* 449-453.

Ryan, E.B., Weed, K.A. & Short, E.J. (1986). Cognitive-behavior modification : Promoting active self-regulatory learning styles. In J.M. Torglsen & B.Y.L. Wong (Eds.). *Learning Disabilities : Some New Perspectives.* New York : Academic Press.

Schleser, R., Meyers, A.W., & Cohen, R. (1981). Generalisation of self-instructions. *Child Development, 52,* 335-340.

Vygotsky, L. (1962). *Thought and Language.* Cambridge, Mass, M.I.T. Press.

Whalen, C.K. Henker, B., & Hinshaw, S.P. (1985). Cognitive-behavioral therapies for hyperactive children : Premises, problems, and prospects. *Journal of Abnormal Child Psychology, 13,* 391-410.

16

Applied Social and Developmental Psychology :

A Viable Interface for Preventive Mental Health

T.S. SARASWATHI

The most significant trend in psychology, particularly on the international scene, during the last decade, has been the growing involvement of psychologists in almost all aspects of health and medical care. Though recognition of this trend has received only marginal attention in the Indian subcontinent, a clear beginning has been made, as can be seen from the creation of a cell for behavioural and social sciences in the Indian Council of Medical Research (ICMR), and the appointment of a behavioural scientist, in the World Health Organization's South-East Asia Regional Office at New Delhi. All the same, there is reason to feel concerned about the marginality of attention paid to health psychology and preventive mental health when compared with the intense reactions and efforts aroused for example, by the threat of AIDS.

Within the sphere of physical health, particularly in the public health care delivery system, considerable activity is taking place related to holistic health, well-being and health promotion stimulated in part by the WHO and UNICEF emphases on the importance of life style in maintaining and enhancing health (Goldston, 1986). The idea is also beginning to catch on in the area of mental well-being.

The presentation that follows is based on the recognition of the role of behavioural factors in illness and illness prevention, and the fact that health indicates a positive quality of life rather than mere absence of illness. The emphasis is on a gestalt approach to preventive mental health (Goldston, 1986). By prevention is meant deliberate and positively aimed intervention prior to the occurrence of mental disorders (Long, 1986). The goal is identification and eradication of the causes of mental disorders and the establishment of a health-conducive environment (Coleman, 1976).

The organizing principles of the ideas presented are as follows :

(1) Prevention and wellness programmes provide attractive alternatives to many aspects of the present dismal mental health care system, and psychologists must take a lead in informing the public and public health officials of the ways in which the health and mental health care systems can be structured to best effect a comprehensive wellness oriented system over time.

(2) The knowledge base that is needed for a culture relevant understanding of psychopathology is rooted in the ecological context of people's lives and social psychology can make significant contributions in this area of epidemiological studies.

(3) A developmental perspective is imperative in preventive mental health research and intervention as

 (a) this provides a "future orientation in which early intervention is considered important for the improvement of future mental health status" (Maddux, Roberts, Sledden, & Wright, 1986; p. 25);

 (b) each period of life is accompanied by its characteristic set of stressors and the optimal social supports for each developmental stage must be identified; and

 (c) the poorly understood and appreciated human and financial costs of mental illness call for early intervention and mental health promotion, i.e., before the damage is done, and idea that has been well understood by now in the area of physical illness and health.

Knowledge-base Required for Preventive Mental Health

Given the premise that an ounce of prevention is worth a pound of cure, we are confronted with the challenge of building a knowledge-base that can provide reasonable answers to the questions *where*, *what*, and *why* of psychopathology.

Our current knowledge-base related to the complex interactions among genetic, biological, behavioural and environmental factors need to be strengthened. It is here that social psychologists can play a key role as members of inter-disciplinary investigative teams.

The development of a knowledge-base for prevention requires systematic interdisciplinary communication and co-ordination. The insights of clinicians, and information obtained through research findings generated by epidemiological, biomedical and behavioural sciences, could be utilized by health service providers in designing and implementing prevention programmes. This implies linkages among researchers, policy-makers and service providers (Long, 1986). The task on hand assumes Himalayan proportions when we contrast what we know with what we do not know.

As elucidated by Long (1986), research needs to identify groups of individuals at increased risk for developing mental-emotional disorders, particularly the potential victims of multiple stressors, such as poverty, unemployment, genetic heritage, history of mental illness in the family and family instability. Research also needs to focus on providing an understanding of the "associations between mental and emotional status and such variables as skill acquisition, diminished pain, stress reduction, and increasing coping capacities. . ." (Goldston, 1986, p. 457).

Albee (1986) succinctly states that ". . . epidemiological studies find clear correlations between most forms of psychopathology and one or more of the following :

(a) emotionally damaging infant and childhood experiences;
(b) poverty and low self-esteem;
(c) powerlessness and low self-esteem; and
(d) loneliness, social isolation and social marginality" (p. 891).

Some of the strategies recommended for off-setting the identified risks include : family planning and genetic counselling; developing stress related coping skills; fostering early trusting relationships; establishing social support networks; and providing access to community resources for the management of transitional and developmental crises (Goldston, 1986; Long, 1986).

A Developmental Perspective

The adoption of a developmental perspective reflects the importance of the need for identification of developmental crises, as they are generally the antecedent stressors for a wide variety of mental disorders; the perspective also facilitates early and appropriate intervention (Long, 1986). Further, early developmental intervention proves to be effective in the formation of health attitudes and beneficial behaviour patterns regarding diet, exercise and hygiene (Maddux, *et al.*, 1986). In what follows, mental health risk factors associated with one stage of life, namely childhood, are discussed to serve as an exemplar.

Psychological Maltreatment of Children : A Threat to Mental Health

"Psychological maltreatment of children and youth consists of acts of omission and commission which are judged by community standards and professional expertise to be psychologically damaging. Such acts are committed by individuals, singly or collectively, who by their characteristics (e.g., age, status, knowledge, organizational form) are in a position of differential power that renders a child vulnerable" (Proceedings of the International

Conference on Psychological Abuse of Children and Youth, 1983, p. 2 Cited in Hart & Brassard, 1987). The importance of adopting a developmental perspective in prevention and promotive mental health programmes is best exemplified in the case of childhood maltreatment and its consequences to mental health.

Emotional and behavioural problems caused due to direct and severe forms of psychological treatment may manifest itself in the form of learning disorders in childhood (e.g. lying, depression and aggression) and psychological distress in adulthood. Psychological maltreatment may also interact with and exacerbate the effects of social pathologies like poverty and deprivation (Hart & Brassard, 1987).

The need to define and study psychological maltreatment in its ecological context is pertinent, because the organization of the community setting affects the behavioural pattern of its members. Information in this regard would provide valuable information on the processes conducive and detrimental to mental health, thereby providing a basis for preventive intervention (Holtzman, Evans, Kennedy, & Iscoe, 1987; Kelly, 1977).

In programmes directed toward children, health providers can focus on parents and other caregivers as they determine much of the child's environment and behaviour. Efforts can be directed at sensitizing parents to adopt desirable child care practices and other behaviour patterns (Maddux, *et al.*, 1986). In order to ensure optimal conditions for child growth and development, caregivers can be provided physical supplies (e.g., prenatal and postnatal care), psycho-social supplies (e.g., opportunities to develop intellectual and social competencies), and socio-cultural supplies such as day care facilities (Coleman, 1976; Zax & Spectar, 1974).

As in the case of risk factors that are likely to predispose and to precipitate psychopathology in childhood, stressors characteristic of each developmental stage can be and must be identified.

What Next? Some Recommendations

Some recommendations have been presented herein that may serve to ensure an active, aggressive and meaningful role that can be played by psychologists, in evolving feasible preventive mental health programmes in our public health system. The recommendations pertain to policy and programme planning, creating public awareness, research and training drawn from various sources as indicated.

Policy and Programme Planning

* In the present context, wherein there is a national committment linking development to psycho-social well-being, especially for children (Hasan, 1979), it is imperative that professional psychologists and professional organizations in psychology participate actively in mental health programme planning, development, and implementation (Goldston, 1986).
* Since mental health falls at the cross roads of many disciplines, an active effort must be made to evolve an interdisciplinary approach characterized by a sense of mutual respect and enthusiastic co-operation, and directed toward the shared goal of mental health and well-being, by professionals in the behavioural, social, and medical sciences.
* Organizational structures at the local level, which could serve as the focal point for programmes for women and children, should be strengthened.
* Prevention and treatment measures for mental disorders can be made an integral part of preventive health care strategy, founded on community based service and in keeping with local needs (Hasan, 1979).

Creating Public Awareness

* Following the model of effective propaganda related to planned parenthood, especially through use of television as a medium, it is important to create

public awareness regarding preventive and promotive mental health.

* People need to be sensitized to the importance of early identification of mental disorders and their early referral.
* Solutions to existing problems, if they are to be real and lasting, must be worked out in consultation with the population (Hasan, 1979). Only then will resulting services have its support and be put to maximum use.

Research

* Research must be directed toward identifying groups of individuals, especially chilren, at increased risk for developing mental health problems and toward building a knowledge-base regarding the complex interactions among the biological, social, and environmental influences detrimental to psycho-social well-being, as well as the existing social supports that act as buffers.
* Funding support must be ensured for epidemiological, biomedical, behavioural and clinical research aimed at preventive mental health, to assess and evaluate existing programmes of prevention, and to replicate effective preventive programmes particularly those related to existing community support systems.
* Commissioning of reports and literature reviews related to public health, mental health, communal violence, stress management and related topics would enable the field to assess the state of the art and to give direction and identify priorities.

Training

* The possibility of including public health training in at least selected branches of psychology at the pre-doctoral, doctoral and post-doctoral level of training needs to be seriously examined (Olbrisch,

Weiss, Stone & Schwartz, 1985), as also the possibility of including a strong base of behavioural sciences in the training of public health personnel (Goldston, 1986).

* Individuals in daily contact with children such as parents and teachers, can be trained to identify children at risk of mental disorders and to provide mental health services. Community workers/para-professionals can be trained to provide physical and emotional support to parents of disabled children and to assist them in meeting the special needs of these children (Hasan, 1979). Such a training will naturally adopt a "culturally sensitive modality of mental health services" (Roger, Malgady, Constantine, & Blumenthal, 1987, p. 565).
* Non-professionals like housewives, students and mid-wives could be involved in providing mental health services. This would serve the two-fold purpose of utilizing untapped assets and atleast partially overcoming the dearth of professional services (Zax & Spectar, 1974).

Conclusion

The global Medium-term Programme of the World Health Organization (WHO) for the period 1984-1989 cited four major activities in which psychologists can play a central role :

(1) the development of mental health policies and the promotion, co-ordination, evaluation, and support of programmes throughout the world;

(2) the improved understanding and utilization of psycho-social factors in the promotion of health and hyman development;

(3) the prevention and control of alcohol and drug abuse; and

(4) the prevention and treatment of mental and neurological disorders (WHO, 1983; cited in Holtzman *et al.*, 1987).

In the Indian context, the plea remains pertinent a decade later and can serve a mutually enriching purpose of strengthening the social relevance and professionalization of psychology, as also the mental health programme that is struggling to find a firm footing.

REFERENCES

Albee, G.W. (1986). Toward a just society. *American Psychologist*. *41*, 891-898.

Coleman, J.C. (1976). *Abnormal Psychology and Modern Life*. Bombay : Taraporewala (Reprinted 1987).

Goldston, S.E. (1986). Primary prevention : Historical perspectives and a blue print for action. *American Psychologist*. *41*. 453-460.

Hart, S.N., & Brassard, M.R. (1987). A major threat to children's mental health : Psychological maltreatment. *American Psychologist*. *42*. 160-165.

Hasan, K.Z. (1979). Child mental health in primary health care. *Assignment Children*. 47/48. 91-101.

Holtzman, W.H., Evans, R.I., Kennedy, S., & Iscoe, I. (1987). Psychology and health : Contributions of psychology to the improvement of health and health care. *International Journal of Psychology*. 22. 221-267.

Kelly, J.G. (1977). Community psychology : Ecological approach. In B.B. Wolman (Ed.). *International Encyclopedia of Psychiatry, Psychology, Psychoanalysis and Neurology*. Vol. 3. (pp. 264-270). New York : Aesculapius.

Long, B.B. (1986). The prevention of mental-emotional disabilities. *American Psychologist*. *41*. 825-829.

Maddux, J.E., Roberts, M.C., Sledden, E.A., & Wright, L. (1986). Developmental issues in child health psychology. *American Psychologist*. *41*. 25-34.

Olbrisch, M.E., Weiss, S.M., Stone, G.C., & Schwartz, G.E. (1985). Report of the national working conference on education and training in health psychology. *American Psychologist*. *40*. 1038-1041.

Roger, L.H., Malgady, R.G., Constantino, G., & Blumenthal, R. (1987). What do culturally sensitive mental health services mean? *American Psychologist*. 42. 565-570.

Rosenberg, M.S. (1987). New directions for research on the psychological maltreatment of children. *American Psychologist*, *42*. 166-171.

Tarnowski, K.J. (1991). Disadvantaged children and families in pediatric primary care settings : Broadening the scope of integrated mental health service. *Journal of Clinical Child Psychology, 20*, 351-359.

Zax, M., & Spectar, G.A. (1974). *An Introduction to Community Psychology*. New York : Wiley.

17

Emerging Perspectives in Stress and Health

AJIT K. DALAL and **GIRISHWAR MISRA**

People go through a wide variety of stresses in their lives which include both, every day hassles, like noisy neighbourhood, as well as tragic happenings, like bereavement and heart attack. These life stresses put heavy demands of the coping resources of people. Over the past few decades social and psychological researches have focused on the effects of such stresses on health and illness status. Traditionally these studies were conducted mostly by the mental health professionals to develop some understanding to guide them in clinical practices. These earlier studies focused on how people react emotionally to major crises, which reactions are adaptive, and how such reactions change over time (Lehman & Wortman, 1985). The theoretical advances made by the work of Selye (1976) and Lazarus (1984) have aroused much interest among cognitive and social psychologists to understand psychological and physical health related consequences of stressful life events. This change is clearly perceptible in most of the researches in the last two decades or so.

Psychological stress is one of the most productive ar[ea] of research at present. It is well evident by the researc[h] presented in this volume. This section, however, does n[ot] intend to review these researches. It purports to identi[fy] some future trends, suggesting some new directions i[n] which many research possibilities exist.

Stress and its Health-Related Consequences

Chronic illness is found to be a major factor in developing, as well as, in recovering from various diseases. Stress reduces body's immune efficacy, sets in certain physiological reactions, like increase in blood pressure, heart rate and skin conductivity, and also increases secretion of acids harmful to health in the long run. The affective and cognitive consequences of stressful experiences are found to be as varied as depression, anxiety, denial, morbid thoughts, inability to concentrate, withdrawal and performance impairment. Beginning with the seminal work of Selye (1966, 1976) and Lazarus (1984), stress research has yielded enormous data to substantiate the argument that stressful events lead to several health problems. The general assumption being that moderate level of stress will lead to adaptive responses, but stress above a threshold point will have debilitating health consequences (Taylor, 1991).

Though this assumption found general support in many research studies, the correlations between measures of stressful life events and mental and physical health are found modest at the best. One interpretation of this finding was that stress as measured in terms of life event changes could be less relevant to actual experience of stress, than the way an individual appraises and copes with changing events, made up of different components, each needing a separate coping strategy. For example, in a crowding situation it could be invasion of privacy, loss of identity, or competition for scarce resources, or all these factors could be the source of stress. In such cases, those who have greater flexibility to move from one coping strategy to another are much better off than those who lack this flexibility. People take time to understand the multifaceted nature of the stressful situation and about appropriate coping strategies. Stress research has not been able to grapple with this enormous complexity at theoretical and methodological level.

Religious Beliefs and Life Stress

It has been known for long time that religious beliefs influence both the appraisal and coping with life crises. Religion plays important role in all life domains, more so in the Indian cultural context. Religion provides meaning to human suffering and makes it easier to face the crises. For example, in the case of severe accident victims, only those respondents who could find some meaning in their suffering were better adjusted than those who could find no such meaning (Bulman & Wortman, 1977). Religious beliefs provide the basis for reconstructing the tragic events, finding some positive meaning and working out coping strategies. Dalal and Pande (1988) and Dalal and Singh (1992) found that accident victims and patients having some chronic diseases frequently attribute their health problems to metaphysical factors, such as God's will, fate and karma. However, no clear linkages were found between metaphysical beliefs and health recovery.

The dominant Hindu world view is that this world is full of suffering, and that miseries are integral to the worldly existence of all human beings (Radhakrishnan, 1926). Worldly desires are presumed to be the main cause of all this suffering and the only way out is to realize one's true self. Thus, one is advised to look within to understand the causes of suffering and it is through changing one's cognitions that one can effectively deal with life stresses. This thinking provides the basic frame of reference within which stressful experiences are interpreted and follow up measures are taken (Paranjpe, 1986). Surprisingly, there is little empirical work to throw light on the role this belief system plays in dealing with life stresses. As Ramachandra Rao elaborated, *Gita, Yoga Sutra* and *Charak Samhita* bring out highly developed strategies to manage tragic experiences and to alleviate suffering. Except in few sporadic efforts (e.g., Pande & Naidu, chapter 7), Hindu view of life is rarely subjected to empirical test at least in the tradition of western academic psychology.

Another belief system which has very much influenced the lives of people is the theory of *Karma*. This theory explains human pain and suffering in terms of one's own deeds of previous lives. Three types of *Karmas* are envisaged : *Prarabdha*, *Sanchita* and *Agamin*. The *Prarabdha Karmas* are viewed to be those *Karmas* of the previous lives which have started unfolding and one has to suffer as a consequence. These are like arrows in the air, there is no escape from its consequences. On the other hand, *Sanchita* (accumulated) and *Agamin* (futuristic) *Karmas* are those, the manifestations of which can be changed in future. The theory of *Karma* thus, facilitates the *acceptance* of the present suffering as unavoidable but gives *hope* that one can preclude suffering in future through righteous deeds. The affective, cognitive and behavioural correlates of belief in the theory of *Karma* are yet to be investigated, particularly, its role in buffering health related consequences of chronic stresses. One always has a sense of dismay while scanning the literature that stress psychologists have, except making passing references, shown little interest in taking it as a major research endeavour. The result is that we know very little about the implications of religious ceremonies and rituals in which people frequently engage while passing through difficult times, and even less about the role of traditional healers, and that of religious institutions in alleviating suffering. These healers and their institutions provide a whole range of psychological services, parallel to counselling and psychiatric services of the West. In India, there are 5 million traditional healers offering a wide range of services, but these services and their effectiveness are rarely subjected to systematic research.

Myth and Reality of Social Support

Social support is one of the constructs which is extensively studied. The focus has been on the kind of social support people in stress have and the way in which this social support attenuates the debilitating effects of stressful events. An over-evident finding is that the more the social support the better the person is equipped to cope with tragic events. For example, in a 9-year follow up study on a large sample of respondent living in California (Berkman & Syme, 1979) showed that a number of network and support indicators were associated with reduced mortality risk. In Indian setting, where people have large networks, social support is considered one of the major psychological resources which a person has to deal with emotional and social problems arising from the crisis.

Even a cursory glance at the state of research will reveal that the research endeavours have concentrated on the consequences of receiving social support for the recipient. Motives and support efforts of the providers are relatively ignored. Also there is little effort to examine when even well-intended social support become unsupportive, or have negative consequences. Social support may fail for many reasons. One, people are often guided by their own desire to help rather than by the need of the recipient. In their earnestness be helpful, some members of the family are overindulgent, take decisions on behalf the person in distress undermining their own adaptive skills and efforts to effectively cope with the situation. Sometimes, such emotional indulgence is resented by the victims who may see it as a threat to their sense of autonomy, self-esteem and personal control. They resent being pushed around by the demanding well wisher, even if it is purported to be for their good. Two, many times people are more keen to prove that their helping efforts did work, benefitting the recipient. In this, they fail to take notice of the feelings and expectations of the person being helped. As people make more and more investment in providing support, they come to share success and failure of the coping efforts. In their anxiety to avoid any blame for 'failures' in such a situation, the help providers may endeavour to curtail the freedom of the victims, aggravating the victim's sense of helplessness. Three, in a crisis situation the other family members may be more anxious and distressed than the perosn who is directly affected. Thus, in the process of providing support they may transfer some of their own anxiety, making it more difficult for the person to cope. Fourthly, the support group which believes in a just world may inadvertently attribute the negative events to the victims. Particularly, belief in the theory of *Karma* imputes that the person has done some wrong deeds in this or previous births to deserve the suffering. Thus, people are held causally, if not morally responsible for their predicament. Such explanations, instead of comforting the person make him or her wary of the support providers.

Most of the above explanations of the failure of social support are at the best tentative. The import of the negative side of social support is yet to be clearly understood and subjected to empirical testing. Work in this area is important for any meaningful counseling to the family and social network about the kind of support that will work and the kind of comments they should refrain from making. We still need to know how the social support network can be used more effectively in avoiding the adverse consequences of stressful events.

Methodologial Shift

The enormous complexity of stress experiences and coping efforts, and the failure to get consistent findings suggest that our understanding in this field is more likely to progress by studying reactions to specific situations. Such a shift is clearly noticeable in research. Rather than engaging in general surveys of stress events, the shift is toward case studies where specific stress experiences are the focus. This approach has many exciting possibilities of understanding the repertoire of coping skills which a person possesses or develops to deal with a crisis event. Also, this approach does facilitate comparisons of response patterns for different events. One can be hopeful that this shift in methodology will result in more sophisticated research in which by taking carefully matched comparison groups, comparative analysis of different life crises would be possible (Lazarus, 1986).

It seems more logical to use ipsative methodology in this area of research, i.e., doing an in-depth study by taking a smaller sample. This is a kind of compromise between large surveys and case studies, thus making it possible to repose greater confidence in the generalizability of the findings. Such ipsative methodologies provide opportunity to the respondent to more systematically explore their inner world in a reflective mode. In this respondents are encouraged to trace their own anxieties, stresses, inadequacies and related experiences, and the coping efforts made. These kinds of exploratory interviews were found to be a useful approach to understand health-related consequences of chronic stresses (Dalal, 1994). There is vast scope of improvising and employing this kind of exploratory-reflective methods in stress reseach. The fine-grained data so obtained should help in appraising the effectiveness of different coping strategies at different stages of a crisis.

The methodological innovations are necessary to establish clear linkages between stress, coping and health. What coping efforts protect and which one promote health. The idea is to differentiate between maintenance and growth oriented coping. What happens in the case of high situational uncertainty? Our knowledge to answer these questions is still very limited and most of our best answers are also just tentative. It is hoped that creative methodologies will remove some of these cobwebs in our understanding.

Culture and Health

It has been demonstrated that the processes of health and illness are regulated by a number of factors including environment, diet, exercise, alcohol consumption, smoking, availability of public health care measures and quality of medicine. However, this list of factors contributing to health and disease processes will remain incomplete unless we attend to culture. There is growing realization that culture is intimately related to the health status of the people. Life expectancy and diet vary across cultures. The higher life expectancy in rich countries is perhaps linked to sound public health measures and good medicine than to diet. Within rich countries also we find variations in health status. There are also differences in the amount of stress experienced by people in different cultures. People in the fast changing cultures experience greater stress than those living in relatively stable cultures. The rate of mental hospital admissions also vary across cultures. Life events are perceived as more or less stressful depending on the way culture and socialization peredispose a person to look at them.

A multitude of forces influence our health and our ability to prevent and treat illness. Increasingly health is being viewed as synergy of the forces of self, nature and others rather than an individual's state or characteristic. This view is contrary to the medical model which considers pathogens as the root of all the diseases. It seems that understanding the role of culture in the maintenance of health and development of disease will help us in a long way in preventing disease in future. As research reveals the implications of cultural tendencies, we can also examine cultural influenees to help us treat people of different cultures in a muct better way.

Once we realize the role of culture in determining the meaning and expression of health we must rethink and modify our methods of assessing and treating diseases. In order to evolve suitable assessment strategies, knowledge of culturally appropriate construals of health and disease must be taken into consideration. Explication of culture-specific systems of healing is also necessary to develop effective methods of both assessment and treatment. There is growing research evidence that culturally sensitive tools, measures and treatment methods are vital to improving our ability to effectively address the health needs of people from diverse cultural settings. Research in the field of health psychology has to respond these issues if we intend to contribute to the well being and quality of life of the people.

REFERENCES

Berkman, L.F., & Syme, S.L. (1979). Social networks, host resistence, and mortality : A 9-year follow up study of

Alameda county residents. *American Journal of Epidemiology, 109*, 186-204.

Bulman, R.J., & Wortman, C.B. (1977). Attribution of blame and coping in the "real world" : Severe accident victims react to their lot. *Journal of Personality and Social Psychology, 35*, 351-363.

Caplan, R.D., Naidu, R.K., & Tripathi, R.C. (1984). Coping and defence : Constellation versus components. *Journal of Health and Social Behaviour, 25*, 303-320.

Dalal, A.K., & Singh, A.K. (1992). Role of causal and recovery beliefs in psychological adjustment to a chronic disease. *Psychology and Health, 6*, 193-203.

Dalal, A.K., & Pande, N. (1988). Psychological recovery of the accidents victims with temporary and permanent disability. *International Journal of Psychology, 23*, 25-40.

Lazarus, R.S. (1966). *Psychological Stress and the Coping Process*. New York : Springer-Verlag.

Paranjpe, A.C. (1984). *Theoretical Psychology : Meeting of the East and West*. New York : Plenum.

Radhakrishnan, S. (1926). *The Hindu View of Life*. Bombay : Blakie.

Selye, H. (1966/1976). *The Stress of Life*. New York : McGraw Hill.

Taylor, S. (1991). *Health Psychology*. New York : Random House.

Index